THE COMPLETE FILMS
OF THE
MARX BROTHERS

THE COMPLETE FILMS

A CITADEL PRESS BOOK

OF THE
MARX BROTHERS

ALLEN EYLES

Published by Carol Publishing Group

ACKNOWLEDGMENTS

For their assistance in researching the careers of the Marx Brothers for this book, I would particularly like to thank Paul G. Wesolowski, David S. Parlett, David F. Cheshire, Bernard Hrusa-Marlow, Alvin H. Marill, John Behrens (CBS Program Information), Pat Billings, David Trevor-Jones, and Petri Nevalainen. As usual, my wife Lesley provided valued support. For past help, I remain grateful to David S. Parlett, Kevin Brownlow, Kingsley Canham, Paul Chown, John Cutts, Chester Erskine, George Folsey, Ted Gilling, John Hickey, Jim Kearley, Doris McChesney, and Barrie Pattison.

Sources of information and quotations include:

Cocktails for Two by Sam Coslow. Arlington House, New Rochelle, New York, 1977

Colliers (May 15, 1937, "Don't Call Me a Stooge" by Kyle Crichton)

Film Dope

Flywheel, Shyster, and Flywheel: The Marx Brothers' Lost Radio Show, edited by Michael Barson. Pantheon Books, New York, 1988

The Freedonia Gazette, the Magazine Devoted to the Marx Brothers, edited and published by Paul G. Wesolowski. Darien 28, New Hope, Pennsylvania.

Growing Up With Chico, by Maxine Marx. Prentice-Hall, Englewood Cliffs, New Jersey, 1980

Groucho and Me, by Groucho Marx. Dell, New York, 1959

Groucho, Harpo, Chico and Sometimes Zeppo: A Celebration of the Marx Brothers, by Joe Adamson. Simon and Schuster, New York, 1973

The Groucho Letters. Simon and Schuster, New York, 1967

The Groucho Phile, an Illustrated Life, by Groucho Marx. 1976

Harpo Speaks! by Harpo Marx (with Rowland Barber). Avon, New York, 1961

"Hello, I Must Be Going": Groucho and His Friends, by Charlotte Chandler. Doubleday, New York, 1978

Hollywood Quarterly (April 1947, "American Classic" by Richard Rowland)

I Blow My Own Horn, by Jesse Lasky (with Don Weldon). Simon and Schuster, New York, 1957

I'll Cry Tomorrow, by Lillian Roth. Frederick Fell, New York, 1954

The Marx Brothers, by Kyle Crichton. Doubleday, New York, 1950.

The Marx Brothers, by William Wolf. Pyramid, New York, 1975

The Marx Brothers Scrapbook, by Groucho Marx and Richard J. Anobile. Darien House, New York, 1973

Mayer and Thalberg, The Make-Believe Saints, by Samuel Marx. Random House, New York, 1975

Movie Comedy Teams, by Leonard Maltin. New American Library, New York, 1975

On the Other Hand: A Life Story, by Fay Wray. St. Martin's, New York, 1988.

Penguin Film Review (no. 7, 1948, "American Classic" by Richard Rowland)

S. J. Perelman, a Life, by Dorothy Herrmann. Simon and Schuster, New York, 1988

The View From the Sixties by George Oppenheimer. David McKay, New York, 1965

The book is illustrated with publicity photographs (many obtained from the Stills, Posters and Designs Department of the British Film Institute in London, and from the late Bo Johan Hultman) that were issued for promotional use by Metro-Goldwyn-Mayer, Monarch Film Corporation, Paramount, RKO Radio, 20th Century-Fox, United Artists, and unidentified sources. Additional key photographs courtesy of Paul G. Wesolowski.

A Citadel Press Book
Published by Carol Publishing Group
Citadel Press is a registered trademark of
Carol Communications, Inc.
Editorial Offices: 600 Madison Avenue, New York, N.Y. 10022
Sales & Distribution Offices: 120 Enterprise Avenue, Secaucus, N.J. 07094
In Canada: Canadian Manda Group, P.O. Box 920, Station U, Toronto, Ontario M8Z 5P9
Queries regarding rights and permissions should be addressed to Carol Publishing Group, 600 Madison Avenue, New York, N.Y. 10022

Carol Publishing Group books are available at special discounts for bulk purchases, for sales promotions, fund raising, or educational purposes. Special editions can be created to specifications.
For details, contact: Special Sales Department, Carol Publishing Group, 120 Enterprise Avenue, Secaucus, N.J. 07094

Designed by A. Christopher Simon

Manufactured in the United States of America

10 9 8 7 6 5 4 3 2 1

Library of Congress Cataloging-in-Publication Data

Eyles, Allen.
   The complete films of the Marx Brothers / Allen Eyles.
      p. cm.
   "A Citadel Press book."
   Filmography: p.
   ISBN 0-8065-1301-2
      1. Marx Brothers. 2. Comedy films—United States—History and criticism. I. Title.
   PN2297.M3E85   1992
   791.43'028'0922—dc20
                                                                 92-26998
                                                                    CIP

CONTENTS

The Marx Brothers fooling around on the agent's office set of their promotional short for *The House That Shadows Built* (1931).

INTRODUCTION

With seven feature films released between 1929 and 1937, Groucho, Harpo, and Chico Marx created a body of work that has ensured them a permanent place as outstanding comedians. *The Cocoanuts*, *Animal Crackers*, *Monkey Business*, *Horse Feathers*, *Duck Soup*, *A Night at the Opera*, and *A Day at the Races* were immensely popular in their time and they remain popular today. (Later films have their moments but will not bring the team new converts.)

Groucho, Harpo, and Chico brought to the screen material that had been perfected in vaudeville and theatrical musical comedy. Their brazenly irreverent humor suited the mood of audiences in the harsh climate of the Depression and, with Irving G. Thalberg's help, they found a way of making it more palatable for a while when times improved.

Unusually for a comedy team, the Marx Brothers offered a variety of styles and humor (and they

Minnie Marx, the mother of six Marx brothers.

Groucho (left) and Harpo outside the house where they lived on East 93rd Street, New York, in late 1899.

each looked funny in a different way). There was Groucho, with his agile manner and mind, more than a match for everyone but his brothers. There was Chico, with his dense humor based on a phony accent and farfetched puns. There was Harpo, with his silent mischief. (And, for a while, there was Zeppo, who never really got going.)

It is enough that they made us laugh, that (like one of Arnold Bennett's characters) they were devoted to the great cause of cheering up all of us. But there was a distinctive side to their comedy. Groucho was once quoted as saying: "We hold the theory that we shouldn't be repressed. When we see a pompous fellow in a high silk hat swelled up with his own importance and sniffing and sneer-ing at folks as they pass, we do exactly what the rest of the world would like to do. We heave a ripe tomato at the hat. If we suppressed that desire, we would not be normal." Like good surrealists, the Marx Brothers lived positively, according to the dictates of desire. That sense of liberation, of nonconformism, communicates itself as vividly as ever.

On their own, nothing the Marxes did after 1937 would have given them more than a minor footnote in comedy. Watching them in later ma-terial, there are still rewarding moments—espe-cially when these can be traced back to their earlier work—and one admires their persever-ance: to the end of their lives, Chico never lost his inimitable way with a piano, Harpo could still drop knives from his sleeve with perfect timing, and Groucho could revive his old wisecracks.

Thirteen films as a team and various solo appearances do not always seem enough. In various revues and acts, performers have tried with varying success to impersonate the Marx Brothers and give us more. It is an interesting phenomenon but this book is about the real thing. An overview of the Marx Brothers' career is followed by commentaries on their thirteen feature films as a team.

The Marx Brothers in Hollywood—Chico in rare hatless pose.

THE LIVES OF THE MARX BROTHERS

Before making their first feature film together in 1929, Chico, Harpo, and Groucho had been performers for twenty or more years, working their way up from the lowest vaudeville houses to the Palace on Broadway and going on to become a sensational success on the legitimate stage.

Minnie Schoenberg, the mother of the Marx Brothers, arrived in New York from Germany when she was fifteen. Three years later, she married another immigrant, a Sam Marx from Alsace. Their eldest son, Manfred, died in infancy. Leonard (later Chico) was born on March

Groucho (standing) at seventeen and Gummo at fifteen. At this point, Harpo was a bellhop in a hotel, Chico was playing piano in nickelodeons, and Zeppo was an infant.

Top to bottom: Groucho, Harpo, Gummo, and Lou Levy as The Four Nightingales.

The Four Nightingales in 1909. Left to right: Gummo, Lou Levy, Groucho, Harpo.

22, 1887. He was followed by Adolph (later Arthur, finally Harpo) who was born on November 23, 1888. Then there was Julius (to become Groucho) on October 2, 1890. Two more sons arrived some years later: Milton in 1897 (nicknamed Gummo, he did not appear in any of the Marx films), and finally Herbert (nicknamed Zeppo) in 1901. (There has been some confusion over their birth dates, as film studio biographies took four or five years off the ages of Chico, Groucho, and Harpo.)

The Marx family settled in the predominantly German Yorkville section of Manhattan. Minnie's parents, who lived with them, had been traveling entertainers in Germany—her father a ventriloquist-cum-magician, her mother playing a small harp after his performances for the audience to dance. Minnie's brother, Al Shean, was the entertainer of her generation and the big celebrity of the Marx clan, being half of the famous Gallagher and Shean act. It was through Minnie's efforts that Al originally became a vaudeville star, for she badgered the bookers and got him dates just as she was to do for her sons.

Groucho went into show business in 1905,

Fun in Hi Skule (circa 1912). That's Groucho as elderly schoolteacher Mr. Green in center with Dorothy Yale. Harpo is pointing his finger at them, and behind him, by the blackboard, is Chico. Gummo is seated at far right.

joining singing acts that would contrive to leave him stranded and penniless a thousand miles from home. Gummo began his performing career shortly after, helping out an inept ventriloquist by becoming his speaking dummy. Chico was doing fine by himself as a piano player. Minnie decided that Groucho and Gummo would be better off as a singing act, and she teamed them with a female singer she engaged to create the Three Nightingales. The addition of a boy named Lou Levy made them the Four Nightingales. They toured the country for the next few years, and Harpo was brought in to replace the woman in the act in 1909 or 1910.

Then, when Minnie and a relative also joined in, they were the Six Mascots. Groucho played the guitar during the act while Gummo and Harpo performed on mandolins. There was no great demand for their services, but they kept on

Groucho in his Napoleon costume outside the Walnut Street Theater in Philadelphia during the run of *I'll Say She Is* in 1923.

Zeppo, Chico, Groucho, Carlotta Miles, and Harpo in a pose for the Napoleon and Josephine sketch of *I'll Say She Is*.

working. Minnie gave up performing to manage the group.

They began to emphasize comedy above the music, and they developed a skit, "Fun in Hi Skule" or "School Days," largely modeled on the routines that were all the rage elsewhere. Groucho played an elderly schoolteacher, Mr. Green, and spoke with a German accent. Harpo wore a red wig for the first time and threw his "gookie" expression, the puffed-cheek, pop-eyed look that he'd picked up as a child from the facial appearance of a man rolling cigars in a shop window. At this time, Harpo was still speaking lines. There were some women in the troupe and Chico joined in as well. He added a piano piece to their brash routines, which already had hints of their later work and much the same riotous spirit as the biology class of *Horse Feathers*.

15

Chico, Zeppo, Groucho, and Harpo in the stage production of *The Cocoanuts*.

A little envious of Chico's piano, Harpo experimented with a harp and soon had it in the act. More horseplay slipped into the show whenever Minnie wasn't looking, and the musical half was largely abandoned in favor of more comedy. They received a complimentary review in *Variety* (February 24, 1912) for their "school act"—especially Harpo, his harp-playing in the middle of the act "giving a classy touch to the whole." In one new scene (Harpo related in his 1961 autobiography, *Harpo Speaks!*), he had a line in which he announced himself as the garbage man. Groucho retorted: "Sorry, we don't need any." (Indicative of how Groucho would store gags for later use is the way it came up again while Groucho was in London in 1965. He told a reporter: "This morning I was awakened by a great din and told it's the dustman. I told him to get lost. Who needs dust?")

It was at about this stage in their career in 1914 that a fellow performer, monologist Art Fisher, handed out their lasting nicknames along with the cards he was dealing in a poker game: "Harpo" for obvious reasons; "Chico" for his amorous pursuit of "chicks" (so it should have been spelled "Chicko" and should be pronounced as though it was); "Groucho" either for his grouchy disposition, always scenting disaster, or because he kept his money for safety in a "grouch-bag," a leather pouch worn around the neck; and "Gummo" either from the gumboots or shoes with gum soles that he invariably wore. They still retained their given names in official billing. (Herbert was still in school and "Zeppo" was a

The Four Marx Brothers pose in costume for the party
sequence from the stage production of *The Cocoanuts*.

Groucho with some of the bellhops from the stage production of *The Cocoanuts*.

later family gift that has been variously explained: as coming from zeppelins, from a well-known performing chimp called Zippo, or from an earlier nickname, Zebbo, when he worked on a farm.)

The troupe was still not offering a very distinguished show, and Chico's enthusiasm did a lot to keep them going. They were good, but they needed the overhauling that Al Shean gave their work in 1914. He reshaped and built up their existing material and directed them in *Home Again*, a musical tabloid, or short musical comedy, for vaudeville.

It opened with a ten-minute piece of rough-house humor between Harpo and Chico and a suspicious policeman set on the piers of the Cunard line. This introduced Harpo's routine of the stolen cutlery cascading out of his sleeve at an inopportune moment, as when he is shaking a policeman's hand (it forms part of the first two Marx films and Harpo used it in stage and television appearances to the end of his career). Harpo had also stopped speaking, because Uncle Al had given him next to nothing to say, and he remained silent professionally after that. About this time he also adopted the familiar plug hat, underslung pants, and the trench coat that were to stay with him through his films, stacked up with valuable props and likened by French critic André Martin to "the caverns of Ali Baba." And he introduced the bulb-shaped taxicab horn which sounded when someone bumped into him or when he had something to "say." What was to be his familiar screen image had been evolved largely through trial and error. Chico was equally firmly a dialect comedian.

The docks sequence was followed by scenes at "Henry Schneider's Villa on the Hudson Three Weeks Later," with Groucho playing old man Schneider. (When the war broke out, the name was changed to Henry Jones, then later became Henry Hammer.)

Home Again was favorably received in *Variety's* issue dated February 12, 1915, where it was noted:

The fun-making is taken care of by three of the Marx brothers. Julius . . . is an excellent German comedian. Leonard Marx is the Italian, who plays the piano in trick and other ways, also has comedy scenes with his brother, Arthur Marx. . . . This Arthur Marx is marked as a comedian for a Broadway show, just as certain as you are reading this. He is a comedian who doesn't talk. Arthur plays the harp and piano, getting laughs from the handling of both. He and his brother, Leonard, have some new kind of rough-house fun . . . that made the Royal [Theatre] audience howl. In fact, Arthur made the house laugh any time he wanted them to. . . . Julius Marx does a song and dance by

Groucho as Captain Spaulding in the original stage production of *Animal Crackers*.

Theater on Broadway. *Billboard* (February 22, 1915) reviewed the Monday matinee:

Twelve people assisted the Four Marx Brothers to make good the reputation that had preceded their act from the Bronx to Times Square, and they abundantly cleaned up. Their tabloid ran forty minutes, and during that time the audience was either rocking with laughter or electrified with applause. The harp playing Marx brother performed wonders with his sweet-toned instrument and gets credit for being the first person this writer has ever seen who could get rollicking fun out of handling a harp. He is a comedian of rare talent. Praise must freely go, as well, to the piano playing Marx brother for similar ability to get comedy from his musical instrument, and the whirlwind dancing by the boy and girl, who were outside the Marx family pale, must be credited with assisting valiantly to rolling up the hit of the show for this corking good offering.

Margaret Dumont and Groucho in the Du Barry sketch from the end of *Animal Crackers* on stage (omitted from the screen version).

himself, and there is a pretty mechanically arranged finale that is helped along by some more comedy by Arthur. The fourth Marx brother, Harold [*sic*], does straight, looking extremely well.

After a complaint about Harpo spitting ("That should go out immediately"), *Variety* concluded: "*Home Again* looks like the best tab New York has ever seen, and it's an act big time could depend upon for a feature."

Indeed, only a few days later they were playing a week on the bill at the celebrated Palace

Harpo posing with some of the girls in the hotel lobby set of the screen version of *The Cocoanuts* (1929).

nouveau riche family to break into society. Then, in 1919, the Marxes had a rare setback when they put on a legitimate musical show called *The Street Cinderella* by Jo Swerling and Gus Kahn. It failed after a few performances.

Still keen to expand their horizons, the Marxes decided to try moviemaking. With a budget of some $6,000, which they and others contributed, they embarked on a film of their own, written by Jo Swerling and called *Humorisk*. Its title at least was a parody of Fannie Hurst's melodrama of mother love, *Humoresque*, which had been made into a top film attraction by Frank Borzage in 1920.

Humorisk was filmed partly out of doors on a vacant lot near a vaudeville theater in Fort Lee, New Jersey, at which the Marxes were appearing, and partly in a studio on Tenth Avenue in New York. Harpo was the romantic lead, called Watson, who wore a top hat and slid down a chute into a coal cellar. Groucho was the villain and ended up dragging a ball and chain. The leading lady was Mildred Davis, who was soon playing the heroine in Harold Lloyd comedies like *Safety Last*. (She also became Mrs. Harold Lloyd.)

Posed shot from the auction scene of the film *The Cocoanuts* (1929). Watching Harpo's antics with Margaret Dumont are Mary Eaton (blonde at left), Oscar Shaw, Chico, Zeppo, Groucho, and Basil Ruysdael.

Zeppo became part of the team in 1918 when Gummo, feeling that he lacked the performing skills of his brothers, joined the army. At the time, Zeppo was contentedly working as a motor mechanic, but his mother, Minnie, insisted that he join the act so that it would still be the Four Marx Brothers. However, he was given the straight man's part and never had a chance to develop a comedy style of his own.

Al Shean wrote another show for the team, *N' Everything*, about the ludicrous attempts of a

Apparently, two reels' worth of footage was completed and test-shown, with disastrous results. The film was abandoned, and the footage soon lost forever.

By 1921 the Marxes were performing a new musical "revuette" called *On the Mezzanine Floor* which played the Palace for the week of March 14 after a tour of New England. This had two scenes. The first presented a theatrical manager being besieged in his office by the Marxes playing Chaplin imitators. The second was a tryout of a play brought by a visitor to the manager's office in the first scene. Around this time, Groucho also moved part way to his familiar character, substi-

Margaret Dumont and Groucho in the film version of *Animal Crackers* (1930).

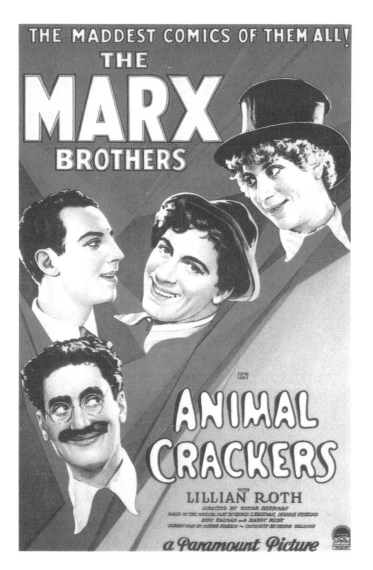

tuting a greasepaint mustache for a crepe one when he arrived late for a performance, and persisting with the substitution despite the objections of the theater's manager.

The team did two seasons with the show, which later became known as *On the Balcony*. They took it to the Coliseum Theatre in London's St. Martin's Lane in 1922 and got off to a bad start with an English audience that had come, for the most part, to catch a troupe of acclaimed Russian dancers (including Leonide Massine) who were concluding their run at the Coliseum with a week alongside the incoming Marxes. The balletomanes hissed at the Marxes and threw pennies, prompting Groucho to step forward and say, "We've come a long way—the least you could do is throw silver."

However, the Marxes' work was well liked by some of the press. Without managing to sort out one brother from another, the London *Times* declared:

It is not always that a much-heralded American turn comes up to expectations, but it may be said

Chico at the piano of the Savoy Hotel during their London visit in January 1931, watched by Chico's wife Betty, Groucho's son Arthur, Marion Marx and her husband Zeppo, Groucho's daughter Miriam, Groucho's wife Ruth, and Groucho. Harpo took a later boat and so was probably not available for this publicity shot.

Groucho (left) with some of the writers assigned to *Monkey Business* in Hollywood: Solly Violinsky, S. J. Perelman (perched on fender), Will B. Johnstone (light suit), and Arthur Sheekman.

at once that the claims to comic gifts out of the ordinary for the Marx Brothers was amply justified. For the best part of a half an hour they kept the audience in one continuous roar of laughter . . . a word of appreciation should be said in passing for the smart and resourceful gentleman who plays the Hebrew part; for the skillful pianist who can extract so much fun from his fingers; and for the speechless partner whose work on the harp is as good as anything of its kind we have yet had at the Coliseum. . . . The Marx Brothers are very welcome.

For the second week of their booking, they reverted to *Home Again*, which went down much better with audiences (now minus devotees of the dance), and they took it to the Alhambra Theatre in Leicester Square as well.

Back in the United States, the Marxes for one reason or another fell out of favor with the powers in the vaudeville world and had to look elsewhere. Chico negotiated their appearance in a tatty musical show called *I'll Say She Is* which

Zeppo, Groucho, Chico, Gummo, and Harpo pose together in this 1931 shot.

opened on June 4, 1923, at the Walnut Street Theater in Philadelphia, using existing sets as a cheap experiment in giving audiences something to watch in a season when theaters normally closed for lack of air conditioning.

I'll Say She Is offered a series of sketches built around a flimsy plot: A poor little rich girl promises to marry the man who gives her a "thrill." It used the established routines (such as Harpo's cascade of stolen silverware as the policeman comments on his honest-looking face; piano and harp interludes by Chico and Harpo) and sketches (the theatrical agency routine from *On the Mezzanine*, this time with Groucho, Chico, and Zeppo presenting imitations of a popular singer and dancer of the time, Joe Frisco). As Groucho later said: "We had fifteen years of surefire comedy material, tried-and-true scenes that had been certified by vaudeville audiences from coast to coast."

New material was devised by a newspaper cartoonist, Will B. Johnstone, and embellished by the team. This included a Napoleon skit that ended the show and was the hit of the evening.

The Marxes' talent kept *I'll Say She Is* running an incredible seventeen weeks in Philadelphia. A three-week stay in Kansas City was also remarkable. The show toured for nearly a year before daring a Broadway opening at the Casino Theater on May 19, 1924. According to legend, it attempted to sneak in on the evening that the main critics would be attending a more important opening but that was postponed, and they went somewhat grudgingly to *I'll Say She Is*, only to be won over completely by the Marxes.

The eminent George Jean Nathan welcomed it as a revue that, for a change, didn't attempt to copy sophisticated British examples but had its roots in American musical shows. "If there was ever a poorer musical show than *I'll Say She Is*, I don't know its name. But if ever there was a poor music show turned into a corking one by its

A 1931 shot of Chico, Groucho and Harpo without their makeup.

Groucho and Harpo race young Jackie Cooper on the Paramount lot circa 1932. Carole Lombard sees them off.

February 17, 1933: the Marx Brothers put their handprints, footprints, and names in cement at Grauman's Chinese Theater in Hollywood. That's Grauman at left wrestling with Zeppo. (The picture has been inscribed "For Marshall Best Wishes From Harpo Marx," written upside down above the writing in cement.)

Chico, Harpo, and the hapless victim of the mustache-trimming sequence from *Monkey Business* (1931).

Groucho, Harpo, Sid Grauman, Chico, and Zeppo pose on the forecourt of Grauman's Chinese Theater.

clowns, its name is the name of this one. . . . In such low comedians as they, we get again the sweet and fragrant rosemary of the old American burlesque show." Nathan recognized that their antics were not new but declared: "With a trick of the voice, a flip of the brogan or a new brand of whimsical mustache they convert these venerable grandpas of comic hokum into what seem to be newborn babes."

Among other rave reviews was that of Alexander Woollcott in *The New York World:* "As one of the many who laughed immoderately throughout the greater part of the first performance given by a new musical show, entitled, if memory serves, *I'll Say She Is*, it behooves your correspondent to report the most comical moments vouchsafed to the first nighters in a month of Mondays. It is a bright colored and vehement setting for the goings on of those talented cutups, the Four Marx Brothers. In particular, it is a splendacious and reasonably tuneful excuse for going to see that silent brother, that shy, unexpected, magnificent comic among the Marxes, who is recorded somewhere on a birth certificate as Arthur, but who is known to the adoring two-a-day as Harpo Marx." In Woollcott's reckoning, Groucho came second, Chico a poor third, and Zeppo could have been the property man.

Groucho was still being called Julius in the press coverage, and while Harpo and Chico were often referred to by their nicknames, they were billed as Arthur and Leonard on the official publicity.

The script of the Napoleon scene was included

The Marxes' impressions in cement remain in the
prominent view on the lefthand side of the
forecourt at Grauman's (now Mann's) Chinese
Theater in 1991.

Director Norman McLeod (Macko) and assistant director Charles Barton (Echo)
pose with the Marxes during production of *Monkey Business* (1931).

27

Groucho with Thelma Todd in a publicity pose for *Monkey Business* (1931). When Thelma Todd was found dead from carbon monoxide fumes in a garage one morning in December 1935, some of Groucho's lines to her as gangster's wife Lucille Briggs in the film seemed to have been prophetic: "You're a woman who's been getting nothing but dirty breaks. Well, we can clean and tighten your breaks but you'll have to stay in the garage all night."

Groucho with first wife Ruth and children Miriam and Arthur. As Ruth Johnson, she had been Zeppo's stage dancing partner when she met Groucho. The marriage lasted from 1920 to 1942.

THE 4 MARX BROTHERS

"Horse Feathers"

DIRECTED BY NORMAN McLEOD

A PARAMOUNT PICTURE

by Groucho in his book *The Groucho Phile* (1976). Groucho's Emperor repeatedly tries to catch Josephine misbehaving with the three gentlemen in waiting (Harpo, Chico, and Zeppo) by setting off for distant parts, then returning unexpectedly. Departing for Russia, he tells the Empress: "Farewell, my Queen. Beyond the Alps lies more Alps, and the Lord 'alps those that 'alps themselves." François (Chico) offers to marry not only Josephine but the Emperor as well. "Why, that's bigamy," says the Empress. "Yes, and it's bigamy too," declares François. When Groucho returns, the Empress is sitting on the lap of Harpo's Gaston to hide him, and Groucho kneels and kisses Harpo's hand in mistake for Josephine's and tries to reclaim his rubbers, which Harpo is wearing.

This sequence was later remodeled as the Du Barry scene in the stage *Animal Crackers*. Although it was never put on film, lines and situations were reclaimed for future movies, especially

Horse Feathers. The Marx Brothers never abandoned good material.

I'll Say She Is played 304 performances at the Casino, followed by a seventeen-week tour. During the run, the Marx Brothers became the toast of Broadway not just for their performing skills but for the inventive ways in which they freshened up the script or dropped it entirely to make up lines between themselves or talk to the audience.

Harpo found time to visit Hollywood and appear in a movie. He took a small part as the Peter Pan or genial idiot-boy of a Basque village in *Too Many Kisses*, a Famous Players–Lasky (Paramount) production released in January 1925. This contemporary romantic comedy starred Richard Dix and Frances Howard.

The leading stage producers—Ziegfeld, the Shuberts, Charles Dillingham—competed to put on the Marx Brothers' next show. But the Marxes wanted Sam H. Harris, who had been partnered with George M. Cohan and Irving Berlin, and who had an enviable record of stage hits. Initially, he proposed another show with a revue format, but the team demanded a properly scripted play.

It was probably Harpo who suggested that George S. Kaufman should write it, as they had met at poker games and at the Algonquin Round Table. Kaufman preferred writing with a collaborator and chose Morrie Ryskind, who worked uncredited as a creative assistant.

In devising *The Cocoanuts*, Kaufman and Ryskind provided the Marx Brothers with a fresh start so that they no longer had to depend on their old vaudeville routines. It was Kaufman's idea to base the show on the recent Florida land boom. And it was Kaufman who created a society dowager to be the butt of the team's humor and who spotted the ideal woman for the part in Margaret Dumont when she was portraying a social climber in another play. Groucho came to regard Kaufman as "the best writer for me of them all," and declared, "I think he was the wittiest man I ever met." Oscar Eagle was the play's director. Sammy Lee did the choreography.

The Cocoanuts opened badly in Boston but was reworked there and in Philadelphia, with the Marxes becoming more disciplined and attentive, so that it arrived finely honed at the Lyric Theatre in New York, where it was greeted rapturously on opening night, Tuesday, December 8, 1925, and won unanimously favorable reviews.

The Marxes were soon improvising and ad-libbing. Harpo interrupted one of Groucho's big scenes by chasing a blonde across the stage, honking his horn, and got such a laugh it became a regular feature of the show. Groucho inserted a query to the audience, "Is there a doctor in the house?" and when one obligingly stood up, he asked, "Enjoying the show so far, Doc?" (This exchange was later worked into the football game of *Horse Feathers*.) Such moments were widely reported and provided good publicity.

Like *I'll Say She Is*, the show became one that attracted repeat attendance as fans knew that no two performances would be exactly alike. The humor was so strong that songs provided by Irving Berlin did not have a chance. (He is often said to

have written "Always" for *The Cocoanuts*, only to have it turned down, but there is considerable doubt as to whether it was ever intended for that show.)

The Cocoanuts did well for a while in the hot summer of 1926, boosted by an official revamping with a "summer edition" that included new dialogue and new songs. But the Lyric was a large theater to fill—with 1,406 seats—and attendance fell off, so that the production closed in early August after thirty-five weeks. It went on tour in mid-September and played major cities for the next two seasons, including a nine-week run at the Erlanger in Chicago, before making a brief return visit to Broadway at the Century from May 16, 1928.

That summer Harpo set sail for Europe to stay at a villa on the French Riviera with Alexander Woollcott, Beatrice Kaufman (wife of George S.), and Alice Duer Miller. Harpo met Somerset Maugham, H. G. Wells, and George Bernard Shaw, and he recollected in his autobiography, *Harpo Speaks!*:

> One day Shaw and I drove to Cannes, where a friend of his, Rex Ingram, was directing a movie called *The Three Passions*. We only wanted to watch the shooting for a while, but Ingram had other ideas. He shanghaied us and put us to work as extras. In our one and only joint appearance before the camera, George Bernard Shaw and I shot pocket billiards in a poolroom scene. I'm sure the scene was cut from the picture. No audience could ever mistake us for extras, lost in the crowd. The way we shot pool we could only be taken for what we were—a couple of ringers, a couple of sharpies.

George S. Kaufman had stayed behind to direct *The Front Page* and was persuaded by Sam H. Harris to write another show for the Marx Brothers. This time he invited Morrie Ryskind to work on it as a full coauthor. The result was *Animal Crackers*. The setting was a mansion on Long Island, the home of Margaret Dumont's Mrs. Rittenhouse. Groucho was a phony celebrity, Captain Spaulding, with Zeppo as his secretary.

Harpo and Chico were musicians. The songs were provided by Bert Kalmar and Harry Ruby and included "Hooray for Captain Spaulding" and "We're Four of the Three Musketeers." (The latter was part of the concluding Du Barry scene, derived from the Napoleon sketch of *I'll Say She Is* and regrettably omitted from the later film version.) Oscar Eagle again directed. The dances were staged by Russell Markert.

The show opened at the 44th Street Theatre (1,323 seats) on Tuesday, October 23, 1928, to rave reviews, giving the Marx Brothers their third stage hit in a row. They again took liberties with the script. There is a now classic story of Kaufman watching a performance and turning amazed to a companion, remarking: "I think I just heard one of the original lines."

While the run continued, Paramount signed the Marxes to make a film version of *The Cocoanuts* at its New York studio, at Astoria on Long Island. The William Morris Agency wanted $75,000 for the play and the Marx Brothers. Studio head Adolph Zukor thought this excessive until Chico went to work on him, buttering him up and successfully suggesting the team was worth $100,000 since the show represented a lifetime's work in developing and polishing their routines.

Paramount had begun making talkies at Astoria to capitalize on the voice-trained talent in New York. In the case of *The Cocoanuts*, it simplified matters by merely filming what had been the play with some slight adaptation by Morrie Ryskind. This was difficult enough, for the actors had to speak within range of microphones hidden in the props and with the cameras largely deprived of mobility inside soundproof booths. Proper soundproofing had yet to be developed (monk's cloth was being hung on the walls) while Groucho's rapid-fire delivery was particularly difficult to record clearly.

Oddly, Paramount assigned the direction of *The Cocoanuts* to two inexperienced figures (apparently all the studio's regular directors were busy, and the company felt it could take a chance with such proven material). They were a Frenchman named Robert Florey (who has strongly denied Groucho's later stories that he didn't understand the script) and Joseph Santley, a former Broadway star who had just directed a short and was primarily concerned with the musical side.

The head of production, Monta Bell, tried telling Groucho that he couldn't use his greasepaint mustache and that he couldn't talk to the audience as he did on the stage. Groucho later claimed that it took a showing in a local movie theater of a test sequence of him with the painted mustache to demonstrate that audiences would accept it. Bell's concern was that light would be reflected off the greasepaint rather than that audiences would see that the mustache was phony in close-up, and some talcum powder was dusted on to reduce the shininess. (This applied to Groucho's eyebrows as well, a point overlooked years later in *Copacabana*, where light reflects off them during his musical number.)

The Marxes worked on the film version of *The Cocoanuts* in the daytime over a two-month period early in 1929 while performing on stage in *Animal Crackers* each evening with matinees on Wednesdays and Saturdays (because of the matinees, they only filmed four days a week). Two of the original Broadway supporting cast were rehired—Margaret Dumont, and Basil Ruysdael as the detective—but the romantic singing roles originally handled by Mabel Withee and Jack Barker went to Oscar Shaw and Mary Eaton, who received variable but often equal-size billing after the Marx Brothers. (Eaton and Shaw had been teamed before, in 1927's *Five O'Clock Girl*, scored by Bert Kalmar and Harry Ruby.) "Mary was lovely, Shaw was strictly no-talent" was Groucho's accurate summation in *The Groucho Phile*.

The technical difficulties of shooting had an inhibiting effect on some of the performances, while Paramount executives pressed for the completion of the film as soon as possible as they had a huge program of all-talking pictures to deliver. Robert Florey had neither the time nor the inclination to rehearse the Marx team as they knew the material so well from the stage and did it the way they thought fit, while (according to cinematographer George Folsey) the director may have understood the words in the script but he didn't think they were at all funny. Florey's biggest problem was finding all the brothers when he needed them—especially Chico, who was either in a speakeasy drinking, on the phone to his bookie, or embroiled in a pinochle game. The cameramen's biggest problem was keeping all the Marxes in frame. Having roamed on stage wherever they wanted and improvised on impulse, the Marxes found it impossible to stick to chalk-marked positions. The cameramen just had to do the best they could to follow them.

George Folsey has described one of Groucho's improvisations:

> Let me recall a shot, one of the first we did. We had four cameras on Groucho, who was the hotel desk clerk. One of the cameras had a four-inch close-up of Groucho (no rehearsal, mind you) and Groucho rang for the bellhops. Getting no response, he quickly dived down to the floor and stuck his head out through the opening of his desk. The cameraman didn't know he was going to do this and when he left his picture behind the desk that's the last he ever saw of Groucho. He quickly panned down just as Groucho left the floor and it really was a very amusing but frustrating shot for this poor cameraman.

This is the moment when Groucho, the hotel manager, standing in for Zeppo, the desk clerk, calls "Front!," gets no reply, and drops down to call "Front! Front! Front!" as though calling a dog. The scene was reshot to keep Groucho's movement in frame and comes across smoothly—or as smoothly as any camera movement does in *The Cocoanuts*.

It was during the run of *Animal Crackers* on stage that Groucho met S. J. Perelman, whose satirical pieces in *Judge* magazine had delighted him. (When they were collected together and published under the title *Dawn Ginsbergh's Revenge* in the fall of 1929, Groucho furnished the publishers with a blurb for the dust jacket: "From the moment I picked up your book until I laid it down, I was convulsed with laughter. Some day I intend reading it.")

Animal Crackers closed in New York in its twenty-fourth week on Saturday, April 6, 1929, after 191 performances. It had been slated to move to a smaller theater, but this didn't happen. Days later the Marxes were at the Palace earning

a record sum of $7,000 a week and giving vaudeville audiences a taste of *Animal Crackers*. *Variety* reported:

The Marx Brothers, with their Du Barry scene out of *Animal Crackers*, left 'em limp with laughter. It's perfect nonsense, undeniably ap-

pealing, and as for that scene, one can stand its repetition several times. As a matter of fact, plenty new ad-lib Groucho-isms are in this week, either new for the Palace or, most likely, interpolated patter from time to time during the show's Broadway run. One wheeze is a pip. Benjamin Franklin [played by Frank L. Hall] is

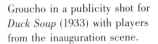

Groucho in a publicity shot for *Duck Soup* (1933) with players from the inauguration scene.

Groucho in a publicity pose for *Horse Feathers* (1932).

introduced to Groucho, who is King Louis XV of 18th Century France, whereupon that musketeer bawls Ben out for not delivering his *Satevpost* [*Saturday Evening Post*] on time.

Margaret Irving's Du Barry was asked by Groucho, "May I call you Du?" The twenty-two minute show concluded with the team singing "We're Four of the Three Musketeers." In their second week at the Palace, Harpo and Chico provided their harp and piano specialties, giving audiences a thirty-five minute show in all. They then went to the outlying Riverside Theatre, where they added the bridge scene from *Animal Crackers*.

With some trepidation, the Marx Brothers watched the film of *The Cocoanuts* open at the Rialto in New York's Times Square on May 23, 1929. They had been dismayed by their first viewing of the picture, which Morrie Ryskind had found "stiff." Paramount chief Jesse Lasky later claimed: "It happened that the print previewed for the Marxes was a mess and the sound was projected carelessly. They were so disgusted they wanted to buy back the negative and destroy it, and they put up quite a howl about it. They could easily have afforded such a luxury, but—protected by our contract—we ignored their protests." Groucho, Margaret Dumont, and Oscar Shaw can be heard jumping cues or stumbling over some of their lines. Technically, the film shows just how bad an early talkie could be (this was one of the pictures from which director Rouben Mamoulian had "learned what not to do" before he made the brilliant *Applause* a few months later with the same cameraman, George Folsey, at the same studios). Paramount was still releasing major silent pictures like *The Four Feathers* and *Thunderbolt* at the time *The Cocoanuts* appeared. The only technically accomplished aspect of the film was the overhead shots of dancers in formation, a device that Busby Berkeley would literally and figuratively take to new heights later on. There seems to have been no alternative silent version of *The Cocoanuts* released, as was normally the case for movie houses not wired for sound—but then Groucho's rapid

dialogue was beyond even the most resourceful of title writers.

The technical defects didn't matter. The Marx humor was there intact, and the critics and the public went wild. It was the prolonged laughter as much as the primitive sound recording that made catching all the dialogue so difficult. For an early sound film, Groucho's delivery was particularly rapid, and he provoked so much laughter that it was practically impossible to hear the next lines. "We had all kinds of complaints about patrons coming back to see the picture two or three times, trying to understand what it was about. It made something like two million dollars' profit, I guess because so many people kept seeing it over to try to figure it out," recalled Jesse Lasky. Along with Harold Lloyd's *Welcome Stranger*, it proved to be Paramount's biggest hit of the 1929–30 season (Lubitsch's *The Love Parade* came third, some way behind).*

Minnie and Sam (known as "Frenchie") were thrilled to see their sons conquer the new medium of film. And Minnie was delighted when the boys got together for a rare family reunion prior to the tour of *Animal Crackers*. On her way home afterward with Frenchie, she suffered a stroke. She died a few hours later, on September 13, 1929, at age sixty-five. Alexander Woollcott wrote "a short history of the magician's daughter who was the managing mother of the four Marx Brothers" for *The New Yorker* and rhapsodized: "She had done much more than bear her sons, bring them up, and turn them into play actors. She had *invented* them. They were just comics she had invented for her own amusement. They amused no one more, and their reward was her ravishing smile."

The Marxes took the *Animal Crackers* show on tour for eight months, opening at the Shubert in Boston on September 22, 1929. A little over a month later, Wall Street laid its famous egg, wiping out Groucho's carefully accumulated savings.

While the show was playing in Chicago, Groucho met another writer who, like Perelman, would make a substantial contribution to his later work. This was Arthur Sheekman, a local news-

*Each of the brother's major features is discussed in more detail later in separate chapters.

Director Leo McCarey, Chico, and Groucho on the set of *Duck Soup* (1933).

Groucho in a deleted moment from the climax of *Duck Soup* (1933).

paper columnist who came to interview Groucho and ended up allowing Groucho to write his column.

For several years, Groucho had been making humorous contributions to magazines and newspapers. With Arthur Sheekman's help, he wrote his first book, *Beds*, which was serialized in *College Humor* late in 1929 before being published in book form in 1930 (it was reissued in 1976).

The Kaiser is none other then Harpo Marx in fancy dress for a party given by Marion Davies. Marie Dressler reprises her outfit as Marthy in *Anna Christie*.

On Monday, April 28, 1930, the Marxes began shooting the film version of *Animal Crackers* for Paramount on the Astoria sound stages. There was little point in tampering with success, and Morrie Ryskind again carried out the minor tidying up of the play for filming purposes, helped by Pierre Collings. Margaret Dumont, Margaret Irving, Louis Sorin, and Robert Greig were retained from the stage version. Lillian Roth was sent from Hollywood to join the cast, and in her autobiography, *I'll Cry Tomorrow*, she recalled her "zany" experience:

> It was one step removed from a circus. First Zeppo, the youngest, sauntered into the studio, about 9:30 A.M. At ten somebody remembered to telephone Chico and wake him. Harpo, meanwhile, popped in, saw that most of the cast was missing, and strolled off. Later they found him asleep in his dressing room. Chico arrived about this time. Groucho, who had been golfing, arrived somewhat later, his clubs slung over his shoulder. He came in with his knees-bent walk, pulled a cigar out of his mouth, and with a mad, sidewise glance, announced, "Anybody for lunch?" Work resumed at mid-afternoon, and then it was five o'clock, and they were finished for the day. Every scene took longer than the director planned, for the ad libs came thick and fast, and the budget soared as the laughs increased. . . .We were running far over schedule . . .

An experienced director, Victor Heerman, was in charge this time, but *Animal Crackers* was almost as stilted as *The Cocoanuts* (not long after, Heerman gave up directing for a quieter life, writing the scripts of *Little Women* and *Stella Dallas*). Still, *Animal Crackers* hardly called for flights of directorial genius: the play was the thing, and the film of the play became Paramount't top-grossing picture of 1930.

It opened at the Rialto in New York on August 29, 1930. A few weeks into the run, a *Variety* reporter monitored a showing and clocked 388 laughs, an average of four a minute (301 for spoken gags, 87 for "situations"). Such breath-taking humor did not register as well in "the sticks" or in some export markets—audiences in the north of England, for example, found the film incomprehensible.

The Marxes hankered to perform before live audiences again, and their agent, Max Gordon, made a deal for them to appear on the RKO circuit. They kicked off at the Brooklyn Albee in early October 1930, and then played two weeks at the Palace on Broadway, headlining a three-hour show. When *Variety*'s reviewer, evidently a veteran follower, as he referred to the team by their real names, covered the third show on the Sunday, all was apparently not well:

> The Marx family closed in an act which appears to be a composite of various bits from their shows. Being their third time out for the day, the Marxes didn't seem overly enthusiastic. As Julius goes—so goes the act. And Julius apparently wanted to be a lot of places at this hour, among which was no hint of the Palace. But Julius can let down plenty and still remain a funny guy. That goes for Arthur (Harpo). Probably what enhanced the lethargic impression was that the act is minus a finish. It's strung together on the pretense of some kind of a betrothal party with Julius (Groucho) in charge, Arthur and Leo (Chico) the musicians, and Zeppo, the youngest brother, as the prospective bridegroom. Seven or eight "extras" dress the full stage. Turn abruptly climaxes on the dropping of the table silver, the finish being signaled by the closing in of the drapes.

However, things had improved when *Variety* took a look at their second week:

> Marx Brothers, the four of them, holding over from last week, were the usual panic with their comicalities in closing spot, flanked by two women who dressed and fed the boys for the usual rollicking results. Mrs. Marx's offspring were spotted in closer and held the rostrum for twenty-five minutes. Groucho copped the biggest results for comedy as the philandering monarch who trumps the Queen for Du Barry,

and both gals are good. Remaining triumvirate of Marxes flit in and out for laughs, getting them. Despite a disconnected series of nonsensical stuff, they go over big.

When they arrived at the RKO Palace in Chicago in early November, there were problems after Groucho fell ill:

"It was the Marx Bros. who drew the house and filled the lobby with standees. . . . With Groucho in the Michael Reese hospital with appendicitis and Zeppo wearing his mustache and clothes, the performance of the brothers lacked spirit. Zeppo was adept at the substitution and when the boys know where they stand it will be okay. At the first show they were inevitably rather listless, uncertain, and didn't do well."

The tour ended on December 18 at the Michigan Theater in Detroit.

Adolph Zukor was eager to sign up the Marx Brothers for more pictures, and he went to work on Chico. Details were finalized by Max Gordon, and the Marxes contracted to make another film for Paramount for $200,000 against fifty percent of the net (excluding the cost of the picture negative). This amazingly generous offer, which gave the Marxes a half-share in the profits, included an option for two further pictures if the first grossed well. On Christmas Eve 1930, Max Gordon rushed down to New York harbor for the Marxes' signatures on the final contracts. They had already boarded an ocean liner, the *Paris*, to sail to Plymouth, England, on their way to another appearance on the London stage, taking Margaret Dumont with them.

They opened on January 5, 1931, with forty minutes of scenes from the stage productions of *The Cocoanuts* and *Animal Crackers* as the star attraction of Charles B. Cochran's 1931 *Varieties* at the Palace Theatre. (West End audiences had a choice, in the first week, of seeing the Marxes live or in the film of *Animal Crackers* concluding its run at the Carlton.) The team played twice daily in London until the last day of the month with Ivy

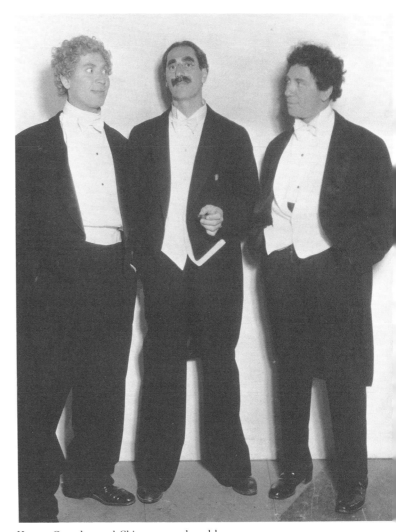

Harpo, Groucho, and Chico seem sobered by their evening dress in this publicity shot for *A Night at the Opera* (1935).

St. Helier and the Melody Maids as supporting attractions, the show being reinvigorated by the addition of Frakson, "the cigarette marvel," and other new acts in the last week. The critic of *The Times* was particularly taken with Harpo (although he was beyond identifying any of the brothers by name): "How pathetically innocuous he looks while an unending cataract of spoons falls from his sleeves!"

Under their new contract with Paramount, the Marxes had agreed to make their next picture, *Monkey Business*, in Hollywood, where the facilities were better. It is tempting to think that the recent voyage to and from England gave them the

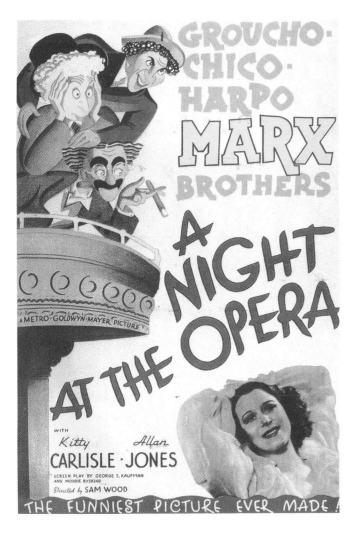

idea of setting the picture aboard an ocean liner. But it appears that Groucho had previously approached S. J. Perelman and Will B. Johnstone to come up with a fresh idea for a radio series after one of the networks had shown an interest in using Chico and him. Groucho liked the pair's suggestion of them playing stowaways living in barrels on an ocean liner and decided, with his brothers, that it would be put to better use as a movie. Paramount had agreed and signed the two writers to work in Hollywood while the Marxes played their London engagement.

The brothers headed west in February and approved the work that Perelman and Johnstone had done so far. They continued working on the script, along with Arthur Sheekman and Nat Perrin, whom Groucho had nominated to provide

some additional gags. The Marxes themselves contributed ideas, Groucho in particular recalling the protocol of life on an ocean liner and the officiousness of the passport and customs authorities.

The well-known wit, drinker, and gambler Herman J. Mankiewicz was producing the picture and Norman McLeod had been selected to direct it. A clergyman's son and former pilot who had been a writer and assistant director before becoming a director in 1928, McLeod had codirected two comedies for Paramount, *Along Came Youth* and *Finn and Hattie*, so *Monkey Business* was a big break for him. He was young and commanding enough to control the team as well as anyone could, but Groucho later labeled him "inexperienced."

While waiting to start *Monkey Business*, the Marxes made a four-minute promotional short for *The House That Shadows Built*, which was a preview of forthcoming Paramount productions of 1931. As the script wasn't ready, the Marxes dusted off the opening scene of *I'll Say She Is*, set in a theatrical agency. This time their imitations were of Maurice Chevalier (then a big star at Paramount) singing "A New Kind of Love," with Harpo dancing and whistling on his turn. This became a scene in *Monkey Business*, relocated to the customs counter, where each tries to get off the ship by presenting a passport belonging to Chevalier and claiming to be him.

Monkey Business went into production in mid-April 1931. No longer having stage-tested material to work with, the Marx Brothers found it difficult to judge how funny the material was and how long to pause for audiences to laugh. *Variety* reported in July, "It is no local secret that the Marxes have had their hands full on remakes and retakes for *Monkey Business*, with several previews necessary, because of a literal embarrassment of riches. The floundering was only natural due to the uncertainty of where and how to spot the laffs." In the end, the film's editors judged it more than well enough. Released in September 1931, *Monkey Business* was Paramount's third biggest hit of the year, surpassed only by the

Maurice Chevalier musical comedy *The Smiling Lieutenant* and the Marlene Dietrich spy opus *Dishonored*.

The team's father, "Frenchie" Marx, appeared as an extra in the docking sequence: he can be seen on shore in a white hat, behind the Marxes, when they are carried off the boat by stretcher and also on the boat itself. (An extra looking very like him features in the similar sequence in *A Night at the Opera* and has often been identified as the Marxes' father; but Frenchie died in Los Angeles on May 11, 1933, long before *Opera* was made.)

Groucho now regarded a stage production as an essential preparatory step for making a film and declared that he hoped the team would be back on Broadway at the end of the year. He, Chico, and Harpo did return to the New York stage—but only for two nights. On Thursday and Friday, August 20 and 21, they appeared at the Cohan Theatre in New York as guest stars in the cooperative revue, *Shoot the Works*. This was a gesture of friendship toward their pal Heywood Broun, newspaper columnist, card-player, and would-be politician. Broun was financing, directing, and starring in the revue, which was mostly written by Nunnally Johnson and had a cast of out-of-work actors that included George Murphy and Imogene Coca. The low-budget show was doing well enough, but the Marxes (minus Zeppo) doubled the takings for the two nights they appeared. With Margaret Irving and Leo Sorenson, they revived their Du Barry skit, waiving any fee and paying their helpers out of their own pockets. Other guest stars, including Helen Morgan, followed, and the revue seems to have had a successful limited run.

When they couldn't do a new Broadway show, the four Marxes went on another tour of the RKO circuit, beginning in October. They were receiving the phenomenal sum of $10,500 weekly, and in Columbus, Ohio, Groucho kidded the press about having a nervous breakdown over their huge salary. To meet the huge crowds there, the Marxes did an extra, fifth, show daily at the RKO Palace between showings of the film *Platinum Blonde* and took the theater's weekly takings to a new high of $27,800. In December, they were

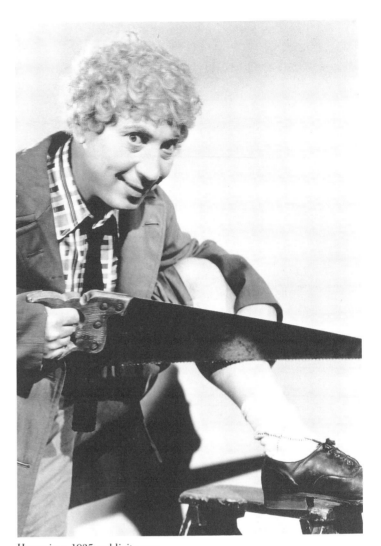

Harpo in a 1935 publicity gag.

back at the RKO Palace in Chicago, where Groucho had been when he was hospitalized a year before. Supported by the film *Fanny Foley Herself*, they brought in just under $30,000, which was only slightly over the break-even point (after paying the Marxes) but considered worthwhile for the boost it gave the theater for future weeks. They ended the year back in New York at the Brooklyn Albee and the Palace.

Since *Monkey Business* had been such a success, Paramount put the same writers, S. J. Perelman and Will B. Johnstone, and the same director, Norman McLeod, to work on another vehicle for the team under the same supervisor, Herman J. Mankiewicz. Bert Kalmar and Harry Ruby, who were now writing comedy scripts as well as songs, also collaborated on the screen-play.

The setting this time was an American college. In her book *S. J. Perelman*, Dorothy Herrmann notes:

> Since neither the Marxes nor Kalmar nor Ruby had ever attended college, it is probable that Sid, who spent most of his college years writing diatribes against university policies, contributed much of the satire on academia in *Horse Feathers*. . . . The spirit of *Horse Feathers* is pure S. J. Perelman. Only a man who was forced to endure four years in a place where he didn't fit in and that refused to graduate him could have made such devastating fun of it.

Horse Feathers started shooting in March 1932, but production had to be suspended for ten weeks after Chico was seriously injured in a car crash early in April. One of his kneecaps was shattered. When he did return to work, he was still only able to hobble around. This restricted his participation in the climactic football game, which was all that remained to be shot when production resumed on Saturday, June 18. Although a double was used in long shots, Chico can be seen limping around in the closer ones.

Harpo and Chico had their usual musical spots, but Abel Green, reviewing the film in *Variety*, noted: "The harp and piano numbers were repeated against the Marxes' personal wishes but by exhibitor demands to the studio. The piano is oke, but the harp reprise of 'Everyone Says I Love You' . . . substantiated the boys' negative opinion that that tended to slow up the comedy." Groucho was particularly opposed to these scenes, and in the film, as Chico is about to play, he tells the audience: "I've got to stay here but there's no reason why you folks shouldn't go out into the lobby until this thing blows over." It was both a joke and what he personally felt. But Groucho himself did a musical turn with the same number on the guitar.

The harp scene certainly didn't do any harm. The film was another big hit, the top attraction of August 1932, helped by a front-cover story on the team in *Time*'s August 15 issue (for which they posed in the garbage chariot used in the football climax). But the Marxes' drawing power was slipping. *Horse Feathers* was not in a list of the year's fifteen box-office champs issued by *Motion Picture Herald*, although three other Paramount pictures were: *Dr. Jekyll and Mr. Hyde* with Fredric March, *One Hour with You* with Maurice Chevalier and Jeanette MacDonald, and *Shanghai Express* with Marlene Dietrich.

On a six-week visit to England, while waiting for Chico to recuperate from his auto accident, Norman McLeod described the experience of directing two films with the Marx Brothers.

> Making comedies is difficult at any time. When the Marx Brothers are in the picture it's sheer murder. The four brothers are as irresponsible off the screen as they are on, and it's a man-sized job keeping them in order. They get the cast and the technicians into hysterics with laughter, and the whole production is held up while they recover. When we were producing a scene for *Horse Feathers*, the four were asked to be on the set at nine A.M. in makeup. Punctually they arrived dancing on to the floor—but they were wearing each other's makeup! Harpo had put on Groucho's mustache, Chico was running round crazily in Harpo's wig, while Zeppo shot off wisecracks in Chico's dialect. Most surprising things are apt to happen when they are around. When they were brought from New York to play in *Horse Feathers*, I was waiting for them in the studio to go over the story. Suddenly they all came trooping in at the door obviously bent on revelry. As soon as they saw me they shouted, "Hello, Mac!" and all four pounced on me, got me on the ground, and tore my pants off! This episode took place in the outer part of the studio, with a dozen or so amused onlookers watching the Brothers tearing round the studio waving my pants.
>
> Harpo is the quietest of the four. He is not dumb, nor is he crazy in real life. He talks comparatively little compared with the others, and has the most kindly nature imaginable. He is always ready to help people who are in trouble. He takes his harp-playing very seriously. Everywhere he goes he carries with him a

Director Sam Wood (in light suit) watches shooting of a scene from *A Night at the Opera* (1935). At far left (in round glasses) is gag man Al Boasberg.

Harpo in a publicity pose for *A Night at the Opera* (1935).

Harpo pauses during shooting of the escape from the ship's brig in *A Night at the Opera* (1935).

Long-suffering Sam Wood with Harpo and Kitty Carlisle on the set of *A Night at the Opera* (1935).

small harp with gut strings. It makes no sound, but he is continually practicing finger movements between scenes. The harp seems to help him to think, for he is nearly always playing it when engaged in serious discussion.

Groucho, the wisecracker with the black mustache, seems to be the "father" of the bunch. It is not generally known that Chico is actually the oldest. Harpo is next, and Groucho third. But Groucho keeps the others in order—as far as that is possible!

One of my greatest difficulties is getting them on the set punctually. Nothing will induce them to get up in the morning. They are always very vague in their movements, and you have to have your eyes open to keep them on the set. One day in the middle of *Monkey Business*, Zeppo came up to me after a scene and said, "You won't be wanting me for a bit, will you, Mac?" I told him he was not in that particular scene, but as he walked off something seemed a little peculiar. "Hey, Zepp," I called. "Where are you off to?" "Oh, just going up to San Francisco for a couple of weeks," he replied. In the middle of a picture—I ask you!

One of their favorite tricks is chasing girls just as they do in their films. If I can't find Chico or Harpo, and I hear shrill whoops from another part of the studio, I know what is happening. An extra girl, a typist, or anyone handy is tearing round for dear life with Chico and Harpo in full cry after her! If Chico catches her, sure enough in a couple of seconds Harpo will poke his crazy face round the corner and toot on his famous motor horn. Then the chase will start all over again.

These two have very odd likings. Nothing makes Harpo happier than to have someone stroke his hands. Chico likes his feet being rubbed! When Chico injured his knee recently I went to visit him in hospital. The first thing he said as I entered the room was, "Hello, Mac, come and rub my feet!"

The four brothers write a certain amount of dialogue for their films, and also make up a great deal of the funny business. Often they get right out of hand and run away with a scene. They forget the "business" of the scenario and carry on making up the action on the spur of the moment. I always let these scenes run until they dry up, and sometimes the funniest part of a scene has never been in the original plan. It may be a backhanded compliment, but sometimes Groucho is so funny as to be a nuisance. He goes on and on "gagging," and when we see the scene through it seems a shame to cut out so many laughs. The one thing Groucho cannot learn is to keep within the camera limits. If we are photographing a scene with the camera fairly close, and the microphone just above his head, we put chalk lines on the floor to mark the limits where he walks out of range of the camera. He gets so carried away with the scene that in a moment he has forgotten all about the chalk lines, and is bounding off across the set imitating monkeys on the furniture and fooling around yards from the camera and the mike.

They're a great bunch to work with, but they're a tough proposition. It's bad enough making a picture anyway, without having actors who steal your pants, and clamber over the camera.

Even before the release of *Horse Feathers*, Paramount was anxious to get the third film under the team's contract into production. No less a director than Ernst Lubitsch was interested in working with them. He had an idea for a scene in which Groucho would be discovered in a closet of a lady's boudoir by her husband. Asked what he was doing there, Groucho would reply that he was waiting for a streetcar, and at that very moment a streetcar would arrive for Groucho to climb aboard.

In August, Paramount announced that the Marxes' film with Lubitsch would be a burlesque of mythical kingdoms called *Oo La La*. However, the company was in bad financial shape, struggling to meet the payments to mortgage holders on the huge theater chain it had built up. Chico began considering many radio offers for Groucho and himself.

As a result, Groucho and Chico went into radio with a Monday evening half-hour show that was broadcast in the East and South on the NBC Blue Network beginning November 28, 1932. Initially

Director Sam Wood in serious mood with the Marx Brothers.

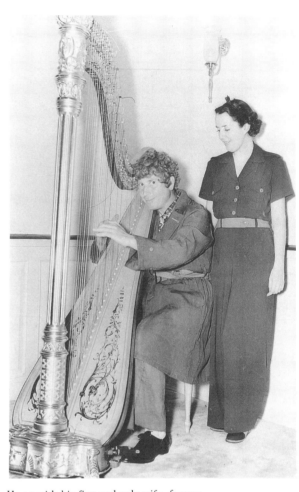

Harpo with his first and only wife, former actress Susan Fleming. They married on September 28, 1936.

Groucho, Chico, and Harpo hit the hay for a publicity shot for *A Day at the Races* (1937).

43

it was called *Beagle, Shyster, and Beagle* and starred Groucho as shyster lawyer Waldorf T. Beagle and Chico as his assistant Emmanuel Ravelli (the name he had used in *Animal Crackers*). Nat Perrin and Arthur Sheekman wrote the scripts, and Groucho and Chico shared $6,500 per episode. After three episodes, the name of the show was changed to *Flywheel, Shyster, and Flywheel* following a complaint by an attorney named Beagle. The show went out live from New York until January 1933, when the Marxes returned to Hollywood, expecting to start the new picture for Paramount, now called *Cracked Ice* and written for them by Bert Kalmar and Harry Ruby. The radio show continued to be transmitted from the West Coast.

On January 26, Paramount Publix went bankrupt and was put into equity receivership. A separate company, Paramount Productions, was formed to take over and continue the filmmaking side of its operations. The Marx Brothers suspected that they might never receive their share of profits from *Monkey Business* and *Horse Feathers*, and they refused to make the new picture on the grounds that their contract had been reassigned without their approval and they had not received an accounting of profits on the two earlier movies.

But the team was not through with pictures. The Marxes accepted an invitation from Sid Grauman to put their handprints in cement outside Grauman's Chinese Theater on February 17. They then formed The Four Marx Brothers Inc. on April 4 and announced their future plans. They would join up with a new company formed by their old Broadway producer, Sam H. Harris, along with Max Gordon, their agent, and Sam Katz, who would provide the backing. They would film the 1931 Broadway smash hit *Of Thee I Sing*. Written by George S. Kaufman and Morrie Ryskind with songs by George and Ira Gershwin, it was a musical satire on politics that made fun of the presidency, and it had won the Pulitzer Prize. The team wanted Norman McLeod to direct it. The Marxes would also star in a new Broadway show and afterward make a film of it.

Kaufman and Ryskind began writing a screen

adaptation of *Of Thee I Sing*, giving Harpo the role of a mute Vice President. Groucho and Chico went to New York in late April to continue with *Flywheel, Shyster, and Flywheel*. George Oppenheimer and Tom McKnight were now supplementary writers on the radio scripts. It was while Groucho and Chico were in the East that their father, Sam "Frenchie" Marx, died at seventy-two in Los Angeles. His body was brought to New York for the funeral.

Standard Oil decided to drop Groucho and Chico's radio show after the May 22 episode. According to Michael Barson, in his introduction to the published scripts (*Flywheel, Shyster, and Flywheel: The Marx Brothers' Lost Radio Show*), the program went out too early (7:30 P.M.) to attract a large audience. As he notes, some later episodes of the series heavily raided the earlier Marx stage shows and movies for their material, while others featured jokes that would be incorporated into their next film, *Duck Soup*, when Perrin and Sheekman provided additional dialogue. Barson interviewed Perrin, who recalled:

> We only had a couple of rehearsals for *Flywheel* on the day it was broadcast—everything was done live at the time—but Chico had trouble making even those. He'd always be late, and usually I'd have to stand in for him on the read-throughs. When he finally *did* show up, he'd be reading Ravelli's lines and Groucho would tell him to stop. "Deacon," he'd say to me—he always said I looked like a crooked deacon because of the steel-rimmed glasses I wore—"show him how the line should be read." My Italian accent was better than Chico's, you see. But Chico didn't care. All he really cared about was the horses and cards, especially bridge. He was a very undisciplined guy, but he negotiated all their deals, and he was the one who mingled with the movers and shakers.

The Marx Brothers postponed their plans for independent filmmaking and reached an agreement with Paramount to make the last film under their contract, now called *Duck Soup* (after being known as *Cracked Ice* and *Grasshoppers*).

Lubitsch was no longer available. He had turned his attention to directing *Design for Living*, from the Noël Coward play. The Marxes went after Leo McCarey, who had directed Kalmar and Ruby's previous script, *The Kid From Spain*, and who had signed with Paramount. Though McCarey's reputation as a feature film director was slight at that time, he had brought Laurel and Hardy together and supervised and directed some of their shorts. He knew comedy, and the Marx Brothers knew he did.

Shooting started on *Duck Soup* in early July. (Something of Lubitsch remained in the mythical kingdom burlesque: the name of one of the countries, Sylvania, was previously used in his 1929 musical romance, *The Love Parade*.)

The Marxes' respect for Leo McCarey did not improve their behavior. As he told *Cahiers du Cinéma*:

The most surprising thing about this film was that I managed to avoid going crazy. I really did not want to work with them: they were completely mad. It was nearly impossible to get all four of them together at the same time. One was always missing! Yes, they were the four craziest people I ever met, which didn't stop me from getting a good deal of pleasure out of shooting one or two scenes in the film. As my experience in silent films had been a very great influence, it was Harpo that I liked best. But this film wasn't ideal for me; in fact, it's the only time in my career—as far as I can remember, at least, where I had to get the humor from the dialogue: with Groucho, it was the only humor you could get. Four or five writers provided him with gags and comebacks. Personally, I didn't contribute a thing. [These are not McCarey's actual words but a translation of the French translation.]

The film brought back Margaret Dumont and dispensed with Chico and Harpo's musical interludes, coming in at a fast seventy minutes running time. It was released in November, just after the studio's latest Mae West picture, *I'm No Angel*.

Based on the Marxes' past box office perfor-mance, there were high hopes for *Duck Soup*. It started off strongly. The real fans were coming, but the general public weren't so enthusiastic. It had been booked for a four-week run at the Rivoli in New York but was taken off after a poor third week (although it did return to Loew's State for a week at Christmas). In some places—Denver, Boston, Baltimore—*Duck Soup* did big business, but it was rated a disappointment in Los Angeles, San Francisco, St. Louis, Pittsburgh, and Phila-delphia. Yet these bookings were only a letdown compared to the business racked up by the earlier Marx comedies and set against the performance of the Mae West film, which was being held over and rebooked everywhere. The runs of *Duck Soup* were still profitable, the film was still making money, and it was far from a flop, judging by these initial engagements.

After five pictures, the Marx Brothers' humor was being taken for granted. They were no longer fresh and unpredictable. The biggest audiences were flocking to fresh novelties. Mae West was the new top attraction and *I'm No Angel* Para-mount's biggest hit of the year. Emanuel Cohen, who had taken control of production at Paramount in late 1932, showed no interest in retaining the Marxes' services. Even before *Duck Soup* had opened, the team reiterated its plans for inde-pendent production with Sam H. Harris. Max Gordon had yet to join the new venture, *Of Thee I Sing* was still the most likely first picture, and the Marxes with Harris were to arrange half the financing. They would use United Artists, the haven of independent producers, as their distrib-utor.

In November, Harpo set sail for Moscow, having been invited to perform in the Soviet Union, just then being officially recognized by the United States. Giving a press conference in Moscow on December 16, he declared that the Marx Brothers' first picture for United Artists would be a Russian story "turning the five-year plan topsy-turvy." Nothing more was to be heard of this idea.

Harpo spent a month performing in Russia—a week in Leningrad, two weeks in Moscow, and a week touring the smaller cities. In Moscow, he was introduced by the eminent film director Vsevolod Pudovkin and was honored when, for his final performance, the foreign minister, Maxim Litvinoff, became his straight man, shaking Harpo by the hand to dislodge the cascade of knives from his sleeve. Besides the knife-dropping routine, Harpo blew bubbles from a clarinet, did his letter-ripping and ink-drinking routine from *The Cocoanuts*, and, of course, his harp solo. He docked in New York on January 9, 1934, passing Chico in mid-ocean on his way to perform in London.

The Marxes' plans for independent film production remained in embryo—once described by Groucho as "a small town on the outskirts of wishful thinking." Lack of finance was undoubtedly the main problem. For a year or more, the team's careers faltered.

In March 1934, Zeppo decided it was time to quit and became an agent. Understandably dissatisfied with his meager roles, he had talked of leaving for several years. He had joined the team too late to establish a distinctive comic contribution of his own, if indeed there had ever been room for one.

In the same month, Groucho and Chico began a new radio series called *The Marx of Time* for Amoco, in which they made satirical comments on news events around the world. Groucho was Ulysses H. Drivel, an "eagle-eyed newshound," while Chico played a character called Penelli. This was broadcast from New York on Sunday nights but lasted only seven or eight weeks.

In July, Gummo came from New York (where he had been in the garment industry) to join Zeppo in Los Angeles and take care of Groucho, Harpo, and Chico's affairs within the new agency.

While in the East, Groucho played the leading role in a summer stock revival of Ben Hecht and Charles MacArthur's hit comedy *Twentieth Century*. It was a discreet test of his ability to perform roles outside his familiar character. Groucho's portrayal of the conniving, penniless Broadway producer Oscar Jaffe was at the Lakewood Playhouse, Skowhegan, Maine, opening on August 13 following a week of rehearsals. (John Barrymore had played Jaffe in the just-released film version.)

It was at this lull in the Marxes' careers that Chico's contacts with leading figures in the film world really paid off. He often played bridge with Irving G. Thalberg, the noted young Metro-Goldwyn-Mayer producer whose image was that of a refined and serious filmmaker (although his current schedule included an adventure melodrama called *China Seas* as well as *Mutiny on the Bounty*). What he was not noted for was an interest in comedy or comedians.

However, Thalberg told Chico what the Marx Brothers were doing wrong. They were using poor material, making hodgepodge, patchwork movies that were badly paced and didn't appeal to women. Thalberg declared that the boys needed to become more sympathetic, have the audience rooting for them, appear in believable plots supported by a romance and musical numbers that would attract females. Even more important, Thalberg was prepared to put his ideas into practice and make pictures with them at MGM, despite the objections of studio chief Louis B. Mayer, who thought the Marxes were all washed up. Thalberg offered the team a three-picture contract with the added inducement of a fifteen percent share of the gross. They jumped at it, signing on the dotted line on September 19, 1934.

When Groucho, Harpo, and Chico went to discuss Thalberg's ideas with him in more detail, they were kept waiting for four hours before the appointment was rescheduled for the next day. Thalberg then saw them an hour late and promised not to keep them waiting in future. When he next did so, according to legend, they tried to teach him a lesson by lighting cigars and blowing smoke under his door until he appeared to see if there was a fire, and on another occasion they barricaded his door with filing cabinets and desks so that he couldn't get out. After that, he began story conferences with them on time, but then disappeared to deal with an urgent matter on another picture and did not return for hours. One time, when he finally arrived back at his office, he found the three Marxes sitting naked on the floor, roasting potatoes on a big blaze they had started in his fireplace. He laughed and phoned the commissary to send up some butter.

Essentially, Thalberg was proposing a return to the musical comedy format of *The Cocoanuts* and *Animal Crackers*, but with a stronger plot and more believable characters, including those played by the Brothers. He called together all his writers and asked them for a fresh idea for a Marx comedy. James Kevin McGuinness, who had been working on *China Seas*, suggested that the appeal of the Marxes lay in the way they attacked dignity, and nothing in the United States was more dignified than the Metropolitan Opera House. Thalberg, delighted at the suggestion, put McGuinness to work developing a storyline in which the Marxes created havoc at the opera. When he had finished, Thalberg gave his outline first to Bert Kalmar and Harry Ruby, who knocked it into some sort of comic shape, then turned to the writers of earlier Marx Brothers hits, George S. Kaufman and Morrie Ryskind.

When the first draft of the screenplay was turned in, Groucho became nervous, reminding Thalberg that the team's first two films from shows by Kaufman and Ryskind had been such hits because the gags had been thoroughly tested before a live audience. Since *Monkey Business*, he had wanted to pretest their film material before audiences. It is to Thalberg's credit that not only did he agree with Groucho but he enthusiastically arranged for the team to take five major comedy scenes from the script and play them as a stage show in movie houses. This was a completely new idea, expensive and complicated to arrange, but it was a good business proposition. The Marx Brothers recovered most of the cost by drawing huge audiences at higher than usual prices while the publicity for the forthcoming picture was invaluable.

Following a month of rehearsals on the MGM lot, a four-week tour on the West Coast of *A Night at the Opera* started at the Salt Lake City Orpheum on April 13, 1935, and then visited Seattle, Portland, and Santa Barbara. The Marxes performed a seventy-five-minute show four times a day between a movie presentation. Including musical interludes, it had twelve scenes in all.

The threesome was supported by Allan Jones, who had been assigned the romantic lead after a small singing role in Jean Harlow's *Reckless*, but the other principal players in a cast of forty were not used in the film (they included the blonde Dorothy Christie in the Margaret Dumont role and Dewey Robinson as the detective Henderson).

The show opened with Groucho and Dorothy Christie in a stage box. Groucho's first line was "Well, toots, how do you like the show?" As he later reminisced: "I was understandably nervous the opening afternoon and it didn't come out quite that way. There was a slight variation and about an eight-minute laugh because she had very large breasts. It wasn't done deliberately. I stumbled over the word. It took some time before we could get the show going."

Morrie Ryskind watched all the performances with Al Boasberg, who was a renowned specialist at adding gags. Laughter was timed with a stopwatch to see how long the audience needed to respond to each joke. In a generally favorable review of the production at Salt Lake City, it is interesting to read: "During one scene, the steerage deck on board the ship, Chico and Harpo perform on the piano and harp to the great delight of the audience. It was only after repeated encores that the show was permitted to continue." This does indicate that the musical interludes, dropped from *Duck Soup*, were appreciated by audiences.

One sequence that wasn't working at all well, the overcrowded stateroom, had started out as one of Al Boasberg's ideas. At one point, the writers were going to drop it entirely, but Thalberg had it retained, declaring that it was difficult to make the scene work convincingly on stage with simple flatdrops to represent the setting. The Marxes kept trying variations. Early in the scene as subsequently filmed, Groucho orders two fried eggs, two poached eggs, two scrambled eggs, and

Maureen O'Sullivan and Allan Jones pose with the three Marx Brothers on the set of *A Day at the Races* (1937).

Harpo demonstrates the gookie on the set of *A Day at the Races* (1937).

Harpo and Chico receive last minute instructions before a take on *A Day at the Races* (1937).

two medium-boiled eggs for the stowaways in his stateroom from a steward in the corridor outside. "And two hard-boiled eggs," calls out Chico. Not to be outdone, Harpo sounds his horn. "Make that three hard-boiled eggs," amends Groucho. It was Chico and Harpo's additions that made it work. The audience roared with laughter. (The additions had antecedents. In *Monkey Business*, when Groucho ordered the captain's lunch, Chico added: "Hey, two." And, in *Duck Soup*, when Groucho radios for help and adds, "If you can't send help, send two more women," Harpo holds up three fingers, and Groucho changes the request to "Send *three* more women.")

A cut sequence from *A Day at the Races* (1937) in which Chico and Harpo respond as bellboys to Groucho's call for a bottle of Scotch to share with his midnight date, Flo Marlowe. Harpo created havoc by squirting the seltzer everywhere. The scene was replaced by that in which Chico masquerades as a house detective with Harpo as his assistant.

Groucho (lower left) jokes with Carole Lombard at a gathering of the new stars of radio's *The Circle* in early 1939. Also seen: Cary Grant, Lawrence Tibbett, Chico, and Ronald Colman.

Thalberg and director Sam Wood came to watch the show during its final week in Santa Barbara. Wood was an experienced director with no great reputation for comedy; but he knew how to put a picture together, and he had twenty takes done each time to make sure of a shot that worked. Al Boasberg was watching as well when shooting started on June 3 to ensure that the full comic potential of every scene was realized. According to Groucho and Harpo, Sam Wood's sole instruction to them on every take was: "I want you to go in there and sell 'em a load of clams." As usual for a director of a Marx picture, Wood had to endure a lot of horseplay. Walter Woolf King, who played the villainous Lassparri, recalled:

Sam Wood was a hell of a nice guy, but they made his life miserable. I don't think he even wanted to do the picture. He was under contract to Metro and he had just a hell of a time with them, because they were never around when he wanted them or was ready to shoot. Chico would be over in the dressing room with a dame or

Cut section from the wallpapering scene in *A Day at the Races* (1937) in which Chico covered Esther Muir (as Flo Marlowe) in paste. Apparently, Muir retired from the screen shortly after this film.

49

Groucho would be some place else and he couldn't get them to cooperate.

For Kitty Carlisle, the film's leading lady, the Marx Brothers

> were very serious and they were big worriers. Groucho would come up to me from time to time and ask me, "Is this funny?" Then, totally deadpan, he'd try out a line. I'd say, "No, I don't think it is funny," and he'd go away absolutely crushed and try it out on everyone else in the cast. Harpo would work well until about eleven o'clock. Then he'd stretch out on the nearest piece of furniture and start calling at the top of his voice, "Lunchie! Lunchie!" The only one that didn't worry was Chico. He was always in his dressing room when it was time to film a scene, either with a card game or a lady . . . *any* lady.

Allan Jones remembered Chico as the main source of trouble:

> We never could find him when it was time to shoot a scene, and usually he was found on the phone making bets, or playing pinochle with some of the stage hands on the set. He was always in bed. . . . But with all that he was a lovable person.

Besides Wood, the other actors were butts of the team's practical jokes. Allan Jones recalled that on the first day of shooting they sent two dozen roses to Kitty Carlisle, C.O.D. from him. And Walter Woolf King remembered an incident from the film's climax: "We had a scene where I got in the box on the stage. They had it on a rope and it just flew up in the air. So they started to take my pants off in the box. I had to fight for my life! It was all done in fun, but they were quite a group."*

The Marx Brothers' irreverence extended to the studio trademark of Leo the Lion roaring inside the scroll labeled "Ars Gratia Artis." However, they were only allowed to kid it for the trailer—in

*These quotes are from interviews in *The Freedonia Gazette*.

which first Groucho replaced the lion with dubbed roars as he opened his mouth, then Chico, and then Harpo, whose mouthings are silent until he has a brainwave and sounds his motor-car horn instead.

A Night at the Opera became a smash hit in November 1935, and the Marx Brothers were truly back in the motion picture business. Part of the film's drawing power must be attributed to the immense popularity of "Alone," which became the only hit song ever introduced by a Marx picture. With the huge number of extras in many scenes, *A Night at the Opera* had been an expensive production, shooting for fifty-five days and costing $1,057,000. According to Sam Marx, the studio's story editor of the time (and no relation to the brothers), it made only a modest profit of $90,000 from its first five years of worldwide release. (This jumped to $661,000 following a 1948–49 reissue.)

While the stage tryouts had indicated what was funny, the attempt to build in pauses to accommodate audience laughter was probably a waste of time. *Variety*'s reviewer, who evidently liked the film well enough to see it twice, specifically commented on this with regard to Groucho's lines: "The impossibility of timing gags for the screen to perfection was shown at the Capitol [New York] where, on two different shows, the audience responded in a different manner."

Had Groucho, Harpo, and Chico missed Zeppo? In its issue of November 25, 1935, the *Hollywood Reporter* reported: "The Marx Brothers in all seriousness proposed yesterday to Alexander Woollcott that he become the fourth Marx Brother in their next MGM picture. Woollcott ponders."

Around this time, surrealist Salvador Dali sketched images for an imaginary Marx Brothers picture called *Giraffes on Horseback Salad*. He had befriended Harpo and presented him with a harp that had barbed-wire strings.

After *A Night at the Opera*, the Marxes were next seen in separate, minor screen appearances.

Harpo appeared in an MGM short in Technicolor, *La Fiesta de Santa Barbara*. This was a nineteen-minute musical revue, built around the Santa Barbara Mission at fiesta time, that also featured such stars as Gary Cooper, Robert Taylor, Warner Baxter, Leo Carrillo, Edmund Lowe, and Buster Keaton.

In May 1936, Groucho and Charlie Ruggles were sunbathing on the beach in Coronado when a Paramount film crew turned up to shoot a scene for a gangsters-and-gambling tale, called *Yours for the Asking*, which starred George Raft, Ida Lupino, and Dolores Costello. The unit wanted to shoot where Groucho and Ruggles were sitting. They couldn't be bothered to move and so became unpaid background extras.

Chico made a brief appearance as himself in a fictional short, *Hollywood—The Second Step*, an MGM one-reeler about a young actress trying to succeed in Hollywood.

After seeing the warm response to *A Night at the Opera*, the MGM top brass wanted a second Marx Brothers picture put into production quickly, in the spring of 1936. Thalberg had several major productions claiming his attention: *Romeo and Juliet*, *The Good Earth*, and *Camille*. But he started the ball rolling.

Will B. Johnstone, signed to develop a story for the Marxes, arrived from New York in mid-December 1935. Carey Wilson and George Oppenheimer were put to work with Johnstone. Because of the urgency, Harpo cancelled a European trip and came out from New York to discuss the new project before Christmas. Groucho called off his vacation plans to join the talks. Chico was, as usual, nowhere to be found. Before the year ended, George Seaton and Robert Pirosh, two young writers who had done a final polish on the romantic scenes of *A Night at the Opera*, had also been put on the film, which was given the temporary title of *Step This Way*.

It was Seaton and Pirosh who suggested a sanitarium as a suitable arena for Marxian antics. Thalberg liked the idea but wanted a contrast, which was provided by the racetrack sequences. This was the start of *A Day at the Races*.

There were limits on the kind of material Thalberg would allow. George Oppenheimer, in his reminiscences, *The View From the Sixties*, recalled a satirical opening scene he devised with Seaton and Pirosh that Thalberg vetoed:

This was the time of the wholesale invasion of America by Austrian and German psychoanalysts, all of whom claimed to have been students of Freud. We decided to open the picture with a convention of Austrian analysts in a hotel ballroom. When we meet them, they are bearded, in white coats with stethoscopes about their necks, waltzing with one another to the strains of "The Blue Danube." Then Groucho, an American quack, aptly named Dr. Quackenbush, calls the meeting to order and addresses it. The medical business, he tells them, has been rotten—and why? Because doctors have been wasting too much time looking for cures rather than new diseases. Now he personally has invented a disease that will increase business overwhelmingly. He has called it "Rittenhouse" after his sponsor, benefactor and perpetual patient, Mrs. Rittenhouse. He introduces Margaret Dumont . . . [and] then proceeds to describe the symptoms of his disease in such lurid detail that Mrs. Rittenhouse faints. Hastily Groucho cries out to the assembled quacks, "Is there a doctor in the house?" A man rises in the rear of the hall to announce that he is a doctor. Groucho looks at him indignantly and orders, "Throw that man out."

To Thalberg, the humor was too sophisticated for a mass audience. Clearly times had changed. The sequence parallels in spirit the opening scenes of *Horse Feathers* and *Duck Soup* and would have caused no problem during their Paramount period.

Another change was necessary for legal reasons. The name Quackenbush had to be altered to Hackenbush because, surprising as it seems, the country was teeming with doctors called Quackenbush but none called Hackenbush.

Once again Thalberg encouraged the Marxes to take highlights of the script on the road, this time to the Midwest, opening at Duluth's Lyceum on July 14, 1936, after two weeks of rehearsals in Los Angeles. The trio was accompanied by Mar-

Groucho and Chico in conference with Buster Keaton who contributed gag ideas to *At the Circus* (1939).

Chico, Harpo, and Groucho in a publicity shot for *At the Circus* (1939).

Groucho poses with uncle Al Shean during a break in shooting *At the Circus* (1939). Shean appeared in several MGM films of this period: *Love, Love and Learn; Too Hot to Handle; The Great Waltz; Joe and Ethel Turp Call on the President;* and *Broadway Serenade.*

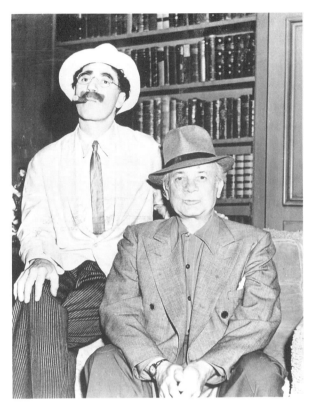

Chico watches as director Edward Buzzell demonstrates a dance movement with Margaret Dumont on the set of *At the Circus* (1939).

It was Margaret Dumont who was actually fired from a cannon in *At the Circus* (1939) but MGM put out this publicity shot featuring Groucho in his ceiling-walking outfit with Florence Rice, Harpo, and Chico.

This shot sums up the essence of the opening scene *Go West* (1940) in which Groucho is swindled by the combined force of Chico and Harpo.

garet Dumont but neither of the film's romantic leads, Allan Jones and Maureen O'Sullivan, went along. Gagman Al Boasberg made notes at all the performances. The hour of scenes from *A Day at the Races* ended up at the Golden Gate Theater in San Francisco in mid-August.

Once again the writers and performers learned by trial and error. As Lawrence Weingarten, one of Thalberg's production staff, recalled in a contemporary article:

> Groucho's creative methods are peculiar. He repeats his wisecracks over and over again until, slightly different each time, they assume a final form. The historic example of this occurred in *A Day at the Races*. Groucho took off his watch, preparatory to washing his hands, and placed it on a nearby table. Seeing someone glance at it, he picked it up and dropped it in the water. The first time he exclaimed, "Better have it rusty than lost," but when we tried this out it didn't get the reception we expected. He changed it to: "Better have it rusty than stolen," but that was still unsatisfactory. It was only really satisfactory when it assumed the final layout: "Better have it rusty than missing."

Shooting started on September 3, with Sam Wood again in the director's chair and Al Boasberg advising on what timing had worked best on the stage tour. Then Thalberg, whose health had always been precarious owing to a weak heart,

Groucho in his going West outfit from *Go West* (1940). He was repeatedly called for costume tests while MGM delayed production.

Chico and Harpo on the train during the climax of *Go West* (1940).

caught a cold which developed into pneumonia. He died at 10:16 A.M. on Wednesday, September 16. He was thirty-seven. Sam Wood broke the news to the cast and crew on the set of *A Day at the Races*.

Production was as chaotic as ever. As the film's cameraman Joseph Ruttenberg has recalled:

Oh God, the Marx Brothers were difficult! For one thing, you never knew what they were going to do, so you had to have a camera on each one of them. With the long-shot camera, that added up to four cameras and lighting for four cameras is pretty dull. And they never did anything the same way twice, so matching shots were impossible. They drove the director crazy. They were fun, too. Harpo was a bookmaker on the side and would try to drum up business among the crew. He came to me and asked me if I wanted to bet. Won every single time! He must have been sorry he mentioned it after a while. Groucho was very quiet offstage, serious, and Chico chased girls.

Thalberg's guidance was missed in the final editing stage. The musical interlude at the water carnival is far too protracted, helping to make the film noticeably longer than *A Night at the Opera* despite the regrettable elimination of Groucho's introductory song, "Dr. Hackenbush," by Kal-

The three Marx Brothers with romantic leads Diana Lewis and John Carroll in a publicity pose for *Go West* (1940).

mar and Ruby. (Fortunately, Groucho later performed the song for a record.)

A Day at the Races was released in June and did good business, but nothing like that achieved by *A Night at the Opera*. The earlier film had introduced a new kind of Marx comedy, but *Races* was simply copying the formula.

In *The Marx Brothers Scrapbook*, Groucho told

Richard Anobile: "When Thalberg died, at that moment I knew that the Marx Brothers wouldn't make any more good pictures because the people who would replace Thalberg were second-rate talents. Yeah, he was good. He was the only first-class producer Hollywood ever had." In fact, the Marx Brothers had been among the stars he wanted to keep under personal contract for the independent company he was about to establish at MGM.

Another significant loss came with the death at forty-five of Al Boasberg, on June 18, 1937, from a heart attack. At the time of his death, Boasberg had embroiled Groucho and Chico in a plagiarism suit. The brothers were found guilty by a jury of copyright infringement in using material from two other writers in a September 1936 radio broadcast. Groucho and Chico claimed the script had been supplied by Boasberg as his own work. Faced with the possibility of a year's imprisonment, they asked the court's advice on the best jails. They were each fined $1,000.

Groucho's own writing activities had resulted in a new film called *The King and the Chorus Girl*, released by Warner Bros. in March 1937. He had done the screenplay with Norman Krasna much earlier (it had been optioned by Paramount in 1935), but it now had added spice in mimicking the event that had rocked the British monarchy: the abdication of King Edward VIII to marry Mrs. Simpson. The film, produced and directed by Mervyn LeRoy, depicted a king (played by French star Fernand Gravet) who married a commoner (Joan Blondell), and it featured a singer under contract to LeRoy named Kenny Baker. Some of the advertising carried a small picture of Groucho's face with cigar surrounded by the words "He wrote it!" (The Marx Brothers were a great favorite of Edward when he was the Prince of Wales—perhaps because of the running joke in *The Cocoanuts*—and, during the period of official mourning on the death of his father, Edward had slipped surreptitiously into a box to watch Harpo perform in London, and then invited him to a reception. Groucho told reporters in Chicago in July 1936 that he and his brothers

hoped to be in London for Edward's coronation. *The King and the Chorus Girl* was too sensitive to be shown in Britain for several years and even then had to be released under a change of title as *Romance Is Sacred*.)

Without Thalberg, the Marxes were unsure of the next step. There was an enticing proposition to work with proven stage material (even if they had not been the ones to prove its worth). In October 1937, they reached an agreement with RKO Radio to make film versions of two Broadway hits, the current *Room Service* and—not forgotten from their earlier plans for independent production—Kaufman and Ryskind's *Of Thee I Sing*. RKO paid the then record sum of $255,000 for the screen rights to *Room Service* (it remained the all-time high for the studio). Zeppo negotiated a fee of $250,000 plus a percentage for the team's services, with a further $350,000 for *Of Thee I Sing*.

A farce by John Murray and Allen Boretz, *Room Service* had opened on Broadway on May 19, 1937, and become a smash hit, going on to rack up five hundred performances. Staged by George Abbott, it concerned the efforts of a penniless theatrical producer (played by Sam Levene) to put on a play by a new young author (Eddie Albert) and keep his cast together in a hotel despite efforts to evict them made by the hotel chief (Donald MacBride).

The Marxes insisted that Morrie Ryskind adapt the play for them. As Ryskind told Richard Anobile in *The Marx Brothers Scrapbook*,

I had misgivings about this because, and I explained this to them, I felt the only good things for the team were those things written expressly for them. I told them I wasn't sure if I could shape the play to their characters. In itself it was a very funny play but their characters had to be there, for I knew that when an audience came to see the Marx Brothers, it was them they came to see, not a film.

Ryskind would seem to have been an ideal choice, having contributed so much to *The Cocoanuts*, *Animal Crackers*, and *A Night at the*

Opera, but a comparison of the stage and screen versions of *Room Service* shows that surprisingly little change was actually made.

Shooting took place in the summer of 1938 and was completed by July 30. The film was released at the end of September. With the Marxes playing actual characters, it was neither a real Marx Brothers comedy nor a real version of the hit play, and this clearly put off much of the potential audience for each. With the huge cost of the play and the Marx Brothers, the budget had exceeded $1.5 million. RKO took a loss of $340,000. (The studio did get further mileage out of the play by turning it into the 1944 Frank Sinatra musical, *Step Lively*. Though the play is often revived on the stage, it has never been filmed straight.)

Groucho concluded: "It was the first time we had tried doing a play we hadn't created ourselves. And we were no good. We can't do that. We've got to originate the characters and the situations ourselves. Then we can do them. Then they're us. But we can't do gags or play characters that aren't ours. We tried it, and we'll never do it again."

RKO had been nervous about proceeding with *Of Thee I Sing*, which would have needed a big budget, and which, as an American political satire, would have had even more dubious appeal abroad than at home. In late August 1938, Zeppo Marx, through his agency, lined up MGM to take over the rights for a reported $100,000, but this was before the poor box office response to *Room Service* was evident. The whole idea was dropped. (There never would be a film of that musical.)

Groucho and Chico next became involved in a new one-hour Sunday radio series called *The Circle*, which was first broadcast on NBC's Red Network on January 15, 1939. Besides the two Marxes, this involved several stars—such as Carole Lombard, Cary Grant, Ronald Colman, and Lawrence Tibbett—in partly scripted, partly ad-libbed debates on subjects of general interest. The Marxes were so adept at this that they remained with the show until the following July, unlike others who weren't so quick off the mark. It was too intelligent to draw good ratings, while the

high cost of the stars was another factor in its termination before the full year originally envisaged.

The Marxes now had a new friend at MGM—Mervyn LeRoy, who had made *The King and the Chorus Girl* and, far more notably, such crime dramas as *Little Caesar*, *I Am a Fugitive From a Chain Gang*, and *They Won't Forget*. LeRoy had been lured to MGM at double his previous salary from Warner Bros. to give up directing and become a production executive. He persuaded the Marxes to sign a new three-picture contract with MGM for $250,000 per picture.

LeRoy was no Thalberg. He produced four films at MGM before deciding he wanted to go back to directing. Two of these—*Dramatic School* and *Stand Up and Fight*—have been justly forgotten. The last was *The Wizard of Oz*, and the first was the Marx Brothers comedy *At the Circus*, which was filmed as *A Day at the Circus*, undergoing a title change in post-production. LeRoy assigned the screenplay to a young writer he had under personal contract—Irving Brecher, who had written radio scripts for Al Jolson, Milton Berle, and others, and had begun his film career contributing additional dialogue to LeRoy's last Warners picture, *Fools for Scandal*. LeRoy also put his singing discovery, Kenny Baker, into the new production.

Brecher clearly used *A Day at the Races* as the model for his situations and characterizations. His one-man efforts were deemed satisfactory for production (presumably by LeRoy): there was no teaming of writers as on all the Marxes' previous pictures, and no stage tour to test the key scenes as on their last two at MGM. Harpo did contribute some ideas for his own role, and MGM assigned Buster Keaton as a gag man to punch up his scenes. The Great Stone Face's suggestions, more suited to his own style of humor, didn't work.

Chosen to direct *At the Circus* was Edward Buzzell, a former musical comedy star who had sometimes worked on the same bills as the Marxes in vaudeville and who first came to the movies as a performer. He had begun directing himself in comedy shorts, given up performing, and become a feature director. That Buzzell's best-known works are *At the Circus* and the next Marx picture, *Go West*, says enough about his other pictures.

Shooting of *At the Circus* was completed on July 14, 1939, and it came out in October. Groucho privately regarded it as a turkey. In a letter to his friend Arthur Sheekman, he confided: "I saw [*At the Circus*] the other day and didn't care much for it. I realize I'm not much of a judge but I'm kind of sick of the whole thing and, on leaving the theater, vowed that I'd never see it again. I don't feel that way about all of our pictures: *A Night at the Opera*, for example, I always enjoyed looking at and, to a lesser degree, *A Day at the Races*, but the rest sicken me and I'll stay clear of them in the future." Groucho's remarks—dismissive of all his Paramount films—serve to indicate how much he had valued Thalberg, and how badly off he felt without him.

The team's next film, *Go West*, had its origins in a Bert Kalmar and Harry Ruby script that placed the brothers in a rodeo setting. This had been in progress for Irving G. Thalberg, but work was stopped after his death. Kalmar and Ruby were now brought back to do some more work on the script, but it was scrapped. Irving Brecher then wrote a new screenplay using a period Wild West setting.

The producer this time was Jack Cummings. At one point the team was going to have a new director as well, the young S. Sylvan Simon, but Edward Buzzell was eventually brought in again.

Groucho, not at all happy with the script, persuaded MGM to test the material on the road. In late April 1940, the Marxes took scenes from *Go West* to theaters in Joliet, Toledo, Detroit, Chicago, and Los Angeles, playing five performances a day, with Irving Brecher and a new writer, Nat Perrin, clocking the shows and making overnight changes.

Shooting was due to start on July 1, 1940, but studio jitters caused a postponement. Groucho wrote to Arthur Sheekman, "I read the script and I don't blame them. If they were smart, they'd pay

us off. . . ." Production finally got underway in August.

Edward Buzzell found working with the team difficult. "They didn't have any enthusiasm at all," he told British interviewer Barry Norman in 1979. "It was just a case of money. They got the money and they made the picture, that's all there was to it. And they ran around like little pixies. But they weren't pixies any longer—they were old men trying to be pixies."

Groucho was looking forward to the end of their MGM contract. He told a reporter, "*Go West* is probably our next to last picture together. I've been acting for a long time and it's been fun, but now we feel like we'd like to do something on our own. Harpo may go on a lecture tour and Chico may take out a band. I hope to keep occupied in various ways."

In fact, Groucho was working on a play with Norman Krasna. Harpo's plans were for a concert tour with his friend Oscar Levant.

The Marx Brothers completed their three-picture contract at MGM with *The Big Store*. The film gave them a new director, Charles Riesner; a whole new team of writers; and another change of producer. Riesner had worked with Chaplin and Keaton (though not for some time).

The Marxes had to share above-the-title billing with singer Tony Martin (at least he came second). The changes did rescue the trio from the depths touched by substantial parts of *Go West*, and it reunited them with Margaret Dumont.

The story came from Nat Perrin and revived the department store setting of an episode of the radio show *Flywheel, Shyster, and Flywheel* (on which Perrin had worked), retaining the same names for Groucho's and Chico's characters—except that Groucho's Waldorf T. Flywheel here becomes Wolf J. Flywheel (Chico's name, Ravelli, originated in *Animal Crackers*, of course). The script came from three writers called Sid Kuller, Ray Golden, and Hal Fimberg. It took almost a year before their work was okayed for shooting.

The title was originally *Step This Way*—which seems to have been temporary until something better came along, having also been assigned to *A*

Day at the Races in the early stages. It was replaced, for a while, by *Bargain Basement*, but that sounded too cheap for an MGM picture and the more spectacular-sounding *The Big Store* was devised. This time, there would be no testing of the material on the road.

Principal photography was completed on April 16, 1941. A depressed Groucho was soon writing to Arthur Sheekman

> . . . we previewed the picture twice—the first time, it went fairly well; then they took out nine hundred feet, previewed it again and it flopped. They are now straightening out the story (this they do with every picture after a preview)—they imagine the audience hasn't laughed because the plot wasn't understood. The fact of the matter is, the audience hasn't laughed because they didn't understand the jokes! However, this is my farewell, and regardless of what the future holds in store for me, I'm happy to escape from this kind of picture, for the character I'm playing I now find wholly repulsive.

He told the press the team had made its last film and was surprisingly frank about it. "When I say we're sick of movies, what I mean is that people are about to get sick of us. By getting out now we're just anticipating public demand and by a very short margin. Our stuff is stale. So are we."

MGM made ingenious use of the team's departure to promote the film. The trailer opens with veteran character actor Henry O'Neill, the embodiment of an official spokesman, facing the camera from behind a desk and announcing: "The Marx Brothers are retiring from the silver screen." Groucho then appears, adding: "That's right, folks, we're on our way." Chico chips in with: "That's right, folks, but where do we go from here?" Harpo emerges from under the desk honking his horn. "And so, to all of you, a fond farewell!" cries Groucho and the three of them wave to the camera. Faint cries of "No! No!" draw them to the window—cut to a huge stock-shot crowd waving. Groucho says, "We didn't know you cared!" Then they preview *The Big Store*, a farewell present to their multitude of fans.

Groucho, Harpo, and Margaret Dumont in a publicity pose for *The Big Store* (1941).

Harpo and Groucho pose with director Charles Riesner during production of *The Big Store* (1941).

Harpo, Groucho, and Margaret Dumont in *The Big Store* (1941).

Harpo made a brief appearance in *Stage Door Canteen* (1943). The soldier is unidentified but the woman is Virginia Field.

Harpo and Lucille Ball rehearsing a routine for a Hollywood Bond Cavalcade variety show as part of the Third War Loan drive in 1943. (In 1955, Harpo would guest on *I Love Lucy* with Lucille Ball.)

Chico, Groucho, and Harpo together again and apparently singing in this group portrait for *A Night in Casablanca* (1946).

Lois Collier and Harpo from *A Night in Casablanca* (1946).

Groucho was right about anticipating public demand. *The Big Store* did what *Variety* summarized as "n.s.g." (not so good) business in its opening week in mid-June 1941: "San Francisco gave it $12,000, meager; Lincoln, disappointing $3,300; Cleveland, so-so $9,000; Providence, fairish $11,000; Buffalo, mild $10,000, and

Pittsburgh, passable $11,500. Exception is Kansas City, where it did over-average at $8,700, supported by the new *Blondie in Society* and Penny Singleton in person on opening days."

MGM therefore had no pressing reason to urge the Marxes to make more films. They had been superseded in audience favor by newer faces: in the same week that *The Big Store* opened, Abbott and Costello were drawing huge crowds to *In the Navy*, and Bob Hope's *Caught in the Draft* was shaping up as a hit. Abbott and Costello's appeal was described as "miraculous" by *Variety* at the end of the year, reviewing their performance in not only *In the Navy* but *Buck Privates*, *Hold That Ghost*, and *Keep 'Em Flying*. Besides *Draft*, Hope had two other smash hits in 1941: *Nothing But the Truth* and *Road to Zanzibar*. Of the older guard, only Chaplin still drew crowds by making his latest film, *The Dictator*, a special event. But the Marxes lacked Chaplin's determination and willpower to continue their screen careers.

And so the three of them went their separate ways. The split-up put the most pressure on Chico. Groucho and Harpo had amassed enough money not to need to work, but for Chico it was different. Having gambled away all his income, he had to keep on working.

He went east to form a band and toured the country, performing a punishing schedule of one-night stands and longer engagements, often a week at movie houses that specialized in live shows with minor picture presentations. Chico remembered his band's debut in Brooklyn in January 1942: "There I was, with sixteen other guys, but I certainly felt lonesome. Every fifteen seconds I'd think I was hearing Harpo blowing that automobile horn, and every other fifteen seconds I'd wish he was." There was a featured male vocal quartet that was billed variably as the Chicolets or the Ravellis.

In *Growing Up With Chico*, his daughter, Maxine Marx, declared:

> The band was a good vehicle for his talents. He would come on stage, tell a joke or two, and then introduce the show. During the course of the

Harpo, Groucho, and Chico pose on the set of *A Night in Casablanca* (1946).

Sig Ruman and Harpo from *A Night in Casablanca* (1946).

program, he would shuffle toward the center spotlight, pretend to conduct the band, tell a few more jokes, take out a banana and start to eat it, and wind up with a solo number. The solo was what the audience generally waited around for, and they loved it: ten unadulterated minutes of Chico shooting the keys and singing the old songs.

Still, it was a punishing routine for a man in his mid-fifties, exacerbated by his other routine of all-night card playing. And even when he could have been relaxing, he entertained the troops at military bases.

In 1944, he dropped the band to costar with Jay C. Flippen in a new revue called *Slap Happy*, which opened at Ford's Theater in Baltimore on May 7 and played in Pittsburgh before a three-week run in Philadelphia. There, in response to mixed reviews, several changes were made to the supporting acts, and the show was retitled *Take a Bow*. As *Take a Bow*, it opened on Broadway at the Broadhurst Theater on June 15 but closed after only twelve performances.

Harpo made his debut as an actor in summer stock playing a version of himself. This was for a production of *The Man Who Came to Dinner*, the 1939 hit comedy by George S. Kaufman and Moss Hart in which an acid-tongued celebrity called Sheridan Whiteside (based on Alexander Woollcott) breaks his leg on a lecture tour and becomes an unwelcome guest in an ordinary home. Another character, Beverly Carlton, was based on Noël Coward, while the frenetic Banjo was a caricature of Harpo. For the week of July 28, 1941, at the Bucks County Playhouse, in New Hope, Pennsylvania, Kaufman played Whiteside, Moss Hart appeared as Carlton, and Harpo—speaking lines for the first time since early vaudeville days—was Banjo.

Woollcott himself was busy trying to reawaken interest in a 1912 play, *The Yellow Jacket*, a story of Chinese life which used the stylized conventions of Chinese theatre. Woollcott was the Chorus and he summoned Harpo to appear as the supposedly invisible Property Man for the week of

August 11, 1941, at the North Shore Playhouse in Marblehead, Massachusetts. Harpo was required to change the sets and props and do special effects (like tossing confetti into the air to indicate snow) in front of the audience. The production starred Fay Wray (in dual roles as the heroine, Plum Blossom, and the hero's mother) and Alfred Drake.

In her autobiography, *On the Other Hand*, Fay Wray recalled:

> Harpo Marx, as the Property Man, would hand the performers their props as needed. When he handed me a bundle of twigs that would represent my infant child, he had such a wild and devilish look in his eyes, that I thought he might be about to do something outrageous. This *is* a wild one, I thought. Just the opposite. He was gentle. He didn't drink; he didn't smoke—which the classic Property Man in Chinese plays is supposed to do constantly. To achieve that effect, he had the cooperation of his devoted wife, Susan. She sat on a stool behind the scenery, smoking and blowing the smoke through a hole in the back of the spot where Harpo was sitting with his props around him, so that the air in that area of the stage was heavy with the haze of cigarette smoke. And Susan was not a smoker, either!

According to Harpo in his autobiography, he thought the play was so ridiculous that he did behave outrageously, blowing smoke bubbles in one scene where he had to do his own smoking after he spotted friends in the audience and creating havoc on the closing night—giving the leading man his leg, spraying flies with a flit gun, and so on—much to the enjoyment of the audience and the anger of Woollcott.

Harpo spent much of his time going around the country entertaining the troops. He recalled in his autobiography, "I traveled two hundred thousand miles and played for half a million troops and defense workers. I performed at camps, airfields, naval stations, hospitals, ports of embarkation, service centers, and war plants. I crossed the continent so many times I lost what little sense of direction I had left." Harpo noted that the audiences were wonderfully responsive, grateful for any kind of entertainment, while he marveled that they could raise a laugh after what they had been through or could anticipate happening to them. Of course, along with his harp playing, the silverware-dropping act was regularly featured. He would arrange for a high-ranking officer to act as his straight man.

Just after returning from a USO tour, Harpo had to pinch-hit for Chico, who was felled by bronchitis in March 1943. Harpo took his place at the head of the band show for engagements at the RKO Palace in Columbus, Ohio (where he actually spoke to the audience, explaining the substitution of himself for Chico), the Stanley Theater in Pittsburgh, and the Earle Theater in Philadelphia.

Harpo made a mute guest appearance in the film *Stage Door Canteen* (1943). The canteen had been established in New York, on 44th Street just off Broadway, by the American Theatre Wing as a club for servicemen to dine and be entertained by the stars. The movie was a fund-raiser for war charities and, besides Harpo, over forty-eight stars of stage and screen donated their services when it was filmed in New York and Hollywood. Katharine Hepburn was prominent as a hostess, along with Helen Hayes, Tallulah Bankhead, and Merle Oberon, while George Raft washed dishes. Katharine Cornell made her only screen appearance.

Harpo popped up briefly between Benny Goodman's "Bugle Call Rag" and Yehudi Menuhin's "Ave Maria." A woman in a phone booth is trying to make a call when she is disturbed by the sound of a horn and finds a fiendish-looking Harpo is inside the booth with her. She shrieks and runs into the crowded canteen past a serviceman who stops the pursuing Harpo and demands that he take off his hat in the presence of ladies. To the amusement of the spectators, Harpo leans on the serviceman so that his horn sounds, then leans again and extracts a pen from his breast pocket. Harpo takes off his hat and bounces it off the floor, gives the man his leg, sits on his knees, smiles at him, and then chases the woman again.

Though not quite as star-laden as the later *Hollywood Canteen* (1944), which was packed with Warner Bros. players, the film was a huge hit, fourth in the box office top ten for 1943, and it raised over $2 million.

Harpo also joined an all-star company making one-night stands for the War Bond Drive and drawing audiences of over 100,000 at some stops. He was seen in a short documentary film, *All-Star Bond Rally*, made to raise further funds and released in 1945.

Groucho, too, spent much time entertaining audiences of servicemen and went on a bond-selling Victory Caravan in April–May 1942. During that year his new book about income tax, *Many Happy Returns*, appeared. Its dust jacket contained a fine example of the imagined insult technique from *Duck Soup*, with Groucho first of all pampering the prospective buyer as "Dear Reader," going on to contemplate him further as a man having a free browse, and ending up by addressing him as "Swine."

Groucho also wrote occasional magazine articles and did much radio work. He was a regular guest on *The Rudy Vallee Sealtest Show* and even starred in his own variety series, *Blue Ribbon Town*, broadcast late on Saturday evenings beginning March 27, 1943, with such guests as Charles Laughton and Lucille Ball. But in June 1944, he was replaced by the up-and-coming Danny Kaye. Early in 1945, he was often to be heard on *Dinah Shore's Bird's-Eye Open House*.

Although none of the major film studios had any interest in the Marx Brothers as a team, it was different so far as independent producers were concerned. Stars no longer under contract to the big companies were a prime source of talent for their pictures. Independent producer David L. Loew, a son of Marcus Loew, specialized in quality films like *The Moon and Sixpence* and *The Southerner*. He persuaded the Marx Brothers to reunite for a comeback film in a profit-sharing arrangement. A contract was signed in the spring of 1945. Much later, Groucho declared: "Chico,

Copacabana (1947). Groucho (as theatrical agent Lionel Q. Devereaux) reads out the schedule under which Carmen Miranda can perform at the Copacabana Club as both herself (Carmen Navarro) and fictitious singer Mademoiselle Fifi.

Groucho with second wife Kay, studying the script of *Copacabana*. She was Kay Gorcey, formerly married to Leo Gorcey of the Dead End Kids. They met on an armed forces tour and married on July 21, 1945. She appeared as a dancer in *Copacabana*. Their daughter Melinda was born in 1946. The marriage lasted three years.

Groucho donned familiar garb to perform the Kalmar and Ruby song "Go West, Young Man" at the Copacabana Club in the film *Copacabana* (1947), playing one of the figures represented by agent Lionel Q. Devereaux (his main role).

"No daring. No imagination. Typical bank clerk." Groucho as worldly-wise waiter Emil J. Keck tries to persuade bank clerk Frank Sinatra and girlfriend Jane Russell to eat the pickled pigs' feet rather than the set lunch in *Double Dynamite* (filmed 1948, released 1951).

Only Harpo looks as though he might be enjoying himself on the set of *Love Happy* (1949).

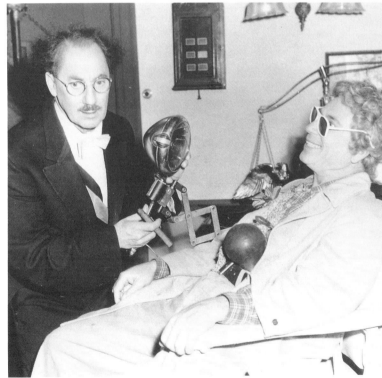

Groucho and Harpo on the set of *Love Happy* (1949).

Harpo, and I wouldn't have teamed up again if Chico hadn't needed the money."

The initial idea behind the film, originally called *Adventures in Casablanca* and ultimately *A Night in Casablanca*, was to satirize the Warner Bros. film *Casablanca* and others of its kind. At one time, the script reportedly called for Groucho to play one Humphrey Bogus opposite a female character named Lowan Behold. As a selling point, David Loew wanted Harpo to speak for the first time on screen, uttering the word "Murder!" for a $55,000 bonus, but Harpo refused.

It was widely reported that Warner Bros. objected to a film using the word "Casablanca" in its title. Groucho issued a long and humorous letter addressed to the Warner brothers in which he observed: "You claim you own Casablanca and that no one else can use that name without permission. What about 'Warner Brothers'? Do you own that, too? You probably have the right to use the name Warner, but what about Brothers? Professionally, we were brothers long before you were." Groucho suggested the whole fuss might be "the brainchild of some ferret-faced shyster, serving a brief apprenticeship in your legal department" and assured the Warners that he loved them: "We are all brothers under the skin and we'll remain friends till the last reel of *Adventures in Casablanca* goes tumbling over the spool."

In fact, as Groucho acknowledged in a private letter to an old friend, "We spread the story that Warners objected to this title purely for publicity reasons. They may eventually object to it, although I don't think so. . . . At any rate, the publicity has been wonderful on it and it was a happy idea. I wish they would sue, but, as it is, we've had reams in the papers."

The Warner legal department seems to have been sufficiently stirred to request a description of the film's plot. At any rate, Groucho circulated an account of the plot, addressed to the Warners: "I play a Doctor of Divinity who ministers to the natives and, as a sideline, hawks can openers and pea jackets to the savages along the Gold Coast of Africa. When I first meet Chico, he is working in a saloon, selling sponges to barflies who are

unable to carry their liquor. Harpo is an Arabian caddie who lives in a small Grecian urn on the outskirts of the city . . ."

Groucho maintained that Warner Bros. then asked for more details of the plot and he obliged: ". . . I play Bordello, the sweetheart of Humphrey Bogart. Harpo and Chico are itinerant rug peddlers who are weary of laying rugs and enter a monastery just for a lark. This is a good joke on them, as there hasn't been a lark in the place for fifteen years. . . . Humphrey Bogart's girl, Bordello, spends her last years in a Bacall house."

According to *Variety* (November 14, 1945), the film's title, still *Adventures in Casablanca*, had been approved by an arbitration board arranged by the Motion Picture Producers' Association.

The film went into production soon after, with the direction entrusted to an old friend of Groucho's, Archie L. Mayo, and shooting was completed on February 14, 1946. It was now known as *A Night in Casablanca*.

For Groucho, at his age, the experience of making such a strenuous comedy proved a trying one. To prevent the film running way over budget, the last few days of shooting extended late into the evening and involved Groucho and his brothers being blasted by a wind machine on a sound stage as they tried to clamber across a ladder from a truck and board an airplane in the climactic chase. Groucho told Chico and Harpo that he was once again retiring from the silver screen, yet he was soon back performing without his brothers, though in parts that were less physically demanding.

First came *Copacabana*. Groucho had lead billing, costarring with Carmen Miranda and Steve Cochran in this musical comedy made by Sam Coslow, song-writer turned independent producer. Coslow had needed a male comedy star to play the manager and boyfriend of the glamorous singer portrayed by Miranda. "I played second banana to the fruit on Carmen Miranda's head" was how Groucho described his role.

In his 1977 autobiography, *Cocktails for Two*, Coslow recalled receiving a letter from Gummo stating that the three Marx Brothers were avail-

Groucho schmoozes with the girl with a bit part in *Love Happy* (1945).

Groucho performs the song "Life Is So Peculiar" with Crosby in *Mr. Music* (1950).

Groucho with Bing Crosby and Charles Coburn in *Mr. Music* (1950).

able to make a film. This gave Coslow the idea of using Groucho, but on his own. Although reluctant to split up the team, Gummo eventually agreed to let Groucho consider the proposal.

Groucho (playing a sailor named Benny Linn) and William Bendix serenade Marie Wilson late at night with "My body lies over the ocean" in *A Girl In Every Port* (1952).

Groucho with Marie Wilson in *A Girl in Every Port* (1952), trying to think of a solution when the wrong twin of two racehorses appears to have been taken for the big race.

The script, centering on the famous Copacabana nightclub in New York, was by Laslo Vadnay, Allen Boretz (coauthor of the stage play of *Room Service*), and Howard Harris (who had been involved in early drafts of *A Night in Casablanca*). Additional dialogue for Groucho was provided by Sydney R. Zelinka (who had also worked uncredited on *A Night in Casablanca*). Veteran Alfred E. Green directed when it went into production in December 1946.

Like many actors who became associated with a particular character or partnership, Groucho longed to prove that he could succeed without the old props and without his brothers. In *Copacabana*, he wore modern, light-rimmed glasses and a proper mustache for his role as Lionel Q. Devereaux, a penniless, cigar-puffing theatrical agent who finally persuades the Copacabana's owner, Steve Hunt (Steve Cochran), to book his girlfriend, singer Carmen Novarro (Carmen Miranda), but only after she adopts a veil and masquerades as a French songstress, Mademoiselle Fifi.

But Hunt then decides to hire Novarro as well, and Carmen has to maintain two separate identities and perform as two different people. Hunt also takes a romantic interest in Mademoiselle Fifi, making Groucho jealous when Carmen comes back from playing Fifi on a date at three in the morning. "I'm going straight to that guy to beat him to a pulp. I don't care if he's sound asleep with his glasses on. Don't try to stop me—there's nothing in the world that can stop me," declares Groucho as he goes through the door. Carmen calls after him: "But he's bigger than you. He could kill you." Groucho comes back, saying "Well, that stops me." On this lame note, the scene fades out.

Eventually, Groucho and Carmen dispose of Fifi, and Groucho comes under suspicion of having murdered her. Groucho flees the police and (shades of *Monkey Business*) attempts to hide in a closet, only to find two cops waiting inside. "They always go for the closet," one of them remarks in the film's most amusing moment. A further twist occurs when it is the cops who become hot and flustered while grilling a Groucho who remains cool and unbothered. They want to know what the "Q" in Lionel Q. Devereaux stands for. "My father used to hang around a pool room," Groucho tells them. But, as this line indicates, the scene doesn't amount to much.

Groucho as Devereaux is really a halfhearted version of the traditional Groucho character. According to Coslow, "Groucho invariably took his lines and injected jokes galore. They were all very funny, but sometimes sacrificed plot to continuity to get a laugh." Rather than disappoint his old audience entirely, Groucho reverted to the familiar frock coat and greasepaint mustache for one musical number.

Although Coslow had written the songs for the film, Groucho insisted on performing an old comedy number called "Go West, Young Man" by Bert Kalmar and Harry Ruby, which they had written as part of their rejected work on *Go West*. Coslow agreed, the rights adding only a modest $2,000 to the cost of the production. Groucho performs it at the Copacabana Club, appearing as himself, a surprise act represented by Devereaux. Cut-ins show Groucho as Devereaux watching and enjoying the performance. Though he gives the song a spirited rendering, the lyrics are weak, and it is no match for "Hooray for Captain Spaulding." When Hunt wants to book Groucho for the Copacabana, Groucho as Devereaux tells him he couldn't afford it.

According to Coslow, Groucho also demanded and received a clause in his contract guaranteeing that he would not have to kiss Carmen Miranda. Perhaps this was out of deference to his young wife, Kay Gorcey, who appeared in the film as a dancer. However, at the end of the film Groucho does kiss Miranda—but only after she has kissed everyone else in the room in the manner of Fifi to prove that she was the French-woman.

Copacabana was only a modest success on its release in May 1947.

Chico was back on the road entertaining. His health was none too good. He had suffered a heart attack on March 19, 1947, after starting a two-

Groucho, the television star.

Jayne Mansfield is reunited with her true love, Groucho (as George Schmidlapp) at the end of *Will Success Spoil Rock Hunter?* (1957).

69

week run at the Fiesta Room of the Nevada Biltmore in Las Vegas. Advised by doctors to slow down, he attempted to retire. But he was always short of money and forced to continue working.

He went to London only a few weeks later as the first big attraction under a new policy at the Casino Theatre, which Bernard Delfont was trying to establish as a rival to the Palladium. Chico played four weeks (from June 9 to July 5) with Gloria Jean and Peggy Ryan also on the bill. His stage charisma is indicated by the report in *The Times* (June 10):

> Chico Marx came on, and the house revived. Without his brothers and without one of the famous film scenarios, Chico Marx captured and held the house. It is always fascinating to look for the means with which a music-hall artist succeeds. Mr. Marx's act is, on the face of it, simple but beautifully planned. He plays the piano, he makes a few jokes: it seems as simple as that. Then you begin to reflect how much depends, for instance, on his curious relationship with the piano. He plays it, in fact, as though he were playing with it. His fingers, which seem at times to have an independent life, have no false reverence for the keyboard: they are now facetious, now admonishing. They run over the keys as if there were a private joke between them, while the pianist professes nothing but a patient disinterest that is extremely comic. As for the verbal jokes, engaging trifles about "making archipeggios," these are colored with something more than the good nature which is ultimately your music-hall artist's trump card. Chico Marx, too, suggests the possession of that humane, if inexpressible, philosophy which the great clowns have. His world is fantastic but composed.

After the Casino, Chico also toured the provinces, appearing at such places as Hull, Dudley, and Coventry, which prompted him to telegraph Delfont: "Eternal gratitude for sending me to Hell, Deadly, and Cemetery." In late August, he was in Frankfurt, Germany, entertaining the occupation troops. He went out to Australia in early June 1948 to star at the Tivoli Sydney in a variety show called *Vive La Venus*. Marx historian Paul G. Wesolowski relates: "While in Sydney he was asked to do a benefit at a hospital for ex-servicemen. When he got there he found out it was actually a nightclub. He had to be convinced that a lot of patients from the hospital frequented the club before he agreed to do a ten-minute show. He told reporters that he wasn't temperamental, that he always performed for servicemen and ex-servicemen, but that he never played clubs." (Newsreel footage of his Australian visit was featured in Philip Noyce's 1978 film, *Newsfront.*)

Groucho had been doing guest spots on radio, including an annual five-minute session on a special show for the Walgreen Drug Company. In 1947, he was partnered with Bob Hope. They abandoned the script and ad-libbed to hilarious effect, giving a watching producer, John Guedel, the idea of starring Groucho in a quiz show that would really be an excuse for him to chat to the contestants and make jokes. This was *You Bet Your Life*, which began as a radio show for ABC. It was an immediate success and won the prestigious Peabody Award for outstanding achievement during 1948. In fall 1949, the show moved to CBS.

Harpo had decided that he could follow Groucho's example and appear in a film on his own. He devised *Love Happy* as a starring vehicle for himself, playing a more sympathetic, Chaplinesque figure who helps a struggling acting troupe put on a show. Short of money as usual, Chico wanted to take part and was given a small role. Frank Tashlin (who had devised gags for *A Night in Casablanca*) wrote the script with Ben Hecht, long a good friend of Harpo's and author of a piece about him in *PM*, the New York newspaper, some years before. A radio writer, Mac Benoff, then worked over the script before shooting began in late June 1948.

The film was made as an independent production by Lester Cowan in association with Mary Pickford. Financing proved difficult. Groucho was persuaded to join the proceedings in a peripheral role so that it could be sold as a Marx Brothers picture.

In 1948, Groucho and Norman Krasna completed a comedy play which they had begun writing in 1941 under the title *Middle Ages*. Now called *Time for Elizabeth* (Elizabeth being the town in New Jersey, not a person), it opened at Broadway's Fulton Theater on September 27 and closed after only eight performances. The leading role, that of an executive for a washing machine company who retires prematurely to Florida only to find that he misses work, was played by Otto Kruger, a suave actor not noted for lightness of touch. The *New York Times* described it as "a childish charade . . . a strangely callow jest to emanate from two of the theatre's maturest workers."

If Groucho had played the principal part then (as he did later in summer stock and on television), the play might well have been a financial—and even a critical—success, but he would have disappointed audiences. The part was not really written to suit him and lacked the wisecracks audiences would have expected. Perhaps Groucho also wanted to see if the play was well enough written to stand up without him. Besides, he was now well settled in California and had plenty of work there.

Chico was in New York for the play's opening. He called a conference with the film trade press there on October 8, before flying to Hollywood to make a few final scenes of *Love Happy*. He declared that once *Love Happy* was completed the team would be planning another independent feature, *The Life of the Marx Brothers*, probably in association with Lester Cowan. According to Chico, he, Harpo, and Ben Hecht owned fifty percent of *Love Happy*, while Groucho had sold his interest to his brothers. There were immense difficulties finishing the picture. Money had to be raised from the companies whose products were featured in advertisements during the climactic rooftop chase.

Groucho left behind the failure of *Time for Elizabeth* and reported to RKO to star in another film without his brothers. *It's Only Money* started shooting in November 1948 with Jane Russell and Frank Sinatra as the romantic leads. RKO studio chief Howard Hughes held it back from release for nearly three years and retitled it *Double Dynamite*—in reference to Russell's physical attributes—before it finally appeared at Christmas 1951.

Chico and Harpo went to England in May 1949 to play separately in leading provincial music halls and join forces to head a variety show at the London Palladium which ran for four weeks beginning June 20. American performers were in huge demand in gray postwar Britain. The Marxes followed in the wake of Allan Jones and crossed paths with Danny Kaye and Burns and Allen.

The difficulties over *Love Happy*, and the crisis in the movie industry generally as attendances slumped, made further independent filmmaking by the Marx Brothers impossible. Both Groucho and Chico went over to the other side, television. Chico made an acting appearance in a character role in January 1950 for the fifteenth episode of CBS's *Silver Theatre*. Called *Papa Romani*, it costarred him with William Frawley and Margaret Hamilton.

Back in January 1949, United Artists had stated that *Love Happy* was completed and ready to be distributed. It had valuable publicity from a feature article in *Life*'s issue of February 7 that year, but it was not until March 1950 that it was released (although there were trade screenings in October 1949). It benefited from the past popularity of the team and the interest in seeing them together again until word of mouth got around that it was neither a full-fledged Marx Brothers picture nor a good picture by any other standards. Ben Hecht had to forego his writing credit in the hope that it could be shown in Britain, where his name was mud following some remarks about his joy when British soldiers were killed in Palestine. (Even so, word leaked out. The film was shelved, and had only a sketchy later release through a minor British distributor.) In his autobiography, Harpo refers to *A Night in Casablanca* as the last Marx Brothers picture and makes no mention of

Love Happy at all. His forgetfulness is understandable.

Groucho took his radio show, *You Bet Your Life*, onto the NBC television network weekly beginning October 5, 1950. He declared: "I'm going to keep my cigar, my leer and any old ad-lib wisecracks I find kicking around. My mustache is my own now. I bought it from the upstairs maid. But the frock coat and the old Groucho who chases blondes will be missing. Even the new Groucho will be missing, but that's only until I can get my spark plugs cleaned." The same show was still broadcast on radio (in fact, listeners heard it a few days before it was seen on television). Excess footage was filmed, enabling the show to be cut down to a half hour and any overly outlandish remarks by Groucho to be deleted.

Almost immediately, Groucho won an Emmy as Outstanding Television Personality of 1950 from the National Academy of Television Arts and Sciences. Ed Wynn and Milton Berle had both won the previous year, the first time the award had been given. *You Bet Your Life* was nominated in the Best Game and Audience Participation Show category but lost to *Truth or Consequences*. The show would be nominated in later years, but it never won. However, it was immensely popular and ran on television for eleven years.

The format of *You Bet Your Life* involved Groucho interviewing a pair of contestants, making gentle fun of them, before they answered questions in a chosen category for various cash amounts, losing half of their winnings to date for a wrong answer. Its appeal lay essentially in Groucho's witty repartee with the contestants. Originally he met them before the show, but after a short while he simply studied background information which gave him ideas for his humorous sallies. The participants were chosen for the scope they gave Groucho. On one show, there was a scientist who explained to Groucho that a single fly could multiply itself a quarter of a million times in a month, allowing Groucho to comment: "Imagine what a married fly would do." In another show, he had himself bound up with a

blonde who was an amateur escape artist and told announcer George Fenneman, "If anyone phones, tell them I'm all tied up."

The format included a secret word—a simple word that any of the contestants might utter by chance and win a prize. A stuffed duck with a Groucho mustache and a cigar descended when the word was spoken. If the contestants failed to win during the quiz, they would be given a consolation prize if they could answer questions like "What great statesman is celebrated on Washington's birthday?"

At the end of 1950, Groucho was a guest star, playing himself, in the Bing Crosby Christmas release, *Mr. Music*. In this dull, overlong comedy, directed by fellow humorist Richard Haydn, Groucho turns up for a student show and performs a comedy song "Life Is So Peculiar," singing and dancing with Crosby, and pausing to tell a joke with Crosby acting as the feed.

When a Chaplinesque type was needed and Chaplin wasn't available, Harpo almost starred in Gabriel Pascal's production of *Androcles and the Lion* at RKO, playing the henpecked, heroic little Christian tailor of ancient Rome whose kindness in extracting a thorn from a lion's paw is rewarded when the same lion refuses to chew him up in the arena. Harpo's test was a great success as far as Pascal was concerned, although according to the eventual director, Chester Erskine, Harpo was chary of taking a speaking role and his voice wasn't suitable for the part. Some sources suggest that Harpo had been signed for the film (and may have even started shooting under the original director, H. C. Potter) before Howard Hughes spotted a hot new performer, Alan Young, on television and decided that he would make the perfect Androcles. Even though it was obvious to everyone else that Young was wrong for the part, Hughes as the studio owner had his way. Despite a starry supporting cast, including Jean Simmons, Victor Mature, and Robert Newton, the film was a critical and box office flop when it was released (after the usual delays associated with Hughes) in 1953.

Chico gained his own television series starring

as the proprietor of an ice-cream parlor and university hangout in a half-hour musical comedy series on ABC, *The College Bowl*, which ran on Monday nights from October 1950 to the end of March 1951. The show was telecast live from New York and presented Chico as the host of the College Bowl, inviting various of his regular customers, including Andy Williams and Barbara Ruick, to perform. Chico spoke his Italian dialect and usually played at least a few notes on the keyboard in each show.

Sometime during the 1950s, Chico also turned up in a short film called *Sports Antics*. Paul G. Wesolowski provides some details:

This newsreel-type film spotlighted unusual sporting events, including an American roller

Chico as the monk advising Anthony Dexter (Columbus) in *The Story of Mankind* (1957).

Harpo as Isaac Newton in *The Story of Mankind* (1957).

Groucho as Peter Minuit buys Manhattan from the Indians in *The Story of Mankind* (1957). The squaw with the obliging back is played by his wife Eden Hartford. The Indian chief is Abraham Sofaer.

73

derby, and at one point Chico comes out of the stands, takes off his jacket, and reveals that he's wearing a roller derby uniform. He skates off, at one point being carried by a group of skaters. While approaching one of the curves, he skates straight toward the camera, slams into a railing, and flips onto the floor. Using a videotape copy and slow-motion, it is possible to tell that it was a cut to a stunt double, but it's very well done on film.

Groucho continued his independent screen career by costarring with William Bendix and Marie Wilson in the farcical *A Girl in Every Port* at RKO, where shooting began on June 11, 1951. S. J. Perelman spent several days on the set, resulting in his magazine essay, "I'll Always Call You Schnorrer, My African Explorer," which proved to be the best thing to come out of the movie.

Groucho had his biggest success as a singer when he recorded "The Four Musicians" and "Blackstrap Molasses" as part of a starry combination that included Danny Kaye, Jimmy Durante, and Jane Wyman, accompanied by Sonny Burke's Orchestra and 4 Hits and a Miss. It reached the hit parade in September 1951.

When *It's Only Money* made its belated appearance in December 1951 as *Double Dynamite*, it hardly proved worth the three-year wait. The plot presented third-billed Frank Sinatra as a meek bank teller who has a big win on the horses that coincidentally matches a shortage at his place of work. His fiancée (Jane Russell) thinks he has robbed the bank to enable them to marry. Groucho featured as Emil J. Keck, a wisecracking and worldly-wise waiter at the Italian bistro they frequent. The Groucho character is fond of quoting old poets and gets to take a bubble bath, but with his clothes on. Groucho and Sinatra team up to sing "It's Only Money" while walking down a street. But the picture was a contrived and tedious farce.

The following month, *A Girl in Every Port* went into release. This was the tall tale of two Navy sailors, the quick-talking Benny Linn (Groucho Marx) and the dim-witted Tim Dunnevan

(William Bendix), trying to make some fast money out of two identical racehorses, one who runs well and one who always comes in last. They keep one step ahead of trouble until the day both horses run in the same race. The unwitting and thoroughly contrived capture of a pair of saboteurs enables the two gobs to end up as heroes. Marie Wilson was a dumb-blonde carhop, while model Dee Hartford was prominent as a stern socialite who disapproves of horseracing. Dee introduced Groucho to her sister Eden, who became Groucho's wife in July 1954.

Groucho was back on the cover of *Time* magazine for its December 31, 1951, issue, but this time without his brothers. It wasn't his brace of new movies that did the trick but his new fame as a television personality with *You Bet Your Life*. He had at last made it by himself and not as one of the Marx Brothers. Harpo was doing milk commercials, and Chico was performing in nightclubs and at county fairs. For some engagements, Chico and Harpo teamed up.

Groucho decided it was time to try out *Time for Elizabeth* with himself in the leading role. In July 1952, he played it in La Jolla, California, and in March 1953, he opened in it at Palm Springs, Florida.

Besides his weekly appearance with his own show, Groucho did some guest shots on the tube. He showed up on *All Star Revue* on October 11, 1952, with Ethel Barrymore and Tallulah Bankhead, then on an hour-long CBS variety special on March 28, 1954, *Presenting Rodgers and Hammerstein*, which was the General Foods Twenty-Fifth Anniversary Show, featuring highlights from the songwriters' shows and Groucho conducting a special session of *You Bet Your Life* with the famous duo as contestants.

Groucho also came face to face with Edward R. Murrow in a live interview on April 9, 1954, from his Beverly Hills home. (Harpo had his turn with Murrow on January 3, 1958, but left all the talking to wife Susan.)

Among Harpo's occasional acting work on television was his memorable appearance as a guest in 1955 on *I Love Lucy*, with Lucille Ball,

Groucho and wife Eden at the premiere of *Peyton Place* (1957). They married in 1956, divorced in 1969, but remained good friends.

mirror gag, with Lucy mimicking Harpo's expressions and movements perfectly until the inevitable slipup which sets the insanity in motion again. The two complement each other perfectly, though Harpo assumes complete command.

On October 9, 1955, NBC presented a ninety-minute variety special in color. Called *Show Biz*, it was a history of music and comedy with Groucho as master of ceremonies and principal comedian. He recalled his early work as a German dialect comedian, burlesqued a beauty parade, and played a comic disc jockey; he also brought on daughter Melinda for duets of "I Hear Music" and "You're Just in Love."

In the summer of 1956, Chico went on a national tour appearing in a character role in *The Fifth Season*, a farce concerning the business and

Groucho with announcer George Fenneman and tray of questions in 1959 photograph for *You Bet Your Life*.

who had come a long way since a supporting role in *Room Service*. In this episode, Lucy impersonated Hollywood stars to impress a visitor with bad eyesight and was left speechless when the real Harpo Marx turned up. As Canadian observer Ted Gilling has recalled:

His scenes with Lucille provided one of the best comic half-hours on American television that season—not to mention a glimpse of the might-have-been. Lucy, on a visit to Hollywood where husband Ricky (Desi Arnaz) is making a film, encounters Harpo in her hotel room. Bent on seducing her, he gives frantic chase, and the fun is on. It could have been chaos, but rarely have two clowns shown such rapport and timing in a television performance. All the Harpo-isms are there: the shake-a-leg, horn honking, horrendous leers, and in one superb highlight the old amatory problems of two garment manufacturers. In *Living With Chico*, his daughter, Maxine, recalled:

> He was charming and endearing on stage, and the audiences loved him. I went to see the show in Boston and was deeply moved, watching Chico in his late sixties taking such a chance and pulling it off. After each performance, he had to lie down. And he amazed the other performers: Before going on some nights, he would be so out of it that he'd ask any actor standing near him to "give me my first line and point me in the right direction." Then he'd amble on stage.

Marx historian Paul G. Wesolowski notes:

> The tour ended in Los Angeles in February 1957 for a two-week run. To help promote the show, all five Marxes appeared on a television show called *Tonight: America After Dark*, hosted by Jack Lescoulie. It was an ancient forerunner of *The Tonight Show*. It was the only time all five Marxes appeared on television. No films or kinescopes are known to exist.

Groucho felt inspired by Chico's example to make an extensive tour of the straw hat circuit with *Time for Elizabeth* in the summer of 1957, during the annual break from *You Bet Your Life*. He appeared at the Playhouse in Ivorytown, Connecticut; the Country Playhouse, Westport, Connecticut; the Spa Summer Theater, Saratoga, New York; the Edgewater Beach Playhouse, Chicago; the Grist Mill Playhouse, Andover, New Jersey; and the Theatre-by-the-Sea, Matunuck, Rhode Island.

Around this time, the prospects of a film biography of the Marx Brothers were at their brightest. A leading producer, Sol C. Siegel, had joined MGM in 1955 with a Marx biopic among his projects. Gummo had negotiated a deal, with Kyle Crichton's 1951 book about the team as source material. Siegel wanted Shirley Booth to play Minnie Marx and contemplated calling the movie *Minnie's Boys*. Groucho declared that he,

Chico, and Harpo would only appear in the finale. Finding players to portray the Marx Brothers was an insurmountable problem and Siegel went on to produce *High Society* and other films instead.

Harpo showed up in a *Playhouse 90* production called "Snow Shoes" on January 3, 1957. The title of this Runyonesque comedy referred to an ever-losing racehorse whose owners, Hard-Boiled Harry (Barry Sullivan) and Sentimental Mousie (Stuart Erwin), are flat broke. They hit on the idea of having the nag hypnotized into winning races by John Carradine's ex-vaudevillian, Felix the Great, and Snow Shoes becomes an overnight sensation. Harpo was originally announced to play Mousie but decided against taking a role in which he would have to speak. He switched with Stuart Erwin, turning Erwin's original part into a silent one in which he (Harpo) could be himself in his traditional comic character, ogling and grinning his way around the racetrack as he plays both the horses and his harp. But it wasn't as much fun as seeing *A Day at the Races* again.

Frank Tashlin had left behind his early days as a screenwriter on *A Night in Casablanca* and *Love Happy* to become a leading writer-producer-director in movies. In his highly witty 1957 CinemaScope-and-color comedy spoofing the world of advertising, *Will Success Spoil Rock Hunter?* (based on the play by George Axelrod), Jayne Mansfield was a screen sex symbol who endorsed a brand of lipstick and became involved with Tony Randall's ad agency exec. But her real love is a man called Georgie Schmidlapp, who turns up at the very end of the picture—played by an uncredited Groucho. "Why didn't you ever try to kiss me?" she asks him. An unlikely question, but Groucho has an answer. "I never could get that close," he responds, inviting contemplation of her huge chest. But he succeeds now, taking her in a tight embrace. After a fruitless encounter with Marilyn Monroe in *Love Happy*, it was gratifying to see Groucho making out with a later sex symbol.

This was a far more satisfactory appearance

than the one he made that same year in the comically inclined Technicolor production of *The Story of Mankind*, based on a work by Hendrik Van Loon. The script by Irwin Allen and Charles Bennett presented a series of historical episodes as a high tribunal in Heaven considers whether mankind deserves to be spared destruction by the H-bomb. Producer Irwin Allen gathered a huge array of fading stars to play in the various vignettes. Along with the bizarre casting of Edward Everett Horton as Sir Walter Raleigh, Virginia Mayo as Cleopatra, and Dennis Hopper as Napoleon, he rounded up all three Marx Brothers and gave a bit part (as an early Christian child) to Groucho's daughter, Melinda. But it was not a screen reunion of the Marx Brothers, as each played in a different episode.

Groucho was burdened with poor dialogue in his appearance as Peter Minuit, the Dutchman who conned Manhattan Island from the Indians. Portraying a squaw called Laughing Water was his wife, Eden. Harpo was briefly magnificent as Isaac Newton, quietly playing a harp in an orchard when a falling apple gives him the Great Idea. Chico had least to do as a monk advising Columbus, played by Anthony Dexter. (It extended a connection between Chico and Columbus, begun in *Monkey Business* when Chico claimed "My father was a-partners with Columbus" and continued when Chico sang about Columbus in Connie Bailey's music lesson during *Horse Feathers*.)

In 1958, Chico was one of the best known of twelve guest stars on a *Playhouse 90* drama, "No Time at All." The script delved into the lives (with flashbacks) of selected passengers on an airplane which develops an electrical fault on a night flight from Miami to New York and loses contact with the ground. Chico played Mr. Kramer, a father afraid for the life of his grown son aboard the plane as it searches for somewhere to land. He had about half-a-dozen lines, looked very aged, but gave a competent performance. He was none too pleased when it leaked out that his services had been obtained on this occasion for a mere $1,000.

Chico also joined Groucho, Bob Hope, Bing Crosby, Ernie Kovacs, and others in a promotional short for the *Saturday Evening Post* called *Showdown at Ulcer Gulch*.

That same year, Harpo provided the music to accompany Evelyn Rudie's narration of an episode of the *Du Pont Show of the Month* that featured an updated version of the Victor Herbert operetta, *The Red Mill*, written by Robert Alan Aurthur and directed by Delbert Mann. Set in a run-down Dutch village, where the red mill only turns when someone is in love, the production featured Donald O'Connor as a visiting American with Shirley Jones playing a local girl.

Guesting on *The Milton Berle Show* (January 14, 1959), Harpo was questioned about his late arrival by Uncle Miltie and described a vertical in-and-out shape. Uncle Miltie asked if Harpo could get him one, and Harpo produced a bottle of Coke. Along with this echo of past mime scenes, Harpo gave his leg to the host, played around hungrily during a commercial message for a Kraft recipe, and made faces through his harp that had a studio audience roaring while Berle was on camera.

Also on television there was one final, fleeting screen appearance of the three Marx Brothers together. This occurred at the end of a telefilm called "The Incredible Jewel Robbery," in the *G. E. Theater* series, which went before the cameras in January 1959 and was shown on March 8. Harpo and Chico starred and Groucho guested (unbilled due to his contract with a rival network), uttering the only word of dialogue in the half-hour show directed by Mitchell Leisen. Although far from successful, the production had a couple of marvelous flashes.

In pantomime (with music on the soundtrack), Chico and Harpo are seen breaking into shops stealing the equipment necessary to disguise an automobile as a police car—all rather tedious and not funny. Then, outside a jeweler's shop selected from a stolen telephone directory, Harpo dons a disguise, including a Sherlock Holmes deerstalker, with his back to the camera. As he turns, the show suddenly comes to life: Harpo has

Late photograph of the five Marx Brothers: Harpo, Zeppo, Chico, Groucho, and Gummo. It seems to have been a visit to Chico at work, since he is wearing makeup.

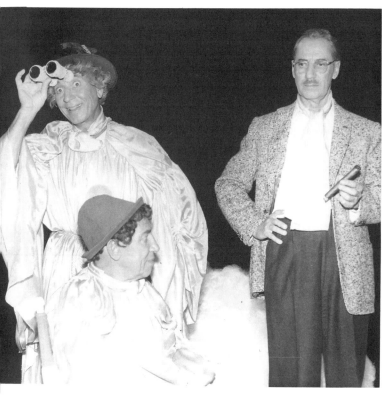

Harpo, Chico, and Groucho on the set of *Deputy Seraph* in 1959.

Chico and Harpo dressed up for their television appearance in *The Incredible Jewel Robbery* (1959).

78

put on a one-piece pair of glasses with attached eyebrows, a fake rectangular mustache, and a cigar, and become Groucho! He paces up and down on the pavement with mischievous alacrity, exactly catching Groucho's walk, before going in to hold up the store. Chico then comes along as a bogus policeman and pretends to arrest him. Fleeing, they have to pick up a woman from a home for the deaf and dumb and deliver her to the maternity hospital. Eventually caught (though not by any imaginative twist of scripting), they are put into a lineup at the police station. Chico is identified as the "policeman," but Harpo escapes, thanks to his disguise. Then, suddenly and for no reason, Groucho enters (not in traditional costume) and lopes up and down the lineup, cigar in hand, and is picked out as the holdup man. Harpo and Chico dash to his side and Harpo gives him his leg. Groucho speaks: "We won't talk until we see our lawyer." Down comes the model duck used on *You Bet Your Life* with the words "The End" on it.

The appearance of the Marx Brothers as a team becomes the climax of the film and its sole justification. It is not about a robbery but about the Marx Brothers, and it was a pleasure to see them giving assured performances, suggesting that they could do more work as a team.

In fact, Chico and Harpo were signed for a proposed television series to be called *Deputy Seraph*, and they did some filming in April 1959. The idea of writers Phil Rapp and Richard Powell was that the pair would play angels who inhabit the bodies of people on earth in order to sort out their problems. Groucho agreed to appear in some episodes. Even though Chico and Harpo would only feature briefly in each episode (the main work being done by actors playing the people they inhabited), it proved impossible to insure Chico for a series.

Chico made a trip to Britain in October 1959 for a television show and a music hall engagement in Bradford. It was his first appearance on British television (for which he was paid approximately £2,000), and he guest starred in a new Sunday night series, *Showtime*, hosted by magician David Nixon. Chico gave a press conference and amused reporters with estimates of having lost $2 million on horses and the gaming tables over the previous thirty years, the reason why he had to continue working. He also declared that the Marxes were still hoping to appear in a film about their lives. But he had two heart attacks in London and was forced to cancel the week of variety in Yorkshire and return to Los Angeles.

Billy Wilder hit upon a great idea for a Marx Brothers feature film. As this arose when he was on peak form after *Some Like It Hot* and *The Apartment*, it could have been quite something. It was while in Manhattan in the winter of 1959 shooting exterior scenes for *The Apartment* and living near the United Nations, at a time when diplomatic crises with Khrushchev and Castro were in full ferment, that Wilder had his Marxian notion.

Wilder broached the idea to his writing collaborator I. A. L. Diamond on the flight back to Los Angeles, and they devised the basic plot before landing. Groucho would lead a mob planning to rob Tiffany's while the police are pre-occupied with security at the United Nations. Harpo would be the safecracker and Chico the outfit's muscleman. After grabbing a load of diamonds, they would rush to a ship, only to be prevented from boarding by an anti-Communist picket line. The police would mistake them for the Latvian delegation and escort them to the country's embassy. Harpo would address the U.N. Assembly in mime, with much honking of his horn, while the interpreters made various conflicting translations.

Wilder declared: "We want to make a satire on the deterioration of diplomatic behavior, on brinkmanship, wild jokes about the H-bomb— that type of stuff." He presented a forty-page treatment to his backers, the Mirisch brothers, who readily accepted the idea. It could have been a *Duck Soup* of the 1960s, but when Wilder had to rule out Chico and Harpo because of their failing health, he decided the project wouldn't work with anyone else. He went ahead and made a different kind of political comedy, *One, Two, Three*, with

6008 3-5   6008 4-5   6008 2-5

Harpo, Chico, and Groucho in publicity shots for *Deputy Seraph* in 1959.

James Cagney. (As it happened, Wilder had to cope with the serious heart attacks of Peter Sellers and Walter Matthau on later pictures, quite apart from a car-racing accident with Horst Buchholz on *One, Two, Three*.)

As an enthusiast of Gilbert and Sullivan since discovering them in the 1920s, Groucho was delighted to star as KoKo in a one-hour color telecast of *The Mikado*, on NBC on April 29, 1960. Although he discarded his cigar and wore a curled Japanese mustache and Japanese costume, his leer and slouching walk were well suited to the lecherous Lord High Executioner who needs someone to execute—but the obvious candidate is the minstrel who loves his ward Yum-Yum. Groucho arranged for his daughter, Melinda, to play a supporting role.

At the end of 1960, Harpo made a television appearance in, for a change, a dramatic role when he starred as a deaf mute in "Silent Panic," an episode of the half-hour *Du Pont Show with June Allyson*, directed by Arthur Hiller. "When a ham actor is handed a thirty-five-page script and discovers that his part appears on thirty-four of those pages, he accepts it," Harpo remarked at the time. "Besides, it's a good part. It satisfies my whim for not talking and at the same time gets away from the Harpo character."

He was seen as Dummy, a friendless and impoverished deaf-mute who finds work pretending to be a mechanical man in the toy department window display of a big store at Christmas. He is the only witness to a gangland murder in the street outside. Hiding from the killers in a lumber yard, he is befriended by the night watchman (Ernest Truex), who gives him coffee. (The idea of a "mechanical man" witnessing a murder had been a striking feature of a minor 1953 crime drama, *City That Never Sleeps*.) Harpo's adopted son, Bill, made his acting debut in a supporting role as a young stranger. His one line, "Lay off there, Pops," enabled him to boast he had a bigger speaking part than his father. For Harpo, the main challenge came in having to play deaf as well as dumb and not react to any sound.

In May 1961, Chico suffered a heart attack at the Friars Club in Hollywood and was rushed to hospital. Later he went home to recuperate, but on October 11, he died of a further one. An editorial in the *New York Times* spelled it out: "While Groucho, Harpo and Chico were all available, there was always an outside chance that they might vandalize the land of cuckoo once more. It can never be. The funniest team of twentieth-century mountebanks is broken beyond repair. Alas, poor Chico. Alas, ourselves."

You Bet Your Life had ended on September 21, 1961, after twelve years. But if NBC no longer wanted it, CBS was willing to take it on and Groucho started a similar show, *Tell It to Groucho*, for the rival network the following January 11. This time the two participants were people bringing personal problems to Groucho— such as a cat lover seeking a husband or someone worried about the lack of laughter in the United States. After talking to Groucho, each took part in a contest to identify images that were flashed on the screen—the quicker they were correctly recognized, the bigger the prize. George Fenneman was again the announcer. But *Tell It to Groucho* foundered within months, ending on May 31. Over two hundred episodes of *You Bet Your Life* were put into syndication under the new title *The Best of Groucho* in the early 1970s.

Groucho also narrated, on screen and off, a documentary about the history of the automobile, "Merrily We Roll Along," for the *Du Pont Show of the Week* in 1961 and began some character acting on television, as Chico and Harpo had done. He played a straight role on *G.E. Theater* in a half-hour episode called "The Hold-Out," shown in early 1962. He was John Graham, the father who opposes the marriage plans of his college student daughter (played by Brooke Hayward, daughter of Margaret Sullavan). She wants to marry another undergraduate (Dennis Hopper, then Hayward's husband in real life), son of a millionaire (Fred Clark). Groucho thinks she should finish her education and her boyfriend should be earning a living before they get hitched, and he refuses to pay for the wedding. As could only be expected from this somewhat conservative series (after all, Ronald Reagan was host), father is proved right. Although he is first seen as old-fashioned and unjust, even by his wife (Dorothy Green), his view prevails and the youngsters see the wisdom of postponing their nuptial plans. (Oh, for the Groucho of *Animal Crackers*, to whom marriage was something foisted on the American people "while our boys were over there"!)

By now, Harpo had run into serious health problems, suffering several heart attacks. He was persuaded to retire for a number of months, and didn't even keep up his practice on the harp. But he became bored and went back to nightclub and television work. He made an appearance in a November 1961 episode of the *Du Pont Show of the Week* called "The Wonderful World of Toys," in which, wearing his traditional costume, he acted as a guide to various toyland settings created in Central Park. And in a 1962 episode of the series *Mr. Smith Goes to Washington*, he appeared as himself, performing in a musicale arranged by Fess Parker's Mr. Smith at the White House.

Groucho, who revived *Time for Elizabeth* again in 1963 at Tucson and Phoenix, starred in April 1964 in a shortened television version, adapted by Alex Gottlieb. Opposite Groucho as the retiring businessman were Kathryn Eames as his wife and his real wife, Eden, in the key supporting role of Vivian Morgan.

Meanwhile, Harpo's health deteriorated. He died, following heart surgery, on September 28, 1964, in Los Angeles.

Groucho carried on as the last performing Marx brother. Though he declined an offer from Federico Fellini to participate in *Juliet of the Spirits* (1965), he made guest appearances on television shows such as *The Hollywood Palace*, *The Dick Cavett Show*, and *The Bill Cosby Show*. As emcee for *The Hollywood Palace* on March 17, 1965, he brought on his daughter, Melinda, to perform with him and with a rock-'n-roll group, then revived his arrival scene from *Animal Crackers*, featuring "Hooray for Captain Spaulding," with none other than Margaret Dumont. She was dead when the show went out: her very last professional engagement had been taped a few days before a fatal heart attack. Also in 1965, Groucho went to England to make a television series based on *You Bet Your life* and called simply *Groucho*. It was not a success.

The publication of selected correspondence to and from Groucho, *The Groucho Letters*, took place in 1967 with Groucho donating the profits to the Golden Key Foundation to further its work in aiding emotionally disturbed children.

Groucho made cameo appearances in episodes of two television series, *I Dream of Jeannie* and *Julia*, and starred in a pilot episode of a proposed series which didn't sell. This was *Rhubarb*, based on the 1951 Ray Milland picture. Groucho played J. Paul Greedy, the richest man in the world.

In 1968, Groucho made a final big screen appearance in Otto Preminger's psychedelic comedy about hippies and gangsters, *Skidoo*. Wearing dark-rimmed glasses, a black toupée, and a rectangular mustache, glued on rather than greasepainted, he played "God," a crime kingpin headquartered aboard a boat with his mistress, played by Luna. (Earlier casting had called for Preminger himself to play God and Faye Dunaway the mistress.) Veterans in the cast were Mickey Rooney, Jackie Gleason, George Raft, Cesar Romero, and Burgess Meredith. The film was a disaster with both press and public. The script and Preminger's heavy-handed direction gave Groucho no scope to be funny in the film, but he came up with an apt comment of his own afterward: "Both the picture and my role were God-awful."

Two years later, Groucho went to New York to attend the opening of a short-lived musical biography about the Marx Brothers, which used the same title as the projected MGM film of the 1950s. *Minnie's Boys* was written by Arthur Marx (Groucho's son) and Robert Fisher. Groucho joined the cast on stage at the first-night curtain call on March 26 at the Imperial Theatre (this followed sixty-four previews). *Minnie's Boys* was based on the Marx Brothers' early life. Shelley Winters was their indomitable mother and Lewis

Groucho addresses an audience at the National Film Theatre in London in 1965.

J. Stadlen the young Groucho. *Variety*'s reviewer, "Hobe," described it as a "stubbornly disappointing musical" and it closed on May 30 after sixty regular performances, with an estimated loss of $550,000.

Groucho and his wife, Eden, had divorced in 1969 (but they remained good friends). In the early 1970s, Groucho hired a former secretary turned actress, Erin Fleming, to answer his mail, and she became his full-time secretary and companion. Following a major heart attack and some strokes, he started performing again, and Erin encouraged him to try out the idea of a one-man show. He accepted an offer from what turned out to be a young student impresario, Tom Wilhite, to perform at Iowa State University in April 1972. Despite Groucho's doubts, his assortment of songs and stories about his life went over ecstatically well with an audience of more than two thousand. They gave him a standing ovation both before and after the show.

He took the show the following month to New York's Carnegie Hall. *An Evening With Groucho* on May 6, his first live performance in New York in more than forty years, was a complete sellout. Many youngsters in the audience came dressed as one of the Marx brothers. The eighty-one-year-old Groucho was introduced by Dick Cavett, Erin Fleming helped him sing a few of the songs, and Marvin Hamlisch played the overture and performed with Groucho. The show was recorded and later released as an album. Then came a trip to France for Groucho to be made a Commandeur dans l'Ordre des Arts et des Lettres in a special ceremony at the Cannes Film Festival—proof, if it were needed, that Groucho's comedy, despite its dependence on the English language, was universally appreciated. Groucho did a further *Evening With Groucho* concert in San Francisco on August 11, 1972, but illness forced him to cancel some other scheduled appearances. He did, however, perform in Los Angeles at the

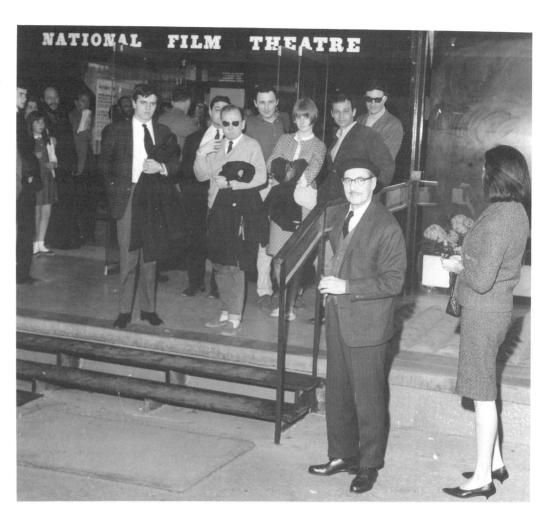

Groucho with wife Eden outside London's National Film Theatre in 1965.

Groucho as the crime syndicate boss "God" in *Skidoo* (1968) with Luna playing his mistress.

Music Center Pavilion during December, three months after the originally announced date.

In 1972, Charlie Chaplin had received an honorary Oscar from Jack Lemmon at the Academy Awards ceremony. When Groucho had offered his congratulations, Chaplin astutely told him, "Stay warm, Groucho, you're next." And two years later, following a proposal to the Academy of Motion Picture Arts and Sciences by writer Nunnally Johnson, Groucho received his special Oscar. Jack Lemmon, presenting the award, declared that "the Marx Brothers were as revolutionary in their approach to humor as Karl Marx was to philosophy." Groucho responded:

I only wish that Harpo and Chico were here to share this great honor—and I wish Margaret Dumont were here, too. She was a great straight lady even though she never got any of my jokes.

She used to say, "Julie, what are they laughing at?" But she was a great straight woman and I loved her. And then I'd like to thank my mother, without whom we would have been a failure. And last, I'd like to thank Erin Fleming, who makes my life worth living and who understands all my jokes.

Groucho's appearance was preceded by a production number that included a scene from *Minnie's Boys* and by a tantalizing glimpse of *Animal Crackers* among a series of film extracts—tantalizing because the film had been officially unavailable since 1958, when the original twenty-eight-year copyright period ran out and was not renewed so that the rights reverted to George S. Kaufman and Morrie Ryskind, the authors of the original play, and to Bert Kalmar and Harry Ruby for the music and lyrics. (Because of different copyright laws, it remained in circulation in Canada and abroad, but was only seen illegally in the United States in poor quality pirate prints.)

Students at U.C.L.A. had formed C.R.A.C., the Committee for the Rerelease of *Animal Crackers*, in December 1973 and organized a petition which gathered 18,000 signatures. Groucho made a personal appearance on campus to lend his support and bring the campaign some added press and television coverage. Other campuses joined in. All this helped convince MCA, which had acquired the pre-1948 Paramount library, that it would be commercially worthwhile putting the movie back into circulation. Negotiations to acquire the rights for $50,000 were completed just in time for a clip to be included on Oscar night.

On May 23, 1974, Groucho attended the gala second premiere of *Animal Crackers* at the United Artists Theater in Westwood, Los Angeles. Then he flew to New York for the big reopening there on June 23 at the Sutton Theater and found it besieged by fans. Police had to be called to control the crowds and get Groucho inside without harm. He had to leave before the end in order to escape safely. *Animal Crackers* began earning substantial amounts in reissue and was later shown in prime time on American television, an amazing achievement for a forty-five-year-old black-and-white movie with primitive sound. *Animal Crackers* is now estimated by *Variety* to have earned $3.1 million in North American theatrical rentals, second only to *Hell's Angels* among all the releases of 1930.

On October 16, 1975, Groucho was honored at the University of Southern California, where he sang and took questions from the audience. Excerpts from his writings were read by Jack Lemmon, Lynn Redgrave, Roddy McDowall, and George Fenneman.

In 1976, Groucho was seen on television with Bob Hope and a raft of comedians in a ninety-minute special called *Joys*. This was a spoof of *Jaws*, in which the various comics were devoured. It was his final appearance before a mass audience. But he did attend a banquet at the Ambassador Hotel in Los Angeles in honor of Zubin Mehta on October 31. He sang the Grace

Groucho with his familiar mustache in his final film appearance as "God" in *Skidoo* (1968), seen here with Austin Pendleton.

Kahn composition "Oh, How That Woman Could Cook."

In March 1977, he spent three weeks in the Cedars-Sinai Medical Center in Los Angeles, having a hip joint replaced with a prosthesis in his right leg. His health remained a matter of concern. When Gummo died of natural causes on April 21, 1977, in Palm Springs, California, it was decided to withhold the fact from Groucho. By this time, his mental health had also deteriorated, and he was unable to take care of himself. He was unaware of a court battle over conservatorship of his person and assets between Erin Fleming, who had become temporary conservator, and Groucho's son, Arthur, who challenged her permanent appointment. The writer Nat Perrin, who was acceptable to both sides, became temporary conservator on April 22 with the approval of the court. In July, Groucho's grandson Andrew was appointed permanent conservator.

Before this, in June, Groucho had been readmitted to Cedars-Sinai for further surgery to strengthen his hip. He spent only one day at home before returning, having contracted pneumonitis, a mild form of pneumonia. For a man of his age and condition the illness was serious. He died in the hospital, aged eighty-six, on August 19, 1977. He was survived by Zeppo, who died at seventy-eight from cancer on November 30, 1979, in Palm Springs.

Some time before Groucho's death, Woody Allen had declared:

I can't think of a comedian who combined a totally original physical conception that was hilarious with a matchless verbal delivery. I believe there is a natural inborn greatness in Groucho that defies close analysis as it does with any genuine artist. He is simply unique in the same way that Picasso or Stravinsky are and I believe his outrageous unsentimental disregard for order will be equally as funny a thousand years from now. In addition to all this, he makes me laugh.

Groucho receives his Honorary Oscar from Jack Lemmon at
the 46th Annual Academy Awards on April 2, 1974. (Photo
courtesy Academy of Motion Picture Arts and Sciences)

THE FILMS OF
THE MARX BROTHERS

Groucho (Mr. Hammer) tries to interest Margaret Dumont (Mrs. Potter) in a map of Cocoanut Manor, the land he will be auctioning. Groucho: "Why, it's the most exclusive residential district in Florida. Nobody lives there."

Harpo, dressed in his party outfit and not amused by the speeches.

The Cocoanuts

1929

Mr. Hammer: GROUCHO MARX. *Harpo:* HARPO MARX. *Chico:* CHICO MARX. *Jamison:* ZEPPO MARX. *Mrs. Potter:* Margaret Dumont. *Polly Potter:* Mary Eaton. *Bob Adams:* Oscar Shaw. *Penelope:* Kay Francis. *Harvey Yates:* Cyril Ring. *Hennessy:* Basil Ruysdael. *Bell captain:* Sylvan Lee. *Dancing bell-hops:* Gamby-Hall Ballet Girls and Allan K. Foster Girls. *Lifeguard/party guest:* Barton MacLane.

Directors: Joseph Santley and Robert Florey. *From the musical play, book by:* George S. Kaufman and *(uncredited)* Morrie Ryskind, *music by:* Irving Berlin. *Screen adaptation:* Morrie Ryskind. *Cinematographer:* George Folsey. *Art director:* Ernst Fegté. *Editor:* Barney Rogan. *Songs ("When My Dream Comes True," "Florida by the Sea," "The Monkey Doodle-Doo"):* Irving Berlin. *Music director:* Frank Tours. *Choreographers:* Chester Hale, Maria Gambarelli. *Assistant directors:* Ray Cozine, Bert Granet. *Associate producer:* James R. Cowan. *Producer:* Monta Bell. *In charge of production:* Walter Wanger. *Presented by:* Adolph Zukor and Jesse L. Lasky. *Production company/distributor:* Paramount Famous Lasky (A Paramount Picture). *Running time:* 96 minutes. *Release date:* August 3, 1929 (New York premiere: May 23, 1929).

Despite its ponderous camerawork and primitive sound recording, its silly plot and dated musical elements, *The Cocoanuts* is a rich and wonderful repository of Marxian humor. Of course, it would have looked better in 1929 when it was on a par with other new movies technically, and before the image on nitrate film had seriously deteriorated in places leaving sections that are visually blemished on modern prints (a few minutes of footage seem to have been lost entirely). In fact, the technical restrictions serve to make it all the better a record of the hit stage play. Because

Zeppo (Jamison) and Groucho greet the new guests at the Hotel de Cocoanut—Chico and Harpo . . .

but the greeting almost develops into a fight.

Harpo gives his leg to a bellboy. In the film, he eats two of the buttons off the man's outfit beforehand.

filming was so difficult, the studio had no incentive to open up the play or do any shooting out of doors despite its Florida setting. (A few buckets of water flung into camera range at the back of a beach set are the only indication of the sea.)

Groucho appears as Mr. Hammer (no first name), the owner-manager of a six hundred-room hotel in Florida. The background is the temporary boom in property values that took place in Florida during the mid-twenties. Groucho also owns some surrounding real estate which he auctions during the film. His name derives from the auctioneer's hammer but it lacks the colorfulness of his later ones.

In most of his films, Groucho has some temporary foothold in society, a position reached by trickery or misunderstanding, and he lives for the moment, a parasite on society. It is a little unusual to find Groucho behaving to some degree like a proper businessman, rushing off to greet some expected guests at the railroad station or seizing an opportunity to cater a banquet. But more often his manner of conducting business demonstrates how indifferent he is to achieving success. Although the season has yet to open (explaining why the hotel looks so empty of visitors), Groucho is virtually broke: "Three years ago I came to Florida without a nickel in my pocket. Now I have a nickel in my pocket." Only one of the present occupants is paying her bill. You would expect this to be Margaret Dumont's Mrs. Potter, who seems so very proper a woman she wouldn't dream of overlooking it, yet it is her daughter who is the model guest (though, surely, mother is paying for her?).

The staff are clamoring for their wages, but Groucho deals with that by a clever play on words that combines a patriotic appeal with the suggestion of a quick bargain. "Wages?" he asks them. "You want to be wage slaves? Answer me that." They don't. "No, of course not!" he answers for them, continuing: "Well, what makes wage slaves? Wages! I want you to be free. Remember, there's nothing like liberty except *Collier's* and the *Saturday Evening Post*. Be free, my friends, one for all and all for me and me for you and three for five and six for a quarter."

As usual, Groucho is attracted to Margaret Dumont for her wealth. Here, as Mrs. Potter (another prosaic name), she is at her most pompous and hidebound, refusing to allow her daughter, Polly, to marry Bob Adams, a mere clerk, until he suddenly achieves success as an architect. (This is not a happy ending: the pleasant Polly, as played by Mary Eaton, deserves better than the oafish hulk of Oscar Shaw's Bob.) Dumont is the first to believe that Bob stole her necklace and, to wipe out the shame of her daughter's past association with him, she arranges for Polly to marry Harvey Yates, of whom she approves because he is "one of the Boston Yates" (whereas in reality he is one of the thieves). Mrs. Potter is never ruffled: when earlier her daughter attempts to correct her assertion that there has never been a scandal in the Potter family by referring to a certain Uncle Dick, she quashes that by declaring, "Polly, it is a well-known fact that your uncle was drunk at the time." And when Harvey Yates has been exposed in his true colors, she makes what she calls "a slight change" in the nuptial arrangements, mereby substituting the now-successful Bob for the now-disgraced Harvey.

As she is so thick-skinned, it is not surprising that Groucho's insults don't usually register or that he can level with her and get away with it (she wonders if he'd love her if she were poor: "I might but I'd keep my mouth shut"). Groucho's romantic patter constantly vulgarizes the notion of love: "Just think, tonight, tonight, when the moon is sneaking around the clouds, I'll be sneaking around you." And "Did anyone ever tell you you look like the Prince of Wales? I don't mean the present Prince of Wales. One of the old Wales. And, believe me, when I say whales I mean whales. I know a whale when I see one." And, of their future together: ". . . an empty bungalow just for me and you, where we could bill and cow—no, we could bull and cow . . ." (Groucho often mixes up his words in this film and *Animal Crackers*.) It was here that Groucho sang a number entitled "A Little Bungalow," cut from the film.

There is one point when Groucho is grappling

Groucho tells Harpo: "Hey, hey, hey, don't throw that! That's only for long distances."

Chico explains to Groucho that Harpo is hungry as he starts eating and drinking the items on the counter.

with her cumbersome bulk where she does complain: "Can't you keep your hands to yourself?" He leaps back with his hands up, crying "Come on, I'll play you one more game! The three of you!" And Dumont does suspect an insult when told her eyes shine like the pants of a blue serge suit, to which Groucho replies: "That's not a reflection on you—it's on the pants." (The insult

93

was an old one, from *I'll Say She Is*.) She is also offended when Groucho locks himself in with her in her room and starts to take off his coat, but he admits to having no real amorous interest, telling her "I'm only playing."

Naturally, Groucho loses no opportunity to expound on his plans for developing the area. To really impress her, he produces a length of pipe. "Look at it, nobody can fool you on a sewer pipe, can they, a woman like you?" Thus at the same time as he flatters her as a woman of experience, he insults her by the type of experience he implies. He goes on to tell her the size of pipe is not yet fixed and householders will be able to vote on it. If there's a tie, it will go to the Supreme Court and Groucho happens to have inside information. "The chief justice is crazy about this type sewer," he whispers in his most outlandish confidence. He leaves her holding the sewer pipe, protesting in vain.

From these examples, Groucho has likened her bulk to that of a whale or three people (the ultimate in this line of development comes in *Duck Soup* where Groucho describes her as occupying enough space for an office block). He has also coarsened love, reducing wooing to animal sex, and, if the sewer pipe is taken as a phallic symbol (as in Dennis P. de Loof's "constructive analysis" of the film), made sex seem dirty and unclean.

Part of Groucho's technique involves answering for the other person (or people, as in his handling of the wage-hungry staff). He assumes that Mrs. Potter would like to know about Florida and proceeds to lecture her. She manages to insert a protest that he's told her before, but he answers that he left out a comma. When she informs him that she hasn't the slightest idea, or clearly the slightest interest, in how alligator pears are made, Groucho is not deterred. "There you are! That's because you couldn't have been an alligator and don't let it happen again. You know that it sometimes requires years to bring the alligator and the pear together. They don't like each other." By now Mrs. Potter is interested and surprised. "No," he affirms, adding, "You know

how many alligator pears are sent out of this state every year and told not to come back? All they can get hold of. Florida feeds the nation but nobody feeds me and that's what I want to talk to you about . . ." Groucho's rapid flights of association come down to his perennial concern with his own well-being.

If Groucho can deal with Margaret Dumont and ordinary individuals who cross his path, he can exercise no control over Chico and Harpo. This provides a very important balance: Groucho would become insufferable without this check on his conduct.

In *The Cocoanuts*, Chico is a guest with no money and no concern about it. Groucho decides to use Chico to make false bids at the land auction and raise prices. Chico manages to grasp the basic idea; but once he's got it he applies it with unyielding tenacity by outbidding everyone else and even raising his own bid. Chico is very belligerent here—in similar situations in later films, he became more affable though still as unshakably stupid. So firmly imbedded is the idea of bidding that when Mrs. Potter offers a thousand dollars for the return of her necklace, Chico calls out "Two thousand!" At the concluding party, Groucho has only to start with "Ladies and gentlemen" for Chico to call out "Two hundred dollars!" It is richly ironic that the one person Groucho tries seriously to reason with and to use should prove so unsuitable.

Chico sports a phony Italian accent and uses this as an excuse to misunderstand words. He explains to Groucho what he thinks "auction" means by recalling that he came across on the Atlantic Auction and suggests that the levees on a map indicate the Jewish neighborhood. The further and more improbable the connection, the funnier it is—in a depressing kind of way. All Chico's misunderstandings obstruct communication: He can't be persuaded that "a lot," a piece of land, could mean anything but too much. In Chico, we see stupidity exalted. Most frustrating of all, he can't be made to realize he is stupid, so he has no reason to be worried about it.

In *The Cocoanuts* there occurs the first extended Groucho-Chico duologue as Groucho tries to conduct an intelligent conversation with Chico but is thwarted at every turn. Groucho is explaining his plans for the development of the area: "Now here is a little peninsula and here is a viaduct leading over to the mainland . . . " "Why a duck?" asks Chico. Groucho tries to explain: "It's deep water, that's vy-a-duck. Deep water. Look, look suppose you were out horseback riding and you came to that stream and you wanted to ford over. You couldn't make it. It's too deep." Chico: "What-a you want with a Ford if you gotta horse?" The "Why a Duck" scene is

Groucho makes love to Margaret Dumont. Groucho: "Say that you'll be truly mine or truly yours or yours truly." Dumont: "Will you keep your hands to yourself!"

undoubtedly the best remembered and most quoted one from *The Cocoanuts*.

Now Harpo is the most complex of the Marx Brothers, a creature of mischief who never hesitates to indulge his every whim and fancy. Though he doesn't speak (and doesn't as yet whistle and mime any messages), he is always eloquent through his expressions and actions and through sounding his horn. There is a quality of zest about everything Harpo does, and his whole-hearted enjoyment of life is infectious. He is easily delighted, easily outraged, easily dismayed. He is unpredictable: sometimes he is devious, sometimes reckless. There is a childlike air about all his actions; he reduces everything to a game. Although he can be regarded as quite a ruthless figure, he is at heart a boisterous child with a keen sense of mischief who never means to give any real offense.

Harpo is keen on petty larceny. Left in charge of the cash register, his first act is to open it and remove a roll of coins. There is an abridged version of his stolen silverware routine with knives dropping out of his sleeve in twos and threes. An engaging hint of his past leaks out when he accidentally reveals an old police notice headed "Silent Red—Wanted by the Police." Chico is more deliberately larcenous, considering picking pockets at the auction and letting Groucho know that he intends to fill his empty suitcase before he leaves the hotel. Groucho, too, is dishonest, recognizing the knives Harpo has dropped as his by the names of the hotels *he* stole them from.

Harpo demonstrates his habit of chasing women as soon as he arrives in the hotel. In *The Cocoanuts* he catches up with his prey—in this case Penelope, the brunette jewel thief played by Kay Francis. After constant interruptions by different Marx brothers and a police detective, she thinks she is alone in her hotel room and there is the magnificent moment when Harpo rises from beneath her bed like a prehistoric monster surfacing from the ocean depths. At this point, the image diplomatically fades.

She has invited this fate by her earlier encouragement of Harpo as part of a plan to make him the fall guy for the theft of Mrs. Potter's necklace. She approaches him in a very flirtatious manner and, obviously viewing him as a simpleton, puts on a superior air. First of all she drops a handkerchief beside him. Harpo picks it up with his foot and pockets it. Penelope is forced to ask him if he's seen a handkerchief. Harpo shakes his head. "I thought I dropped one," she says. Harpo's face seems to say in a very bored tone, "Oh, did you really?" Penelope tells him it doesn't really matter "because what I'm really interested in is you." Harpo nods and gives her his leg, his trick of loading people with it as though it were a detachable object. Penelope starts to lay on the flattery by asking, "Has anyone ever told you that you look like the Prince of Wales?" Harpo nods his head to indicate he's heard it all before. Harpo doesn't know her name but he does know her room number. When she puts her arms around him, he leans on her, smiling and inanely tugging the handkerchief from his breast pocket by his teeth. She walks off and Harpo follows, giving a broad imitation of her swinging hips. There is about Harpo here a fascinating blend of sickly coyness and mischievous impudence.

Otherwise, Harpo's interest is in young women in general, blondes in particular. They have to be unsuspecting to arouse his interest. One glance at him and they read his intentions and run, encouraging Harpo to give chase. The more women the better to Harpo's way of thinking: after he discovers that by ringing the bell on the reception counter he can summon a bellhop, he keeps on ringing it, Chico joins in, and the bellhops multiply.

Harpo does not really regard Margaret Dumont as a woman at all. When he delivers iced water to Mrs. Potter's room, he lies on her bed and with a broad grin pats the cover for her to join him—but this is really to tease her, and sure enough she gets highly indignant. She regards him as some kind of dangerous, unpredictable animal, and during the film is exasperated enough to ask, "What is the matter with the man now?" and similar lines when he invades her room or stag-

gers around drunk at her party. However, when he has recovered her valuable necklace, she instinctively kisses him. Then, oozing with gratitude, she declares that she must kiss him again. Harpo juts out his chin and lower lip, looking ferocious, and threatens to lay her out if she tries any such thing.

Harpo's appetite is another aspect of his character well explored in this film. It ranges from the buttons on the livery of a page boy to a piece of a telephone washed down with the contents of an inkwell. His strange eating habits recur in a few other films; he bites into another telephone as late as *A Night in Casablanca*.

The Cocoanuts also gives Harpo a magical ability to spirit objects away from their owners.

The detective loses his badge to Harpo and, arriving at the final party to keep an eye on things, finds he can't even hold on to his shirt. Groucho loses his necktie, false teeth, and underpants, Bob Adams his watch and handkerchief, the detective his jail keys as well. Groucho takes the joke to surreal lengths by suggesting that Harpo might have taken the third floor of the hotel.

The one thing that Harpo is furtive about is his harp-playing interlude. Here he creeps onto a dais and plays it alone and for his own pleasure.

Harpo and Chico are partners and have routines of their own. One is the fight. In this, Harpo holds Chico at arm's length and prepares to hit him with a massive punch from one fist, then moves forward and kicks Chico with his leg

A blank-faced Harpo offers Mary Eaton a shoulder to cry on after her boyfriend has been falsely arrested for stealing her mother's necklace.

97

instead. This kind of rowdyism is reserved for the most inopportune moments—when the suspicious detective is watching or when they are supposed to be breaking Bob Adams out of jail. Chico explains: "We no fight. That's my friend. We play this way." And Chico makes concessions for his partner. At one moment he declares he is so desperate for money that he would kill for it. He would even kill Harpo. Then he corrects himself: "No, you're my friend—I kill you for nothing."

In *The Cocoanuts*, Harpo and Chico bring off a number of musical parodies of remarkable ingenuity, being developed from the slightest pretext. The detective Hennessy walks up and down contemplating them. They move alongside him and walk back and forth in step, whistling and turning it into a dance routine. Harpo plays with the hotel cash register, pressing the keys so that the drawer keeps coming out, thumping his stomach. In no time Chico is banging the bell on top of the nearby cabinet and honking Harpo's horn and turning it into part of the "Anvil Chorus" from *Il Trovatore*. Then, when an annoyed Penelope labels Harpo a "bum," Harpo savors the word and mouths it to himself, Chico repeats it thoughtfully aloud and his "bum . . . bum . . . bum" becomes like the beating of a drum. They turn into soldiers, Harpo starts whistling, Groucho joins on the end "playing" his cigar as a mouth organ, and the three of them march off screen to the tune of "Yankee Doodle Dandy." Lastly, at the party, Harpo blows a stream of smoke into Groucho's face. "'Tis a breath of old Ireland!" exclaims Groucho in an Irish accent and Zeppo steps forward for all four Marx Brothers to perform an Irish jig. This is one of those rare and gratifying moments when the brothers function harmoniously as a quartet.

While Groucho tries hard to deal with Chico, he doesn't even attempt to argue with Harpo. When his dinner speech drives Harpo to the punch bowl with a ferocious expression of displeasure on his face, Groucho notes: "The one I've got rid of is worth three ordinary ones." Groucho is so disconcerted by his first encounter with Harpo, when

Harpo contrives to slap his face, that Groucho rushes behind the counter for safety. He does make one small effort to deter Harpo from using the hotel's pens as darts to fling at the wall, then gives up and encourages him. It suddenly becomes a fairground sideshow as Groucho starts calling "This way, folks! Three shots for . . ." and rings the bell, handing Harpo a cigar. Harpo's strange eating habits reduce Groucho to an uncharacteristic silence. When Harpo moves over to the pigeon holes and starts tearing up the guests' letters, Groucho is compelled to help him along by handing over some more items and apologizing for the absence of the afternoon mail.

Even in this first film, Zeppo is very much an also-ran. He functions as Groucho's assistant and has most of his scenes at the reception desk. Zeppo does join in the first energetic round of introductions when Harpo and Chico arrive and he is part of the musical burlesque of *Carmen*, "The Song of a Shirt," celebrating its disappearance from the detective's chest. Zeppo might have been given the romantic lead, suitably revised, rescuing it from the leaden hands of Oscar Shaw.

What is regrettable about *The Cocoanuts* is the way the Marxes help Polly and Bob. Consideration for others was never a true Marxian trait.

Groucho likes Polly enough to give her a genial introduction to a song and to sit back while she performs without a single interruption. It seems to have been his idea for Chico and Harpo to rescue Bob from jail (although Bob has to remind him of this). Harpo conks Harvey Yates on the head at the auction so that Bob's bid is so successful and is so moved at seeing Polly left alone on the auction ground, sobbing as Bob is taken to jail, that he comes up and offers her a lollipop and a shoulder to cry on (at least he undercuts the pathos by keeping a Keaton-like expressionless face). And the end of the film depicts the Marxes as foils for the romance: they are shown waving inanely at the camera and yielding the closing shot to Bob and Polly instead of throwing cocoanuts at them as they would later throw apples at Margaret Dumont to end *Duck Soup*.

Groucho makes his appearance at Margaret Dumont's party to general amusement. Groucho: "This costume has been condemned by *Good Housekeeping*." With Zeppo and Kay Francis (Penelope) at left, Cyril Ring next to Dumont.

Harpo's solo.

Animal Crackers

1930

Captain Jeffrey [or Geoffrey] T. Spaulding: GROUCHO MARX. *The Professor:* HARPO MARX. *Signor Emanuel Ravelli:* CHICO MARX. *Horatio W. Jamison:* ZEPPO MARX. *Mrs. Rittenhouse:* Margaret Dumont. *Arabella Rittenhouse:* Lillian Roth. *Roscoe W. Chandler:* Louis Sorin. *John Parker:* Hal Thompson. *Mrs. Whitehead:* Margaret Irving. *Grace Carpenter:* Kathryn Reece. *Hives the butler:* Robert Greig. *Inspector Hennessey:* Edward Metcalf. *Six footmen:* The Music Masters. *Girl:* Ann Roth.

Director: Victor Heerman. *Screenplay:* Morrie Ryskind. *Continuity:* Pierre Collings. *From the musical play, book by:* George S. Kaufman and Morrie Ryskind, *songs "Hooray for Captain Spaulding" and "Why Am I So Romantic?" music and lyrics by:* Bert Kalmar and Harry Ruby. *Cinematographer:* George Folsey. *Art director:* Ernst Fegté. *Music arranger:* John W. Green. *Recording engineer:* Ernest F. Zatorsky. *Production company/distributor:* Paramount Publix (A Paramount Picture). *Running time:* 98 minutes.

Release date: September 6, 1930 (New York premiere: August 29, 1930).

Even though *Animal Crackers* was filmed a year later than *The Cocoanuts*, it is still very restricted cinematically with only slightly less clumsy camerawork and primitive sound recording. Again it is essentially a film record of the hit stage play, though regrettably minus its big costume ball scene.

The film is not opened out but confined like the stage production to Rittenhouse Manor on Long Island. Scenes are shot from one side only, without reverse angles, and often the players are lined up in front of the camera as though they were at the front of a stage. New sets were designed for the film, however, and they form an early instance of screen art deco (the stage production had a classical decor). Theatrical references have been retained (Groucho tells Margaret Dumont's Mrs. Rittenhouse: "You're very fortunate that the Theatre Guild isn't putting this on. And so is the Guild"; and he asks to look at a program to see who he's playing when some confusion arises); Margaret Dumont's expressions are on a theatrical scale as she switches them to order; and, when the tin sheets are rattled to simulate thunder, the impression of watching a stage play is overwhelming. The Marx Brothers make their entrances in turn, as they arrive at Rittenhouse Manor for Margaret Dumont's weekend party opening the social season, and one can almost hear the applause of a live audience as each is announced and descends the staircase.

The love interest has been relegated somewhat compared to *The Cocoanuts* and is in any case much more attractively handled by Lillian Roth in a perky performance as Mrs. Rittenhouse's daughter, Arabella—like *The Cocoanuts'* Polly Potter, a rich girl loving an unappreciated genius, here a young painter called John Parker (played inoffensively by Hal Thompson). The lovers are allowed one song.

Groucho has his most celebrated role as Mrs. Rittenhouse's star guest, the African explorer Captain Geoffrey T. Spaulding. (It's "Geoffrey" on the newspaper headline that is shown, but "Jeffrey" on the cast list that immediately precedes it on the opening titles.) Zeppo is the first Marx brother on screen, as the Captain's field secretary. He joins in the "Hooray for Captain Spaulding" number that the excited guests have started, singing Groucho's conditions for attending. Then Groucho is carried in by four African natives: this and his explorer's outfit are the excessively authentic opening touches that support his masquerade. As the chorus continues the musical greeting, Groucho cavorts around in mad gyrations, twisting his legs like a corkscrew and simulating trudging through the jungle. Then it's down to business, Groucho briskly insulting Margaret Dumont by criticizing her home, trying to sell her an insurance policy, and likening her to an aging horse.

The exposed Harpo goes on a shooting rampage with one of Groucho's rifles. One victim is Robert Greig.

Groucho (Captain Spaulding) arrives at Rittenhouse Manor as the special guest at the party that Margaret Dumont (Mrs. Rittenhouse) is throwing.

Harpo (The Professor) makes his entrance watched by Robert Greig (Hives) and others. Here—but not in the film itself—he throws a "gookie."

It is Dumont who builds up his hunting exploits and he who sneers at her efforts. Her faith isn't even shaken when he faints at the suggestion of a caterpillar on his lapel. Later he romances both her and another prominent socialite, Mrs. White-head, simultaneously (while leveling with them: "You have got money, haven't you? Because, if you haven't, we can quit right now"), proposes bigamy, and then dashes off with some cuties "to sow a couple of wild oats." Which draws the response: "The Captain's so amusing!" and "Isn't he charming?" Groucho is prized as a celebrity and, as such, can do no wrong.

He is an honest phony, compared to the smart set and their retinue. The prominent art critic Roscoe W. Chandler hides the fact that he is a former fish peddler from Czechoslovakia called Abie Cabiddle (on top of that, he is a pompous bore when he gets on the subject of the arts); Mrs. Whitehead and her daughter are a snooty pair, jealously seeking to sabotage Mrs. Rittenhouse's arrangements; Hives, the manservant, who is revealed to have a criminal record, betrays Mrs. Rittenhouse's trust and even chloroforms Harpo on behalf of Mrs. Whitehead, his former employer; and Arabella Rittenhouse is a bit of a snob herself, horrified to learn that an ex-fish peddler is in the house and not above urging her boyfriend to marry her and live off her mother's expense accounts (but she is also rather engaging, thanks to Lillian Roth's bubbling personality, and she is willing to marry beneath her station).

In general, the high society depicted in *Animal Crackers* is shown to be worth very little. As a complete contrast, the Marxes act as they feel, not caring the least what others think. However, Mrs. Rittenhouse is the nicest of all the figures portrayed by Margaret Dumont. Much less stuffy than Mrs. Potter in *The Cocoanuts*, she has a sense of humor, being tickled by a duel of puns between Groucho and Chico. She is not completely stupid, querying some of Groucho's more extravagant statements about his African exploits and rightly accusing Chico and Harpo of being cardsharps when their flagrant cheating in the bridge game becomes too much. She is a little

worried by her daughter's interest in a man of no social position but seems genuinely concerned when it looks as though he is the one who has stolen her precious Beaugard painting, the other highlight (after Captain Spaulding) of her party. When Groucho reaches the point of declaring, in his African reminiscences, "We took some pictures of the native girls but they weren't developed. But we're going back in a couple of weeks . . . " she discreetly concludes the lecture, showing that she is a woman of tact as well as propriety.

Some of her ideas are a bit old-fashioned, of course. "Marriage is a very noble institution," she spouts and Groucho whinnies in contempt (to him, "It was put over on the American people while our boys were over there"). Groucho doesn't grapple with her in the same way as he handled Mrs. Potter and she is quite undeserving of a brutal stomach-punching she receives from Harpo.

She is on the receiving end of some more romantic patter from Groucho: "Mrs. Rittenhouse, ever since I've met you I've swept you off my feet. Something has been throbbing within me—oh, it's been beating like the incessant tom-tom in the primitive jungle. There's something I must ask you. . . . [*Groucho looks upwards, contemplating several ideas*] Would you wash out a pair of socks for me?" She is understandably taken aback but Groucho easily reassures her: "It's just my way of telling you that I love you, that's all."

Retained from the stage production are the pastiche Eugene O'Neill soliloquies and asides based on the playwright's innovative method of expressing a character's inner thoughts. O'Neill's *Strange Interlude* had opened in January 1928 and become a major talking point. It was still running at a rival theater when Groucho made fun of it on Broadway, providing topical satire. But for movie audiences in 1930, the devices must have been startling (the MGM film version of O'Neill's play with Clark Gable came much later). They are featured during his scene with Mrs. Rittenhouse and Mrs. Whitehead. He does let audiences know what's he up to, introducing the parodies with "If I were Eugene O'Neill I could tell you what I really think of you two" and "Pardon me while I have a Strange Interlude." He steps forward as the two actresses freeze behind him to deliver three soliloquies, the last prompted by his reflections on a future with Mrs. Rittenhouse: "You could live with your folks and I—I could live with your folks," after which he breaks off to intone solemnly: "Living with your folks. Living with your folks. The beginning of the end. Drab dead yesterdays shutting out beautiful tomorrows. Hideous, stumbling footsteps creaking along the misty corridors of time. And in those corridors I see figures . . . [*his voice grows deeper and clouded*] strange figures . . . weird figures . . . [*then in his normal voice*] Steel 186, Anaconda 74, American Can 138 . . . "

In no other film does Groucho have so much dialogue (it is the longest of all the Marx pictures). If, as he declares to the audience, "All the jokes can't be good," his material sets an astonishingly high standard of inventiveness. It features many of his most celebrated lines including: "One morning I shot an elephant in my pajamas. How he got in my pajamas, I don't know." In no other film does Groucho twist and manipulate the English language so outrageously. His misuse of vocabulary ranges from repetitions of his trick from *The Cocoanuts* of transposing key words ("Don't you remember Mrs. Beaugard lost a valuable Rittenhouse oil painting worth one hundred thousand dollars?") to dictating a letter to Zeppo for the law firm of Hungerdunger, Hungerdunger, Hungerdunger and MacCormick that is full of standard business phrases but completely without content—and, when Zeppo reads it back, turns out to be lacking a Hungerdunger. "You've left out the main one, too!" exclaims Groucho. (In later years, Groucho claimed to have written this sequence.)

Chico is Signor Emanuel Ravelli, the musician hired to play for Mrs. Rittenhouse. After he descends the main staircase, his first thought is to find the dining room. Eating is as much of an obsession with Chico as it is with Harpo, although

Chico does not share Harpo's exotic taste for objects like telephones and Harpo does not do any eating in *Animal Crackers*. When, in *The Cocoanuts*, Groucho was showing Chico the layout of Cocoanut Manor with Cocoanut Heights, Cocoanut Junction, etc., Chico's only query was: "Where you got cocoanut custard?" When Mrs. Rittenhouse suggests they play cards for the usual stakes, Chico accepts and asks for French fried potatoes as well.

Chico is as dense as in *The Cocoanuts*, but without the surliness. For Mrs. Rittenhouse, he elaborates a scale of fees by which he is paid more for rehearsing than playing and most for not playing at all. He plays "Sugartime" for Mrs. Rittenhouse and her guests, keeps repeating part of it, admits that he's forgotten how it ends and reveals that he once kept on playing for three whole days. Here, as in the bidding at the auction in *The Cocoanuts*, once Chico gets an idea in his head he won't let go. Chico is similarly stubborn about his dishonesty: asked by Arabella to substitute John Parker's copy of the Beaugard painting for the real thing, he refuses to help her when she makes the mistake of assuring him that it isn't stealing. (Later, he and Harpo do make the substitution but their change of heart is not explained.)

Chico never lets Groucho get the better of him. Groucho listens to Chico's scale of charges and asks him, "How much would you want to run into an open manhole?" "Just the cover charge!" replies Chico, unusually laughing at his own joke. "Well, drop in some time," suggests Groucho. "Sewer!" says Chico. "Well, we cleaned that up pretty well," concludes Groucho.

The main Chico-Groucho scene comes late in the film and does not involve Groucho losing out financially like the auction scene in *The Cocoanuts*, although he is ultimately driven into a frenzy by Chico's obtuseness. Groucho is trying to work out who stole the Beaugard painting and Chico laboriously describes the situation as Groucho listens glumly. Chico proposes asking everyone in the house if they took it. Groucho offers a practical objection, which has nothing to

Groucho to Margaret Dumont: "Ever since I met you, I've swept you off my feet." (In the film itself, Groucho exposes the same knee but kneels on the other one.)

Groucho abandons Margaret Irving (left, as Mrs. Whitehead) and Margaret Dumont (right), after proposing marriage to both of them. "Before I get married, I'm going to sow a couple of wild oats."

Harpo is excited at the prospect of receiving a bribe from Louis Sorin to keep secret his former identity as Abie the Fish Peddler.

Harpo examines the check for $5,000 that he and Chico have extracted from Louis Sorin and is about to see if it will bounce (it does).

Louis Sorin (art connoisseur Roscoe W. Chandler) has remarked to Chico (Ravelli), "I see you're admiring my picture, eh?" Chico: "Your picture? Well, it don't look like you." With Hal Thompson (John Parker) and Lillian Roth (Arabella Rittenhouse).

The bridge game with Chico, Margaret Dumont, Harpo, and Margaret Irving. Chico extracts one of many aces of spaces from Harpo's sleeve. (In the film itself, this moment doesn't occur and Harpo's sleeves are rolled up.)

Chico briefs Harpo to come out fighting—his opponent is the unsuspecting Margaret Dumont.

Groucho begins his talk on his African trip: "Africa is God's country—and he can have it."

do with whether the thief would obligingly own up: "Suppose nobody in the house took the painting?" Chico takes a short, logical step forward: "Go to the house next door." Groucho asks: "Supposing there isn't any house next door?" Chico takes another short, logical step forward:

"Then, of course, we gotta build one!" Groucho's interest is suddenly awakened and the pair set about drawing up detailed plans for this entirely irrelevant house. A maid's house is laid out between Chico and Groucho's room and sounds as though it will be as busy as Penelope's bedroom

Chico and Harpo start to fight at Mrs. Rittenhouse's party. (This is no longer in the film and evidently preceded Chico's piano solo.)

Chico and Harpo battling over the piano seat at Mrs. Rittenhouse's party. (This moment is not in the film as seen today.)

Louis Sorin says a few words at the unveiling of his Beaugard painting.

in *The Cocoanuts*. When Groucho returns to the subject of the missing painting, Chico has forgotten all about it.

Chico makes Roscoe W. Chandler admit to being a former fish peddler and Chandler has an interesting comeback: "Say, how did you come to be an Italian?" "Never mind, whose confession is this?" retorts Chico. It is the only time Chico's dialect act is ever questioned. Otherwise, no one in the team's films pays it any more attention than Groucho's greasepaint mustache.

Harpo is the last to make a grand entrance. He is announced as simply "The Professor" but a professor of what—blonde-chasing, perhaps—is never made clear. He is apparently dressed up for the occasion in top hat and bow tie but when the butler takes his cloak he is revealed in his underwear. In context, this is a shocking image that crystallizes the Marx Brothers' contempt for society and for appearances.

His punching of Mrs. Rittenhouse in a later scene is even more disturbing. Harpo is provoked when she declines to play with him, swings a punch at her, misses, and falls over. Chico starts counting him out until a bell rings and then helps set him up for the next round of what has become, quite unknown to Mrs. Rittenhouse, a boxing match. When the bell goes, Harpo charges out, grabs her, and punches her repeatedly in the stomach as she clings to him. This is the most barbaric sight in any Marx film: society, as represented by Mrs. Rittenhouse, literally becoming a punchbag. The image is made tolerable by the way Harpo is obviously lifting Margaret Dumont instead of actually hitting her, but the basic idea is not impaired.

Another reverberative image is that of Harpo using the precious Beaugard painting as a blanket when he sleeps on the garden bench. He takes great care of it *as a blanket*, neatly folding it up after use. When he produces it rolled up from inside his raincoat at the end, Chandler is delighted to have it back and no one is concerned about any damage it may have suffered. The possession of the painting is far more important than the painting itself.

As Louis Sorin (Roscoe W. Chandler) discovers that a fake Beaugard has been put on display in place of the real one, Groucho strips for action: "Leave it to me. I'll throw some light on the subject." The lights go out.

The dictation scene. Groucho reacts to his secretary, Zeppo (Horatio W. Jamison), tells him: "Now, you said a lot of things here that I didn't think were important so I just omitted them."

Margaret Irving tries to get round Harpo by asking him "Isn't there someone you do like? Isn't there someone you love?" Harpo then admits to loving a horse.

Harpo has slapped the hand of Margaret Irving, kissed it better, and now tries to break her arm.

Harpo has chased a blonde through the house and tries to tempt her out of hiding with a lollipop.

One painting has been found and is examined by Groucho, Chico, Lillian Roth, and Hal Thompson.

The Four Marx Brothers arrive on the scene singing "My Old Kentucky Home."

Chico and Harpo are partners and work together in blackmailing Chandler. As in *The Cocoanuts*, Harpo has magical powers by which he spirits away other people's possessions, including, in Roscoe W. Chandler's case, the birthmark on the back of his arm, the very thing that identifies him as the former Abie Cabiddle. Identify confusion is rampant in the Marx Brothers' work.

Harpo develops his blonde-chasing here and repeats his routine of stolen cutlery dropping out of his sleeves in front of the law. He is also approached by another woman who treats him condescendingly like Penelope in *The Cocoanuts*. Here it is Mrs. Whitehead, telling him that she likes little boys like him. Does he perhaps like anyone? Is there someone precious in his life? Harpo nods and produces a photograph of a horse. The woman giggles with amusement while Harpo looks baffled and makes it clear that she is the one who is mad. The Marxes are unshakably sure of themselves; it is others who are wrong.

The ending of *Animal Crackers* on film is curious. The stage version offered the Du Barry scene, a costume ball in which Groucho dressed up as King Louis the 57th, Margaret Dumont was the Queen, and Harpo performed his harp specialty for her. The four Marx Brothers performed the musical number "We're Four of the Three Musketeers." In the film, Harpo faces arrest by a police inspector and uses a spray can to subdue all around him until he is the only one left standing. (This was originally a Flit can, the film's pressbook suggesting tie-ins with local merchants; but the brand name has been crudely scratched out on modern prints.) Harpo starts to pick his way through the bodies, then spots the blonde he has been chasing earlier, and sprays himself to sleep beside her. The film seems to fade away like a dream. . . .

Groucho dances the tango with Thelma Todd (gangster's wife Lucille Briggs).

Monkey Business

1931

The Stowaways: GROUCHO MARX, HARPO MARX, CHICO MARX, ZEPPO MARX. *Lucille Briggs:* Thelma Todd. *Joe Helton:* Rockliffe Fellowes. *First Officer Gibson:* Tom Kennedy. *Mary Helton:* Ruth Hall. *Alky Briggs:* Harry Woods. *The Captain:* Ben Taggart. *Officer:* Otto Fries. *Manicurist:* Evelyn Pierce. *Madame Swempski:* Maxine Castle. *Cab driver at barn:* Ethan Laidlaw. *Passenger/man on dock:* Sam Marx.

Director: Norman McLeod. *Screenwriters:* S. J. Perelman, Will B. Johnstone, and *(additional dialogue)* Arthur Sheekman. *Cinematographer:* Arthur L. Todd. *Assistant director:* Charles Barton. *Producer (uncredited):* Herman J. Mankiewicz. *Production company/distributor:* Paramount Publix (A Paramount Picture). *Running time:* 77 minutes. *Release date:* September 19, 1931 (New York opening: October 7, 1931).

In *Monkey Business*, the four Marx Brothers are stowaways on an ocean liner. It is the only film in which Groucho lacks some kind of a position. He is merely a stowaway like his brothers. Though they are obviously managing quite comfortably in their barrels in the ship's hold, Groucho becomes an outsider like his brothers who runs away when they are spotted and is regarded as odd by other people. At times Groucho is distinctly diminished (although, in reference to his Captain Spaulding in *Animal Crackers* who fainted at the suggestion of a caterpillar on his lapel, he now claims to have fought his way up from wild caterpillars). He is frightened at the mention of a well-known gangster, Joe Helton, and he and Zeppo are so uncomfortable with the pistols they are given by another gangster, Alky Briggs, to use on Helton that they quickly drop them in a handy bucket of water. Just as bad is the moment at the party when Helton and some of the guests laugh at

Groucho's imitation of a bow-legged Southern-er—his performance, which concludes offscreen with the sound of receding horse hoofs, calls for some response from observers, but their amusement has a ring of superiority when perplexed shrugs would be more in order.

But, most often, Groucho manages to assert himself splendidly, and the film does have the pleasing effect of uniting the four brothers from the start. In this case, Zeppo sensibly inherits the duties of the juvenile lead, conducting a light romance with Joe Helton's daughter, Mary (Ruth Hall), and providing the brawn to subdue her kidnappers in the old barn at the end of the film while Chico and Harpo are largely bystanders and Groucho delivers a ringside commentary from the rafters. Throughout this one film, Zeppo finds a valid place alongside his brothers, joining in with them at many key moments and making the romantic banter more tolerable, although at the end he abandons the other three and goes off with the girl.

Though Groucho runs away from the captain, he proves more than able to handle him when they come face to face. At first the captain doesn't realize Groucho's one of the stowaways when he delivers his now celebrated lament: "Do you know who sneaked into my stateroom at three o'clock this morning? Nobody, and that's my complaint." He and Chico follow the waiter into the captain's quarters and sit down to eat, ultimately dealing with the captain's objections by luring him into a closet and locking the door. Although they run away when the first officer arrives, they circle the table and pick up all the food they require before running out.

In this film, Margaret Dumont is replaced by a much younger woman, the voluptuous Thelma Todd, playing Lucille, the wife of gangster Alky Briggs. Groucho hides in her closet and when she asks what he's doing there, his eyeballs rotate lasciviously, his eyebrows jump up and down, he beckons and purrs, "Nothing! Come on in." She is not impressed but she later tries to engage his sympathy over Alky's mistreatment of her. He cuts her off: "I know, I know, you're a woman who's been getting nothing but dirty breaks. Well, we can clean and tighten your breaks, but you'll have to stay in the garage all night." (This line has assumed ironic undertones since Todd was found dead in a garage filled with carbon monoxide fumes on the morning of December 16, 1935, at age thirty; possibly a suicide, probably murder, her unresolved demise has provided one of Hollywood's most intriguing mysteries.)

Groucho responds to Lucille's need for excitement: "Madam, before I get through with you, you will have a clear case for divorce, and so will my wife. Now, the first thing to do is to arrange for a settlement. You take the children, your husband takes the house, Junior burns down the house, you take the insurance, and I take you." Soon she throws herself into his arms and they tango across the room and over the bed, separating so that Groucho, with his eyes shut, inadvertently takes the hands of Alky who has just entered. Groucho quickwittedly assumes the offensive: "Sir, this is an outrage, breaking into a man's home. I'm not in the habit of making threats, but there'll be a letter about this in *The Times* tomorrow morning." Groucho is a master of the emotive phrase: having evoked the sanctity of the home and the power of *The Times*, he turns to the traditional respect for womanhood when Alky threatens to kill him: "That's the thanks I get for freeing an innocent girl who, although she is hiding in the closet at this moment, has promised to become the mother of her children." He then slips into a gruff Southern accent, making for the closet with the utmost dignity: "And with that, sir, I bid you a fond farewell. Good day, sir, good day!"

The scene carries on to be a brilliant demonstration of Perelman's observation about Groucho that "His best quality was the ability to turn in his own wheelbase, with a phrase or movement to set up a whole situation, or to destroy it, or kid it and shift rapidly into another identity or pose." Groucho's lines and delivery are far more varied than in *The Cocoanuts* or *Animal Crackers*. He is constantly changing tack before anyone can pin him down. He is at times sickeningly childish, as when Alky's declaration that he's wise (in the

The four stowaways.

The stowaways pause from being chased around the ship to pick up instruments and break into a swinging jazz number.

Groucho meets some of the ship's passengers: "You girls go to your rooms. I'll be down shortly."

Chico and Groucho follow the waiter into the Captain's cabin and join him for lunch.

Groucho orders the Captain's lunch to be sent up—and his dinner, too.

Harpo joins the puppets in the Punch and Judy show.

Harry Woods (gangster Alky Briggs) is angered by Groucho's friendship with Thelma Todd but comes to admire Groucho's nerve.

Harry Woods's threats to Rockliffe Fellowes (Joe Helton) are interrupting Harpo's concentration on his chess game with Chico, so he hits Woods over the head with his horn.

sense of knowing what's going on) becomes a pretext for a quiz, to see if he knows the capital of Nebraska, which then shifts to a question about the capital of the Chase Manhattan Bank. When Alky allows him a few last words before he's shot, Groucho responds, "Yes, I'd like to ask you one question" and then in a high-pitched semi-gabble asks, "Do you think girls think less of a boy if he lets himself be kissed? I mean, don't you think that although girls go out with boys like me, they always marry the other kind?"

At times like this and when he sucks his finger and smirks childishly, Groucho is hilarious and almost nauseating. He never goes so far in this direction in any other film. This Groucho, one can see, is quite the sort to have sent the captain rude notes (although calling him "an old goat" is a bit tame). He is also unusually callous in this film when he catches an elderly couple, married but not to each other, on the veranda in the party scene and exploits their nervousness and fear of exposure. Had they argued or tried to bluff it out, they would invite rough treatment, but their timidity makes Groucho's verbal harassment somewhat distasteful just as Groucho's insults to Margaret Dumont's characters would not be funny if they understood his banter well enough to be really offended. Normally, Groucho's victims go some way to inviting ridicule and attack by their pomposity or interference, as does the captain: the stowaways are quite content in the forward hatch but he insists on disturbing them. . . .

Chico has comparatively little chance to register in *Monkey Business*. There is a scene in the chartroom where Groucho's attempt to teach him a little history proves as futile as explaining the layout of Cocoanut Manor in the "why a duck" scene in *The Cocoanuts*, Chico mistaking "vessel" for "whistle" and "mutiny" for "matinee." Groucho is so exasperated that he asks, "Do you suppose I could buy back my introduction to you?" and turns to the camera in conclusion: "There's my argument—restrict immigration!" This accepts Chico on his own terms as an Italian.

Chico is again concerned about eating and gets Groucho to order a meal, telling him: "I didn't eat

Rockliffe Fellowes offers Chico and Harpo jobs in his gang. Chico invites him to feel their muscles, and puts forward an arm while Harpo offers his leg.

Harpo and Chico are Rockliffe Fellowes's new bodyguards.

Chico and Harpo have their guns at the ready as bodyguards but are not too sure where their boss has gone. At left, Tom Kennedy (as First Officer Gibson).

When the man tells the barber that he's got a frog in his throat, Harpo starts to look for his missing amphibian.

As bodyguards, Chico and Harpo have mistakenly followed the wrong man and think their boss has put on a beard as a disguise.

in three days. I didn't eat yesterday, I didn't eat today, and I'm not going to eat tomorrow. That makes three days." As usual, Chico always has an answer to everything. Asking Joe Helton for a job for his grandfather putting cheese in mouse-traps at Joe's new mansion, he is informed there are no mice there. "That's all right," says Chico. "He brings his own mice with him."

Chico's keen interest in self-preservation is clearly seen when he and Groucho face one of the kidnappers in the old barn. "Go on, you get him," says Chico. "I'll wait for you outside." "Keep out of this loft!" yells the man threateningly from upstairs. "Well, 'tis better to have loft and lost than never to have loft at all," declares Chico, delivering one of his more ingenious puns. In *Monkey Business*, he is burdened by some very feeble examples, such as those involving heir, air, and hair.

Chico leads Harpo in the mustache-trimming scene in the barber shop. The victim is an officer who settles down for a shave, unaware that two of the stowaways have taken the place of the bar-bers. Under Chico's directions, Harpo snips away at the officer's stylish mustache, trying to even up first one side, then the other, until it has entirely gone. Later, an elderly passenger on the boat has a beard which Chico and Harpo tug vigorously, thinking it is a disguise. Throughout the Marx films, mustaches and beards are regarded as a sign of affectation, to be attacked physically and verbally. Toupees can be added in the case of this film: Groucho whisks one off a man's head at Helton's party. Groucho's own mustache, of course, is patently false and exaggerated, ridiculing real mustaches.

Harpo is at his most savage and ruthless in *Monkey Business*. Although nothing matches his punching of Margaret Dumont's stomach in *Animal Crackers*, there is a much more aggressive sense of devilment about him here. (His costume, too, has become louder, with a strongly patterned shirt.) In no other film is he so violent and unrestrained. When his attempt to get through passport control as Maurice Chevalier fails, he goes berserk and flings papers in every direction.

As various officials try to restrain him, he grabs one and frenziedly rubberstamps the man's bald head. In demonstrating his capabilities as a bodyguard on Chico (at the latter's suggestion), Harpo lets loose a couple of mighty uppercuts that leave Chico looking positively groggy (a complete contrast to his habit in other films of faking punches and playfully kicking Chico instead). When he loses a pet frog, he overhears a little man saying very hoarsely, "I've got a frog in my throat." Harpo promptly upends him, shaking him quite violently, in an attempt to dislodge a frog. When Roscoe W. Chandler in *Animal Crackers* was upended to expose the birthmark which he denied having, he invited the treatment, and in any case was stood on his head rather less vigorously than this innocent bystander.

Harpo's pursuit of women is even more single-minded than before and includes a shot of him on a bicycle in hot pursuit of a woman running across the lawn at Joe Helton's party. He is much more infantile, indulging in such pranks as tricking a male passenger into entering the women's lava-tory. He hears a steward calling "Tag!" and touches him on the shoulder, then darts away, expecting to be chased. He gets Alky Briggs with his hands up and starts a patty-cake routine with him, and he sits down with the children in the ship's nursery, wanting to watch the Punch and Judy show.

Another physically punishing type of situation is introduced in *Monkey Business* and appears in several later films. This involves bodies being pressed on each other. During a chase on deck, Harpo eludes his pursuers. A woman in a deck-chair clambers to her feet rather rapidly, reveal-ing Harpo beneath her. When Harpo rushes off, a very squashed figure of an elderly man rises from the depths of the chair. How this human sandwich came into being is not something one has time to question.

One scene in *Monkey Business* generates the most bizarre confusion between the animate and the inanimate and becomes quite surreal. This is the scene at the Punch and Judy show in which Harpo, joining the two puppets and with frozen

At Joe Helton's party, Groucho advises a guest: "Run for your life. The Indians are coming! Put your scalp in your pocket." (He then takes off the man's toupee and hands it to him.)

Groucho completes his imitation of a Texan by taking the cowboy hat from a guest and walking off bowlegged as Rockliffe Fellowes tries to stop him.

expressions (including his "gookie") and a mask on the back of his head, becomes indistinguishable from the puppets, only giving himself away by his attacks on the ship's officers when their backs are turned. When the socially acceptable ritual violence of Punch and Judy is replaced by First Officer Gibson's attempt to throttle Harpo, the children are not shocked but laugh and clap with delight. When the captain and his first officer pull at Harpo's leg through the front of the booth, Harpo comes out and helps them. The leg comes away (like the hand later when Harpo sits down at the harp before playing his solo). One of the more delicious elements of the scene is the way it manages to totally ignore the actual puppeteer. He is never seen.

Nowhere in the film are there any redeeming touches to help make Harpo "human" or sympathetic, like his gift of a lollipop to the heroine in *The Cocoanuts* or his love of a horse in *Animal Crackers*. In *Monkey Business*, Joe Helton presents to his party guests "the most beautiful thing in the world" and Harpo steps forward, with a nauseatingly coy expression on his face, to take a bow in place of Helton's daughter. Never has he been so grossly impertinent.

As the Marx Brothers' first screen original, *Monkey Business* is much faster than *The Cocoanuts* and *Animal Crackers*, broken down into shorter episodes and using more varied backgrounds. It is a remarkable achievement, for

Harpo is a wandering bustle at the party, here attaching himself to a guest conversing with Rockliffe Fellowes.

The Marx Brothers attempt to clear the passport counter by posing as Maurice Chevalier.

which credit is often tossed to S. J. Perelman, the best-known writer to have worked on their scripts. Groucho quite rightly pointed out, "I was doing this kind of comedy long before I met S. J. Perelman. Everybody has some kind of a curious notion that we were—or I was—deeply influenced by Perelman. That's not true at all. We're good friends but he wrote very little for us. As a matter of fact he wasn't great for us. We had writers—stage writers—that were much better for us than Sid. Now nobody could write a funnier piece than Sid but he wasn't really a constructionist for the stage. . . . The best writers we had were Kaufman and Ryskind." Perelman himself made it plain to interviewers that he worked on only two Marx Brothers films and then only as part of a team. "The Marx Brothers movies were really community efforts. They themselves were so anarchic—they sought advice and help from every possible quarter. It's impossible to trace the actual authorship of those films," he told one interviewer in 1974.

In other interviews, Perelman recalled that Groucho (not the studio) objected to a parody he had written, on the grounds that it would be too obscure for country audiences personified by Groucho as the Barber of Peru—a typical barber in Peru, Indiana. As Perelman explained to British interviewer Tony Bilbow:

> I wrote a scene, the setting of which was a conservatory with music going on in the background: Groucho was reclining in a rather Madame Récamier pose on this chaise longue and Thelma Todd, who was the ingénue, was making mad love to him, when suddenly he sprang up and pulled her into his arms and he said, "Come, Kapellmeister, let the violas throb. My regiment leaves at dawn." Now what I had in mind was a parody of the famous *Merry Widow* in which Prince Danilo looks into the eyes of the little fisher-maiden or whatever she was, and makes mad love to her with the camera moving in a sort of dolly shot with them as they dance. Well, when I submitted this, Groucho thought it was very amusing, but he felt that the rest of the speech demanded that this mythical barber in

> Peru should have a prior understanding of the whole *Merry Widow* legend in order to appreciate this. I didn't feel this. The barber in Peru won, and if you go to see *Monkey Business* you will detect the opening line. They cut out the entire speech but they left that one line: "Come, Kapellmeister . . . "

The parody of *Strange Interlude* could have been dropped from *Animal Crackers* on the same grounds of obscurity, but that had proven itself on stage and Groucho didn't have as much influence on that production. Now it seems he was beginning to take his screen appeal seriously. Of course, O'Neill takeoffs were funny in their own right (and remain funny, even though most viewers now don't know O'Neill's play), and it is quite possible that an extended parody of *The Merry Widow* would have upset the brisk flow of *Monkey Business*.

However, there is certainly a uniquely audacious and outrageous flavor to *Monkey Business*. It goes to extremes of violence and puerile humor like no other of their films. Groucho does not have to practice any subterfuge in *Monkey Business*: he is not pretending to be someone important, he doesn't even have a name, he can be himself. His chameleonic versatility is stretched to the limit, while Harpo becomes more savage and demoniacal. Chico carries on much as before, but the trio become completely unsympathetic. The film's malicious and cutting edge seems to stem from Perelman, as the same qualities are evident in his literary output. (The other screenwriter, Will B. Johnstone, had written *I'll Say She Is*, but seems to have been a more conventional humorist. Arthur Sheekman, credited as the contributor of additional dialogue, showed no great daring in a long and substantial Hollywood career and, according to Perelman, shared Groucho's view that some of his other material was too obscure and took it out.)

Someone seems to have decided that *Monkey Business* went too far. Although Perelman worked on their next picture, *Horse Feathers*, it was much less extreme in tone.

Groucho delivers a commentary as Zeppo and Harry Woods slug it out: "Ending of the first inning. No runs, no errors, but plenty of hits!"

Harpo gets the advantage, for a moment, of one of the kidnappers at the barn, while Chico taunts him: "Thought we were afraid, eh?"

Harpo watches the big fight Napoleon-style while Chico observes from astride a cow in the barn.

Harpo and Chico have delivered ice by hand to Groucho's wall safe. Groucho: "That's a fine way to carry ice. Where are your tongs?"

Horse Feathers

1932

Professor Quincy Adams Wagstaff: GROUCHO MARX. *Pinky:* HARPO MARX. *Baravelli:* CHICO MARX. *Frank Wagstaff:* ZEPPO MARX. *Connie Bailey, the college widow:* Thelma Todd. *Jennings:* David Landau. *Biology Professor:* Robert Greig. *Mullen:* James Pierce. *MacHardie:* Nat Pendleton. *Retiring President of Huxley College:* Reginald Barlow. *Professors in Wagstaff's study:* Edward J. Le Saint and E. H. Calvert. *Bartender:* Edgar Dearing. *Man at bar:* Vince Barnett. *Slot machine player:* Syd Saylor. *Laura, Connie's maid:* Theresa Harris.

Director: Norman McLeod. *Screenwriters:* Bert Kalmar, Harry Ruby, S. J. Perelman and Will B. Johnstone. *Cinematographer:* Ray June. *Music and lyrics (songs "I'm Against It," "Everyone Says 'I Love You' "):* Bert Kalmar and Harry Ruby. *Dance director:* Harold Hecht. *Producer (uncredited):* Herman J. Mankiewicz. *Production company/distributor:* Paramount Publix (A Paramount Picture). *Running time:* 68 minutes. *Release date:* August 31, 1932 (New York premiere: August 10, 1932).

Horse Feathers is the first of the Marx films to really satirize the period in which it was made. It gives college education a vigorous shaking, with comments on Prohibition and the Depression thrown in. Yet the film is more of a hodgepodge than *Monkey Business.* This time, Groucho, Harpo, and Chico have positions in society, even if Groucho is merely the latest in a long line of college presidents and Harpo's job of dog catcher enables him to enjoy himself catching his least favorite animal. Chico is an iceman who sells bootleg liquor on the side, while Zeppo (born ten or eleven years after Groucho) plays Groucho's son, a college student. Chico and Harpo are signed up to play football by Groucho. Alternating with displays of their unusual nonconformism, all of them make some effort to behave constructively and advance the plot so that in the climactic football game they are trying both to indulge their love of mischief for its own sake and win the match for their side. *Horse Feathers*, though largely from the same creative team as *Monkey Business*, is rather broader in humor with fewer audacious moments and memorable bits of dialogue.

University education is a ripe target for the Marx Brothers, readily associated with the kind of pomposity and pedantry that the team detest. The Marxes believe in natural wit, not acquired wisdom, in enjoyment, not enlightenment. Harpo, who cannot even write his name, is not noticeably disadvantaged and has no trouble getting along in the world or being enrolled in college. Groucho, as Professor Quincy Adams Wagstaff, the latest president of Huxley College, quickly shows at his inauguration ceremony what he thinks of higher education and the people who teach it. He ignores the rule against smoking and shaves in the corner of the stage to express his scorn for the full beards of the professors. His song "Whatever It Is I'm Against It" expresses his nihilistic philosophy: whatever the professors have to say, he's opposed to it. Groucho dances around tugging the line of scraggy beards while the students make up a chorus enthusiastically echoing Groucho's words. The professors themselves join in the number, shifting around the stage like sheep, too weak-willed to argue.

When the retiring president of the college interrupts Groucho to say, "I am sure the students would appreciate a brief outline of your plans for the future," Groucho barks "What?" The man repeats himself. "You just said that!" exclaims Groucho, having by this almost infallible method shown professors to be long-winded and repetitive. In a later scene a pair of professors show themselves to be simply yes-men, prepared to agree with anything Groucho says in order to safeguard their academic positions, regardless of what is best for the students.

The only aspect of college life in which Groucho takes any interest is football and, in the mistaken belief that Chico and Harpo are star players, he enrolls them as students so that they can play for Huxley. Harpo puts an "X" on the agreement by which he becomes a college student. It is during this sequence that he does his best to bring education down to his own level by vigorously shoveling books onto a blazing fire in an adjoining study. The shot is dramatically composed and derives its comic effectiveness by the way it escalates from an earlier one in which Harpo was seen placing a volume at a time on the fire, but it is a little unfortunate that his actions parallel the mass burning of books in Nazi Germany.

The fullest attack on education is made by all three brothers during the biology class. The professor in charge, although barely recognizable beneath a feature-obliterating set of whiskers, is played by Robert Greig, the head butler in *Animal Crackers* (and later the embodiment of solemn dignity in many of the Preston Sturges comedies). In *Horse Feathers*, his deep, booming voice and stiff manner are ideal to suggest a dull and pompous professor. Groucho enters to ask, "Have they started sawing the woman in half yet?" indicating his idea of what a biology class should be like. He introduces Chico and Harpo as new students and they bring the professor some fruit as if they were in first grade. Groucho takes over the lesson and points around a diagram of the human body: "The Alps are a very simple people living on a diet of rice and old shoes. Beyond the Alps lies more Alps and the Lord alps those who alp themselves." (The Alps joke is revived from *I'll Say She Is*.) Harpo puts a picture of a horse and then a calendar pinup in front of Groucho's chart. After he shyly confesses to the substitutions, crying like a repentant child, Groucho admonishes him: "My boy, as you grow older, you'll find you can't burn the candle at both ends." At this, Harpo's face lights up with glee and he produces a candle lit at both ends. He has caught the professor out and, like the child who contradicts his teacher on one small point, believes he has disproved the whole lesson. Before long, Chico and Harpo are firing peashooters at Groucho, who just happens to have his own peashooter and replies in kind. The scene has disintegrated into a low vaudeville sketch.

Groucho has to deal with Chico to gain entry to a speakeasy and this leads to the usual verbal misunderstandings on Chico's part that drive Groucho to exasperatedly ask, "Why don't you bore a hole in yourself and let the sap run out?" Groucho has admitted that he doesn't know the password and Chico gives him three guesses and a clue that it's the name of a fish. Chico mistakes Groucho's suggestion of "haddock" for "headache" and otherwise confuses matters, eventually letting Groucho know the right word and opening the door when he says "swordfish." Groucho enters, shutting out Chico, and refuses to admit him when he says "swordfish" because he's changed the password. "Well, what's the new one?" asks Chico. "Gee, I forgot it," replies Groucho, "I'd better come out there with you." And he does, leaving them both locked out. Even if Groucho doesn't intend the door to shut behind him, this last line is rather weak—it's not like him to play by the rules, especially when he does want to remain inside the speakeasy.

Harpo has no trouble entering—he shows a fish with a sword in its throat—and Groucho and Chico are reduced to crawling in on all fours after him. Groucho makes a strong showing when settling up with the bartender. "Can you cash a check for fifteen dollars and twenty two cents?" he asks. The bartender opens his cash register and Groucho adjusts his glasses, waiting very patiently. He takes the money from the bartender and declares that as soon as he has a check for that amount, the bartender will be sure to receive it. But then, instead of moving off calmly, leaving the barman dumbfounded, he runs away before he can be caught.

In this film Harpo behaves as arrogantly as in *Monkey Business*. There is nothing lovable or even likeable about him, although he is not generally as unsympathetic as in the earlier film. He looks a mess; his costume has become far scruffier, making him more uncouth than ever. His trousers are split so that the ends flap as he moves, his coat is slashed, his suspenders dangle loosely, his wig looks like an old mop.

As a dog catcher, he carries out his work with fiendish cunning. He lures one wire terrier into his cart by simply letting it chase him there (he later traps a policeman in the same way). He doesn't restrict himself to strays but rounds up every dog in sight. In view of his dislike for dogs in other films, it is reasonable to suppose that he catches them not for the money but the pleasure. He carries different-sized fake lampposts to attract passing canines and lies in wait for them like a big game hunter. Unfortunately, this establishing scene is missing from modern prints of *Horse Feathers* except for its ending where a down-and-out asks Harpo for help to get a cup of coffee and Harpo produces one, hot and steaming, from his raincoat pocket. It is simply a demonstration of effortless one-upmanship on Harpo's part, like the candle burning at both ends or the hatchet with which he literally cuts a pack of cards or the live seal he produces in Groucho's study to legalize agreements. These sharp visual puns are a well-developed feature of Harpo's work in *Horse Feathers*. Other bits of his behavior are familiar from *The Cocoanuts* but nonetheless effective for that: his outsmarting the cop with just one badge by displaying hundreds of police badges inside his coat, and his hand-over-hand routine up the nightstick the policeman is holding, previously employed on Penelope's cane.

Harpo's hatred of dogs is balanced by his affection for horses. After Zeppo sings a romantic number, "Everyone Says 'I Love You,' " Harpo takes it up, sitting on the edge of the sidewalk, clutching a bunch of flowers and whistling it to the horse who draws his dog cart. He and the horse share a picnic lunch of flowers and salted oats, quite oblivious of the traffic holdup they are causing. The sequence is staged with some care by keeping first the horse and then the line of traffic out of frame, to be revealed in turn for greater comic effectiveness.

Zeppo sings to Connie Bailey, the "college widow," played by Thelma Todd, another woman out for a good time like her Lucille Briggs in *Monkey Business*. He has been neglecting his studies to pursue her. She is working for Jennings, head of the rival Darwin College, to obtain

Groucho (Professor Quincy Adams Wagstaff) concludes the opening musical number at his inauguration as president of Huxley College.

Groucho has entered the speakeasy and locked Chico (Baravelli) out. Chico wants to come in and gives the password—but Groucho has changed it.

Harpo (Pinky) puts a button into the speakeasy's slot machine, pulls the lever, and waits for the jackpot.

Harpo, Groucho, and Chico order drinks in the speakeasy. Edgar Dearing is the bartender, Vince Barnett the customer next to Chico. In the film itself, Harpo dances a jig to indicate he wants Scotch.

Harpo with the posy that he offers his horse.

As the policeman has pointed out his badge, Harpo responds by displaying all the ones he has.

the Huxley football signals before the big game. (The college widow's appearance in the film provides one of several parallels with a successful 1904 stage comedy, *The College Widow*, by George Ade, which may have been a loose inspiration for *Horse Feathers*—see "A Constructive Analysis of Three Early Marx Bros. Films" by Dennis P. de Loof. Ade's play was owned by Warner Bros., which had produced film versions in 1927 and 1930, the latter retitled *Maybe It's Love*.)

Harpo is seen in Connie's room hanging off a coatrack, unnoticed when Jennings takes his coat and departs. Harpo slips down to the floor and sneaks across to kiss Connie on the side of the neck while she thinks Jennings is still there. Harpo is being more cheeky than bashful in stealing the kiss (but he does treat her with respect later, serenading her on the harp). Groucho arrives in an attempt to dissuade her from seeing so much of Zeppo and is soon sitting on her lap, making the sage observation, "I could sit here all day if you didn't stand up." A knock on the door sends Groucho into hiding and Harpo enters, bearing a block of ice (could all the film's ice-carrying be a far-sighted visual pun anticipating *The Iceman Cometh*?).

Harpo leaves, Groucho appears, and Zeppo returns to find Groucho on Connie's lap. Groucho naturally takes the offensive, becoming the outraged father who has caught his son in a shameful place. Zeppo and Groucho leave, Groucho returns, then Chico enters carrying a block of ice as his admission ticket to the proceedings. He throws it out of the window and leaps on Connie, kissing her neck, leaving Groucho to sit glumly at the other end of the sofa. Harpo comes and goes with ice. Jennings returns. "This must be the main highway," remarks Groucho. Peace reigns briefly as Chico is introduced to Jennings as Connie's music teacher and plays his version of "Everyone Says 'I Love You' " and then his own number on the piano. The whole scene is like the comings and goings through the hotel rooms of Penelope and Mrs. Potter in *The Cocoanuts*. Groucho and Chico somewhat surprisingly accept being ordered out by Jennings.

The policeman chases Harpo and ends up in the dog cart.

Groucho with two of his staff (Edward J. Le Saint, left, and E. H. Calvert) and a desk strewn with walnut shells.

Groucho has enrolled Chico and Harpo as students of Huxley College and has a blank sheet of paper for them to sign.

The sequence once extended further than in the prints of *Horse Feathers* now in general circulation. Harpo should reappear, causing Connie to ask, "What do you want?" Harpo points at her. "Are you a good boy?" she asks, and Harpo

Robert Greig (the biology professor) reads about the liver to his class, watched by Groucho.

shakes his head. "You're bashful," she observes, presumably because he hasn't spoken. In answer, Harpo nods, looks bashful, and stands on his head in Connie's lap. She cries for him to get off her and he does, sitting alongside her on the sofa with one foot tucked under him. She tells him to take his foot off the sofa. Harpo shakes his head defiantly and makes his "gookie" expression, so she tries to pull his foot off. Harpo pulls her leg in return. She slaps him, a knock is heard, and he pulls her onto his lap. It is Groucho looking for his hat and rubbers. Connie points in one direction while the hidden Harpo points in another. She seems to be slapping herself as Harpo's hands become playful. "Come now, where's my hat?" asks Groucho and Connie seems to point in three directions at once. Groucho finds his rubbers on Harpo's feet, sticking out from underneath Connie, and mistakes his feet for hers. Eyeing the expanse of muscular leg revealed by Harpo's rolled-up trousers, he comments "We could use you in the football team." Groucho takes off the rubbers and tries to put them on his own feet; but Harpo's are so positioned that Groucho puts the rubbers back on him.

Chico and Jennings enter and Connie stands up, revealing Harpo clutching a block of ice beneath her. Groucho rushes to the window while Chico and Harpo dart out of the door. Arriving below the window, Chico encourages Groucho to jump. Harpo brings out a dog catcher's net to arrest his fall. As Groucho jumps, Harpo hears a dog barking and gives chase, letting Groucho thud to the ground. Like the cut mentioned earlier, this missing footage (partly based on the Napoleon sequence of *I'll Say She Is*) deprives Harpo of one of his best scenes. (Could these have been removed for some forgotten anthology or tribute at the time of Harpo's death and never been reinstated? Or were they simply cut to shorten an already short film for a reissue?)

Harpo and Chico make rough descents of their own after setting out to kidnap the star players of the Darwin team and being locked up in their underwear. Sawing their way through the floor, they crash down at their captors' feet and then onto a ladies' bridge party. The scene starts with a fine example of Chico's obtuseness: having decided to lure the footballers away by telling one of them his brother is ill, he finds that neither has a brother. When one acknowledges having a sister, Chico tells him, "You got to come with us. Your sister, she's a very sick man." When the plan won't work, Chico delegates Harpo to deal with them. Harpo huffs and puffs and looks ferocious, then gives the pair a playful tap on the cheek. They let loose with a mighty uppercut and Harpo lands on the floor, looking very groggy. Instead of retrieving the situation (as Harpo did with the pitchfork in the barn in *Monkey Business*), Chico and Harpo turn tail and run. They are easily caught and Chico suffers the humiliation of being upended and tipped from his outer garments. At least Harpo finds it uproariously amusing and when his turn comes detaches his outer clothing in one go and enjoys himself pretending to be coyly embarrassed in his underwear. It is, however, the first time that Harpo and Chico have met with such a setback. Their two escapes by sawing through the floor follow.

The vital football match between Huxley and Darwin provides the climax to *Horse Feathers*. It has some fine moments. Groucho is unexpectedly chivalrous on behalf of a woman when he excuses himself from a conversation to dash onto the football field and bring down a Darwin player: "That'll teach him to pass a lady without tipping his hat," he declares. And there is the diabolical image of Harpo exacting retribution from one of the two star players who locked up Chico and him: Finding the player lying dazed after a pileup on the field which has dislodged the sausage from the hot dog Harpo was eating, Harpo puts one of the player's fingers in the roll, smears mustard on it, and takes a bite, causing the man to yell with pain. It is another example of the very physical humor, keyed to body-crushing and pain, common to this film and *Monkey Business*.

Harpo's inventiveness with banana peel and a length of elastic help Huxley win the match but the sequence is not that satisfying. The drawback to the scene, as indicated earlier, is that the

Groucho visits Thelma Todd (the college widow, Connie Bailey).
Groucho: "Oh, I love sitting on your lap. I could sit here all day if you didn't stand up."

Groucho finds that Chico has taken his place with Thelma Todd. Groucho: "I was doing all right until you came in."

It's Zeppo's (Frank Wagstaff's) turn with Thelma Todd, which puts Harpo in a frenzy. But no such moment occurs in modern prints of the film.

Marxes are required to act constructively enough to win the game, whereas their real talent is for disruption. Groucho alternates between helping the Huxley team and stretching out on the field for

Harpo looks intent on breaking the leg of Thelma Todd after she has ordered him to take his foot off the couch. Scene missing from modern prints of the film.

Chico tries to calm Groucho as he reacts to the appearance of rival college head David Landau (Jennings), in the Huxley dressing rooms. Groucho: "You've got to fight—I've already taken my coat off."

. . . but Chico and Harpo saw their way to freedom . . .

Star footballers James Pierce (Mullen) and Nat Pendleton (MacHardie) have recaptured would-be kidnappers Chico and Harpo and take the boys' clothes to prevent a further escape attempt . . .

. . . and make a grand slam into a bridge party below before rushing off to take part in the big match. (In the film itself, they do not stop to pose.)

a rest. Chico works hard, giving the Huxley players the signals. Harpo is largely true to character, using the game to have fun and abandoning it to chase off in the wrong direction when he spots a loose dog. Why he gives up this chase to drive his brothers to victory in his garbage chariot is left unclear and highlights the problem of balancing the Marxes' anarchic energy with plot requirements.

In *Horse Feathers*, Thelma Todd's Connie suffers far more, physically, than Margaret Dumont ever did (except perhaps for the stomach-punching of *Animal Crackers*). While out on a canoe ride with Groucho (naturally, she's doing the paddling, with Groucho performing his version of "Everyone Says 'I Love You'" on a guitar that becomes as disposable as a cigarette lighter he threw away in *Monkey Business*), she falls overboard and thrashes about in the water while Groucho responds to her cry of "Professor Wagstaff!" by suggesting she should call him "Quincy" and answers her call for a lifesaver by throwing her a peppermint from a roll of Life Savers in his pocket. This is a parody of Theodore Dreiser's *An American Tragedy*, filmed at Paramount and released in 1931, as Groucho cues us with his line, "This is the first time I've been out in a canoe since I saw the *American Tragedy*." It corresponds to the scene in which the working class boy drowns the pregnant factory girl who stands in the way of his marriage into a wealthy family.

At the very end, Thelma Todd is the bride at a marriage ceremony attended by Groucho, Harpo, and Chico in their tuxedoed best, all three taking her for their wedded wife and leaping upon her (beating the real bridegroom, concealed from our view behind Connie, who is shouldered off

Chico gives the team the signal: "Una duo tre bendee—this time we got left endee." Zeppo then runs with the ball while Harpo spreads banana skins behind him.

Harpo arrives at the big match in his garbage chariot.

127

screen). However, this comic coda is crude and forced, more worthy of the Three Stooges than the Marx Brothers, and omitting Zeppo (unless he was the hidden man).

Originally, there was a big scene following the football match. In the evening, following their football victory, the Huxley students tear the town apart to provide fuel for a celebratory bonfire. Harpo decides that this doesn't go far enough—and, in an escalation of his early pyromania, he sets the main college building on fire. The Marxes then play cards while Huxley burns.

Jennings is trapped on the third floor. Groucho, cigar in mouth, heroically runs into the blaze to the cheers of the crowd. He returns unexpectedly and hands a bystander his cigar. "There's no smoking in the corridors," he explains, and rushes back into the building. He reappears, not with Jennings but with a diploma for Zeppo. "I bet that'll burn Jennings up," he remarks as he retrieves his cigar butt. This sequence does not appear to have been included in the film even in 1932, but a surviving scene still and its description in Paramount's pressbook indicate that it was filmed. Perhaps it just didn't work well enough to be retained in the final cut. Whether the short marriage scene replaces it or followed it is unclear.

Harpo takes the cigar that Louis Calhern offers to Chico and attempts to light it with the telephone.

Duck Soup

1933

Rufus T. Firefly: GROUCHO MARX. *Pinky:* HARPO MARX. *Chicolini:* CHICO MARX. *Bob Roland:* ZEPPO MARX. *Mrs. Gloria Teasdale:* Margaret Dumont. *Ambassador Trentino:* Louis Calhern. *Vera Marcal:* Raquel Torres. *The Lemonade Vendor:* Edgar Kennedy. *Zander:* Edmund Breese. *First Minister of Finance:* William Worthington. *Secretary of War:* Edwin Maxwell. *Agitator:* Leonid Kinsky. *Secretary:* Verna Hillie. *First Judge:* George MacQuarrie. *Second Judge:* Fred Sullivan. *Second Minister of Finance:* Davison Clark. *Prosecutor:* Charles B. Middleton. *Third Judge:* Eric Mayne. *A Palace guard:* Dale van Sickel. *Pinky's horse:* Blanca. [Dennis O'Keefe appears as an extra.]

Director: Leo McCarey. *Screenwriters:* Bert Kalmar, Harry Ruby and *(additional dialogue)* Arthur Sheekman and Nat Perrin. *Cinematographer:* Henry Sharp. *Art directors:* Hans Dreier and Wiard B. Ihnen. *Editor:* LeRoy Stone. *Songs "Freedonia Hymn," "His*

Excellency Is Due," and "The Country's Going to War" by: Bert Kalmar and Harry Ruby. *Music advisor:* Arthur Johnston. *Chief sound mixer:* H. M. Lindgren. *Production company:* Paramount Productions. *Distributor:* Paramount Distributing (A Paramount Picture). *Running time:* 70 minutes. *Release date:* November 24, 1933 (New York opening: November 22, 1933).

Duck Soup may not have been the most popular of the Marx Brothers' films at the time, with either the critics or the public, but it has grown in stature over the years to be regarded as one of their undisputed masterpieces. This is not only because it deals with a big subject—war—but because it was made by a director who was a genius of comedy, Leo McCarey. It is one of the Marxes' shortest pictures and also the sharpest and fastest, strictly attuned to the business in hand of getting the most laughs and dispensing with anything that might slow down its pace, like a soppy romance or musical interludes for Chico and Harpo.

Though it continues a line of "animal" titles, it disposes of the more realistic settings of the previous two pictures. It reverts in broad type to the musical comedy format of *Animal Crackers* and brings back Margaret Dumont. Set in a mythical republic called Freedonia, it introduces a rival one called Sylvania, such fictitious republics and kingdoms being rife in stage plays and films of the period.

As in *Animal Crackers*, Groucho is brought into the picture by Margaret Dumont, here playing Mrs. Teasdale, the wealthiest woman in Freedonia: it is her condition for loaning twenty million dollars to the country to help it out of its difficulties that Groucho's Rufus T. Firefly be appointed president. His inauguration ceremony has a buildup like his arrival as Captain Spaulding in *Animal Crackers* in which various others, including Zeppo as his secretary, Bob Roland, are announced first, and there is the same comic repetition of the chorus of a song, here because Groucho doesn't show up on cue at the end of the Freedonian Hymn (the songs in both cases are by Kalmar and Ruby). In fact, he slides down a handy firepole to one side of the spacious hall and joins on the end of his own guard of honor.

Groucho attains a power and authority far in excess of his earlier roles, even his presidency of Huxley College in *Horse Feathers*. In earlier films, he mocked authority. Here he *is* authority. But he behaves in much the same way. His proposals for running the country, expressed in song, are tyrannical, chaos-inducing, self-interested and wonderfully contradictory. On the one hand "this is the land of the free" but on the other hand "if any form of pleasure is exhibited, report to me and it will be prohibited." And "I will not stand for anything that's crooked or unfair," but "if anyone's caught taking graft and I don't get my share, we stand 'em up against the wall . . . and pop goes the weasel!" Groucho levels with the

assembly: "If you think this country's bad off now, just wait till I get through with it." (Yet Groucho's dictatorship is popular with the people.)

He is once again rude to Margaret Dumont, his benefactor, who describes him as "the most able statesman in all Freedonia." "Well, that covers a lot of ground," responds Groucho and looks her up and down. "Say, you cover a lot of ground yourself. You'd better beat it. I hear they're going to tear you down and put up an office block where you're standing. You can leave in a taxi. If you can't leave in a taxi you can leave in a huff. If that's too soon you can leave in a minute and a huff. You know, you haven't stopping talking since I came here. You must have been vaccinated with a phonograph needle." He accuses her of murdering her late husband, checks that she has inherited the man's entire fortune, and then declares that he loves her.

Groucho's directness contrasts with the deviousness of Louis Calhern's Ambassador Trentino of Sylvania, who plans to gain control of Freedonia by marrying Mrs. Teasdale. He is being helped by a dancer, Vera Marcal, a kind of Mata Hari figure, whom he delegates to distract Firefly while he goes after Mrs. Teasdale. (In fact, Groucho has no scenes alone with her. In the original script, she also took up with Zeppo, but this too has been omitted.)

Groucho takes an instant dislike to Trentino after trying to borrow twelve dollars from him and insults him at the garden party by calling him a baboon. Trentino responds by calling Groucho an "upstart." When the ambassador later tries to smooth things over, Groucho appears amenable, encouraging him to recall the insulting word he used, then slapping him all over again when he comes out with it.

Trentino is using Chico (Chicolini) and Harpo (Pinky) as spies to follow Groucho in the hope of finding something to use against him. When they arrive to make their report, they take every opportunity to turn the occasion into a game. When Trentino asks about Firefly's record, Harpo produces a gramophone record and hands it to him. When he flings it away in exasperation, Harpo shoots it down with a rifle, Chico rings a bell on Trentino's desk and hands Harpo a cigar, shutting the cigar box on the ambassador's fingers. Chico's report on watching Firefly (taken from the first episode of the *Flywheel, Shyster and Flywheel* radio show) is the perfect illustration of his matchless stupidity:

Monday we watch-a Firefly's house but he no come out—he wasn't home. Tuesday we went to a ballgame but he fool us—he no show up. Wednesday he go to the ballgame and we fool him—we no show up. Thursday was a double-header—nobody show up. Friday it rained all day—there was no ball game so we stayed home and we listened to it over the radio.

"Then you didn't shadow Firefly!" exclaims Trentino. "Sure, we shadow Fire, we shadow him all day." "What day was that?" "Shadowday! Some joke, huh, boss?" Chico becomes Freedonia's Minister of War by taking the job that Groucho is no longer offering him. He also takes phone calls for Groucho when he is in the room, telling the caller Groucho isn't there. "I wonder what ever became of me," says Groucho. Chico turns Groucho's quiz question around by giving him three guesses. Groucho tries a couple of guesses before giving up. Chico gives up too. With Chico, lines of thought are run into the ground.

On trial for his life, Chico thoroughly enjoys himself delivering a series of awful puns. He is accused of selling Freedonia's secret war code and plans. "Sure, I sold a code and two pair of plans. 'At's some joke, eh, boss?" he asks Groucho as he slaps the edge of a desk with delight. As with his report on "Shadowday," Chico suggests that he is not really stupid but play-acting. Groucho makes the mistake of referring to Chico as an abject figure ("I abject!") and changes the description to "a pitiable object," challenging Chico to beat that one. After another of Chico's jokes, the judge remarks, "That sort of testimony we can eliminate." "'At'sa fine, I'll

take some," says Chico, and explains: "Eliminate. A nice cold glass eliminate." To Groucho, he adds: "Hey, boss, I'm goin' good, eh?" Groucho gets into the act, offering: "I wanted to get a writ of *habeas corpus* but I should have gotten a writ of you instead."

As usual, Harpo always gets the better of Groucho. He is Groucho's chauffeur and drives off without him every time. Their most ingenious battle of wits comes after Harpo, disguised as Groucho in a long nightshirt, has been attempting to open a safe in Mrs. Teasdale's residence to steal the war plans. When he turns on a radio by mistake, Groucho comes down in his nightshirt to investigate, Harpo runs into a mirror and shatters the glass, falling into a room behind. Groucho has heard the glass shatter and is immediately suspicious when Harpo poses as his mirror reflection. (All the glass has conveniently disappeared.) The obvious solution would be to feel and see if the mirror was there, but Groucho instinctively knows this is a game that must be played by certain rules. He has to make Harpo as his reflection give himself away. He tries out various movements which Harpo matches to perfection. Then, when Groucho swings around in a full turn and flings out his arms, Harpo cheats by not turning at all and merely matching his arm movement at the end.

Groucho then goes off and returns with a white hat behind his back. We see that Harpo has a black hat. They start to circle around each other, passing through where the mirror should be (this makes no difference to the game, of course), changing places, and now Groucho sees that Harpo has the wrong color hat and registers his delight. They complete the circle to resume their original positions and Groucho flings on his hat, pointing triumphantly at Harpo. But Harpo has come up with a white hat and is pointing triumphantly at Groucho. Harpo clutches his stomach in delight and makes a few facial paroxysms before settling down for the game to resume. Groucho is so impressed that, when Harpo accidently drops his hat, Groucho hands it back to him, overlooking the lapse. Harpo is now falling

Groucho (Rufus T. Firefly), president of Freedonia.

Margaret Dumont (Mrs. Teasdale): "Oh, your Excellency!"
Groucho: "You're not so bad yourself."

behind Groucho in matching his actions but not seriously. Then Chico blunders into view, also dressed up as Groucho in a nightshirt. Harpo pushes him away but Chico comes back to be spotted by Groucho. The game is over. Groucho dashes forward and seizes Chico by his nightshirt.

The mirror scene was far from a new idea. It had been familiar in vaudeville, a specialty of the Schwartz Brothers, and had been featured in such movies as Chaplin's *The Floorwalker* (1916) and Max Linder's *Seven Years Bad Luck* (1921). Here the scene gains particular effectiveness because the deception is not being treated at all seriously but only as a game, because the uncanny skill of Harpo in mimicking Groucho's movements makes the impersonation so convincing, and because the sequence is so cleverly developed that it never becomes dull and repetitive. It is also interesting that the entire episode is silent after the breaking of the mirror. Groucho never says anything, not even when he rushes forward to apprehend Chico.

At a deeper level, the scene is a threat to identity. Groucho has to fight with Harpo's mirror image to regain his individuality—if Harpo can go on matching him, Harpo can go on being Groucho forever, or whenever he wants to.

Rather less commendable are Harpo and Chico's two scenes with Edgar Kennedy's lemonade vendor. The film has already shown the pair of them in a wrecking mood in their scene reporting to Ambassador Trentino. As an official and a villain, Trentino deserves all the mistreatment he gets. But Edgar Kennedy, although surly and quick-tempered, is a street vendor minding his business, next to Chico's peanut stand. Trouble starts after Chico becomes annoyed with Harpo when he won't speak (a very curious suggestion that he normally does) and they start to fight, moving onto the lemonade vendor's pitch and disturbing the customer he is serving. He tells them off and they make him even more annoyed by Chico kicking him and Harpo giving him his leg. The vendor's hat falls off and hats are rotated among the three of them so that he does not get his own one back to put on. He becomes so confused he gives Harpo his leg. Harpo squirts him with his own lemonade and burns his hat. End of first scene.

In the second scene the lemonade vendor is intent on revenge. He shows off his new hat to Harpo and helps himself to Chico's peanuts. Harpo tries to stop him and then burns his hat. The lemonade man turns their cart on its side and returns to serve a line of customers. They back away horrified when Harpo rolls up his trousers and goes paddling in the tank of lemonade. The scene does build smoothly and, as a dispute between neighbors, parallels the larger dispute between Freedonia and Sylvania. The final image of Harpo's feet in the lemonade is a splendidly repulsive one. Yet the scenes basically do not work because one feels sorry for the lemonade vendor, even though played by unlovable Edgar Kennedy.

Nor is this the last that Kennedy has to endure. Harpo on horseback spies a woman in her scanties, about to take a bath, and rushes in after her, only to be pushed into the bathroom when her husband, the lemonade vendor, suddenly returns. He insists on taking an immediate bath and settles down in the water on top of Harpo. This recalls the crushing humor of the deckchair sequence of *Monkey Business*. If the vendor had been more patriotic and gone off to fight in the war, he would never have found Harpo in his bathtub.

Duck Soup brings to a climax the love of horses that Harpo demonstrated in *Animal Crackers* and *Horse Feathers*. He pauses before visiting the lemonade vendor's wife to give his horse a feedbag. When he gets home, it is late and a woman is waving to him from the window. The camera then pans from Harpo's boots to a pair of women's shoes to a set of horseshoes at the foot of a bed. In the shot that follows, we see where Harpo's preference lies: the three are asleep but it is Harpo and the horse who are sleeping in the double bed while the woman is in a separate one.

Harpo has become a little more sympathetic than in the last two films. Such moments as his

Groucho clutches Margaret Dumont in fright after being startled by Zeppo (his secretary, Bob Roland).

Chico (Chicolini) and Harpo (Pinky) remove their disguises as they come in to report to Louis Calhern (Ambassador Trentino). Chico: "We fool you good, heh?"

133

Louis Calhern tells Verna Hillie (his secretary) that they are not to be disturbed. Harpo eyes her and starts to follow her out.

Harpo and Edgar Kennedy (lemonade vendor).

Groucho tries to remember the answer to the quiz questions he posed to Chico after Chico gives him three guesses.

Margaret Dumont asks Groucho, offended by a remark of Louis Calhern, to please wait. When he feels her hand on his shoulder, he wheels around, fists up, ready to fight. At right, Raquel Torres (Vera Marcal).

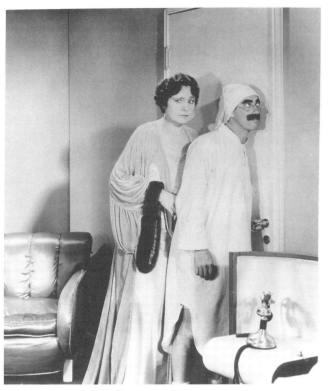

Groucho takes over Chico's defense at his court-martial. "Gentlemen, Chicolini here may talk like an idiot, and look like an idiot, but don't let that fool you. He really is an idiot."

Harpo has awakened the house with a Sousa march on the radio. Margaret Dumont: "What's that?" Groucho: "It sounds to me like mice." Dumont: "Mice don't play music." Groucho: "No? What about the old maestro?"

"Hi-de-hi-de-hi-de-hi-de-ho." The Marx Brothers celebrating "the country's going to war."

"At last the country's going to war" sings Chico, shaking hands with Zeppo, watched by Groucho.

135

War rages. "The enemy have captured Hill 27 and Hill 28 throwing thirteen hillbillies out of work." Groucho and Zeppo.

Groucho calls to all nations for help—three men and one woman are trapped in a building.

discomfort when lemonade has been poured into his trousers (his rueful expression admitting that Edgar Kennedy has temporarily got the better of him as he wriggles about) or his reluctance to be a "volunteer" (when picked out by Chico's crooked method of selection for dangerous work) are ones that make Harpo a creature with feelings that are almost human.

When Trentino threatens war, Mrs. Teasdale arranges for him to meet Groucho again in an attempt to avert conflict. Groucho tells her,

Mrs. Teasdale, you did a noble deed! I'd be unworthy of the high trust that's been placed in me if I didn't do everything within my power to keep our beloved Freedonia at peace with the world. I'll be only too happy to meet Ambassador Trentino and offer him, on behalf of my country, the right hand of good fellowship. And I feel sure that he will accept this gesture in the spirit in which it is offered. . . . But suppose he doesn't? A fine thing that'll be! I hold out my hand and he refuses to accept it! That'll add a lot to my prestige, won't it? Me, the head of a country, snubbed by a foreign ambassador! Who does he think he is that he can come here and make a sap out of me in front of all my people? Think of it! I hold out my hand and that hyena refuses to accept it! Why, the cheap, four-flushing swine! He'll never get away with it, I tell you!

And Trentino arrives in time for another slap on the face before he can utter a word. The ambassador barks "This means *war!*" and storms out. In the following musical sequence, the declaration of war is elaborately celebrated in a dazzling mélange of musical styles.

So, in *Duck Soup*, Groucho by his vanity has brought about a war all on his own. War is depicted here basically as a game of dressing up in various different costumes. Though there are realistic glimpses of tanks, shells, submachine guns, and falling debris, the tone is frivolous. As Freedonia's troops are being badly beaten, a general suggests digging trenches. "Dig trenches!" responds Groucho. "With our men being killed off like flies! There isn't time to dig

trenches. We'll have to buy 'em ready made." Mention of death is immediately brushed aside by a joke. And Chico, pragmatic as ever, has found the perfect solution to Freedonia's predicament: he's joined the other side. But he still comes back to Freedonia where the meals are better.

There is one startling moment when Groucho is gleefully firing his machine gun, only to learn from Zeppo that he is shooting at his own men. "Here's five dollars," says Groucho. "Keep it under your hat. Never mind, I'll keep it under my hat." Yet he is not actually hitting anyone, which would have made the joke intolerable—they are "fleeing like rats."

And war is ultimately decided as if it were a game. Surrounded in a farmhouse, the Marx Brothers subdue the enemy soldiers as they come through the door by a routine of Chico lifting their helmets and Harpo hitting them on the head with a brick (it seems they have run out of ammunition to fight any other way) while Groucho keeps score by moving rings along a curtain rod with the bayonet on his rifle. They catch Trentino in this manner and start pelting him with hard fruit until he surrenders and the war is over—a little too suddenly. The same fruit comes in handy for pelting Mrs. Teasdale when she celebrates victory by starting to sing the national anthem.

The Marxes denied that their film had been a deliberate black satire. And yet the dangers of

dictatorship were apparent when the film was made. Harpo has recalled being chilled when production was delayed on two occasions to listen to radio broadcasts of Hitler ranting. Mussolini was in power in Italy where *Duck Soup* was banned. A weak economy was fertile ground for dictatorship and the United States itself was suffering the worst effects of the Depression, with banks being closed for days. Another 1933 film, *Gabriel Over the White House*, released ahead of *Duck Soup*, not only depicted a corrupt American president but suggested that a dictator could cure the problems facing the country. In 1933 *Duck Soup* was relevant satire. And, while petty dictators abound, it still is.

137

Harpo on the trombone in the opera house orchestra pit.

A Night at the Opera

1935

Otis B. Driftwood: GROUCHO MARX. *Tomasso:* HARPO MARX. *Fiorello:* CHICO MARX. *Mrs. Claypool:* Margaret Dumont. *Herman Gottlieb:* Siegfried Rumann. *Rosa Castaldi:* Kitty Carlisle. *Riccardo Baroni:* Allan Jones. *Rodolfo Lassparri:* Walter Woolf King. *Captain:* Edward Keane. *Detective Henderson:* Robert Emmett O'Connor. *Steward:* Gino Corrado. *Mayor:* Purnell Pratt. *Engineer:* Frank Yaconelli. *Engineer's assistant/peasant:* Billy Gilbert. *Engineer's other assistant:* Jack Lipson. *Police captain:* Claude Peyton. *Dancers:* Rita and Rubin. *Ruiz:* Luther Hoobyar. *Count Di Luna:* Rodolfo Hoyos. *Azucena—gypsy woman:* Olga Dane. *Ferrando:* James J. Wolf. *Maid:* Ines Palange. *Stage manager:* Jonathan Hale. *Elevator man:* Otto Fries. *Captain of Police:* William Gould. *Famous aviators:* Leo White, Jay Eaton and Rolfe Sedan. *Committee:* Wilbur Mack, George Irving, Phillips Smalley and Selmer Jackson. *Policeman:* George Guhl. *Sign scraper:* Harry Tyler. *Immigration Inspector:* Alan Bridge. *Doorman:* Harry Allen. *Louisa:* Lorraine Bridges. *Stage hand:* Fred Malatesta.

Maid: Edna Bennett. *Steward:* Zuke Welch. *Doorman:* Gennaro Curci.

Director: Sam Wood. *Screenwriters:* George S. Kaufman, Morrie Ryskind and *(uncredited) (additional material)* Al Boasberg. *Story by:* James Kevin McGuinness. *Cinematographer:* Merritt B. Gerstad. *Art directors:* Cedric Gibbons, Ben Carré and *(set decorator)* Edwin B. Willis. *Editor:* William Levanway. *Music composer:* Herbert Stothart. *Song "Alone,"* composer: Nacio Herb Brown, *lyricist:* Arthur Freed. *Song "Cosi-Cosa,"* composers: Bronislau Kaper and Walter Jurmann, *lyricist:* Ned Washington. *Dance director:* Chester Hale. *Wardrobe designer:* Dolly Tree. *Recording director:* Douglas Shearer. *Producer (uncredited):* Irving G. Thalberg. *Production company/distributor:* Metro-Goldwyn-Mayer (Loew's Inc.). *Running time:* 96 minutes. *Release date:* November 15, 1935 (opened in Baltimore and St. Louis: November 1, 1935).

138

The opening scene of *A Night at the Opera* is superb. Margaret Dumont, as the wealthy Mrs. Claypool, has been stood up by Groucho's Otis B. Driftwood in a Milan restaurant. To make matters worse, she finds he has been dining with a blonde, not just in the same restaurant but directly behind her. Groucho leaves the blonde with the check while he comforts Dumont with a jovial slap on the back and the most ridiculous flattery possible—that he was only sitting with the blonde because she looked like Dumont. Furthermore, adds Groucho, "That's why I'm sitting here with you. Because you remind me of you. Your eyes, your throat, your lips . . . everything reminds me of you. Except you. How do you account for that?" The humor lies not just in Groucho's verbal dexterity in shifting position but in the confusion over identity so prevalent in the Marx Brothers films: here Dumont is said to look like the blonde; next she looks like herself (as though there were two of her); but then she doesn't look like herself after all.

Groucho has been hired by Dumont to place her in society. It turns out that he has arranged for her to meet the director of the New York Opera Company, Herman Gottlieb. Though not unprecedented, the fact that he is actually doing something to earn his fee is the first small sign of the Marx Brothers conforming to a plot and losing some of their independence. Gottlieb is portrayed by Siegfried Rumann (later Sig Ruman), making the first of three appearances in the world of the Marx Brothers and being driven to a frenzy each time. Groucho introduces Gottlieb to Mrs. Claypool and vice versa and reintroduces them, testing the man's patience and stretching the introductions to absurdity. No sooner has Gottlieb kissed Mrs. Claypool's hand than Groucho imputes dishonesty to men of his pompous appearance and manner by wondering whether all her rings are still on her fingers. Gottlieb is, in fact, after Mrs. Claypool's money like Groucho, but in a more respectable fashion, wanting her to pay the huge salary demanded by obnoxious tenor Rodolfo Lassparri to sing in New York.

Groucho warns Gottlieb that making love to Mrs. Claypool is his "racket" but then generously offers Gottlieb a chance to "take a whack at it"—as though it were some kind of sport anyone can try on her. Groucho merely reminds Gottlieb that he saw her first; then, a stickler for accuracy (so long as it's pointless), he corrects himself: "Of course her mother really saw her first but there's no point bringing the Civil War into this."

Groucho sets out to sign up Lassparri ahead of Gottlieb so that he can take a cut. While Chico is great friends with Harpo as in earlier films, he is also a buddy and supporter of an unknown singer, Riccardo Baroni (ingratiatingly played by Allan Jones, who can sing but makes no attempt to sound Italian). Groucho has forgotten Lassparri's name when he arrives back stage at the Milan opera house and encounters Chico's Fiorello. Groucho can only recall that he's after "the greatest tenor in the world," so Chico negotiates a contract with Groucho for the services of Baroni, whom he regards as fitting Groucho's description. This recalls the mistake Groucho made in signing up Chico and Harpo as football players in *Horse Feathers*.

"Well, you see the spaghetti, don't you?" Groucho (Otis B. Driftwood) tries to point out Herman Gottlieb to Margaret Dumont (Mrs. Claypool) in the opening restaurant scene.

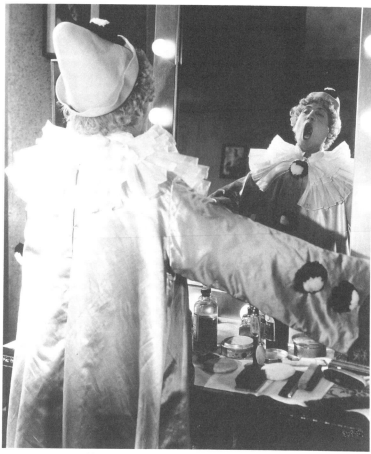

Harpo (Tomasso) is fooling around in borrowed costumes in Lassparri's dressing room.

Groucho's singing is enough to make Margaret Dumont agree to meet him in his stateroom.

Leading from the misunderstanding is one of the finest Groucho-Chico encounters as both warily negotiate the contract. "Could he sail tomorrow?" asks Groucho. "You pay him enough money he could sail yesterday," boasts Chico, displaying his familiar brand of illogic. Groucho takes into account the thousand dollars a night he can wring from the Opera Company and generously offers ten dollars. After Groucho and Chico have made further deductions for themselves and for taxes, etc. (Chico isn't so devoted to his friend that he neglects his own interests), it turns out that Riccardo can break even as long as he doesn't sing too often. This is almost as topsy-turvy as Chico's explaining in *Animal Crackers* how as a musician he earns most by not playing at all.

Groucho hands Chico a duplicate contract. To Chico the word "duplicate" means "five kids up in Canada" (a topical reference to the Dionne quintuplets). "You read it," says Chico, who obviously can't. Groucho: "All right, I'll read it to you. Can you hear?" Chico: "I haven't heard anything yet. Did you say anything?" Groucho: "Well, I haven't said anything worth hearing." Chico: "That's why I didn't hear anything." Groucho: "Well, that's why I didn't say anything." Which takes us as far up that particular cul-de-sac as is possible to go.

With Chico as unperturbed as usual, Groucho struggles on and eventually, by tearing off disagreeable clauses, they end up with two mutually acceptable shreds of paper. Groucho offers his fountain pen "I forgot to tell you," announces Chico, "I can't write." Groucho is not to be outsmarted: "Well, that's all right. There's no ink in the pen anyhow."

Adding considerable pith to the scene is the fact that Lassparri has been lying under Groucho and Chico's feet all through it. Groucho had come along to find the man stretched out cold on the floor and (in a surrealistic dislocation) treated him like a bar rail, calling out, "Two beers, bartender!" leaving Chico to add with characteristic crassness, "I'll take two beers, too."

On the voyage to New York, Gottlieb spitefully arranges for Groucho to occupy the smallest cabin on the boat. This leads to the classic scene in which the tiny stateroom, already occupied by a huge trunk and three stowaways (Chico, Harpo, and Allan Jones), is progressively filled by two chambermaids, an engineer, a manicurist, a huge engineer's assistant, a woman seeking her Aunt Minnie, a cleaner, and four stewards bearing plates of food—just when Groucho is expecting Margaret Dumont at any moment for a quiet tête-à-tête. It's a new development for Groucho to be thwarted like this by circumstances beyond his control but he recognizes the inevitable and actually helps the scene along (rather as he encouraged Harpo by handing him more letters to destroy in *The Cocoanuts*), inviting people to pile into the room and do what they came to do.

The stowaways join the immigrants in the steerage section and here Chico and Harpo seem most contented and relaxed, enjoying the food and the company, and repaying the welcome by entertaining. Chico amuses the children with his tricky piano fingerwork. Harpo follows with some tomfoolery at the piano, spinning the seat and letting it rise to meet him (as in *Animal Crackers*), then playing very badly until he can pretend to catch one hand under the lid. Much as the whole of his body was limp as he dozed during the stateroom scene, here first one hand and then both flop uselessly after being trapped in the lid. He dabs them like paintbrushes on the piano, then flaps them over his young audience who are screaming as merrily at his discomfort as the children watching the Punch and Judy show in *Monkey Business*. Here, though, it is obviously an act to amuse the kids, quite without the sadistic overtones of the earlier picture, and, when he feels he has amused them sufficiently, he drops the pretense and plays his harp.

Harpo performs seriously to an attentive audience. These simple people could not afford a seat at the opera but Harpo's music has no price tag on it (whereas Lassparri contemptuously refuses to sing for nothing to his dockside admirers). Chico and Harpo's music is for the poor to sit around and enjoy at a moment's notice, completely without the formalities associated with going to the opera. Elsewhere Groucho mocks the idea of Lassparri

earning a thousand dollars a night and makes his own opinion of opera clear when he ticks off his carriage driver for getting him to the Opera House in time to hear part of the performance. The film is anti-opera, which was (and remains) part of its popular appeal.

Groucho and Harpo are made much more sympathetic in this film. Harpo's Tomasso has the misfortune to work as Lassparri's dresser and in his introductory scene he is whipped by Lassparri (despite pleading childlike for a truce) for having dared to try on one of the opera star's costumes and then beaten up some more as the man works off a polite rebuff from Rosa Castaldi, the leading female singer who has made matters worse by comforting Harpo. Groucho delivers a love letter to Rosa from the man she really loves, Riccardo, and is thrilled when she kisses him in gratitude.

Gottlieb spots the three stowaways and has them tossed into the brig. They escape and, in taking the place of three famous bearded Italian aviators on board the ship, are forced to go through their tickertape welcome in New York. This impersonation is more logical than the attempts to become Maurice Chevalier in *Monkey Business*, as it allows the stowaways to hide behind false beards and they weren't to know they were taking the place of celebrities. Chico, of course, has an Italian accent of sorts to help him in the masquerade and when forced to speak to the crowds describes how the aviators made their classic flight with a fine demonstration of his false logic: "The first time we get halfway across when we run out of gasoline and we gotta go back. Then we take twice as much gasoline. This time we were just about to land—maybe three feet—when what do you think? We run out of gasoline again and back we go again to get-a more gasoline. This time plenty gas. Then I get a great idea. We no take-a gasoline. We take a steamship! And that, friends, is how we fly across the ocean." It is only when, on his turn to speak, Harpo stalls for time, drinking glass after glass of water until his beard starts to come off, that the three arouse suspicion of being imposters.

The scene draws on at least one actual event. Although said to parody newsreel footage of

141

The stateroom scene.

Chico (Fiorello) entertains the passengers in steerage.

The three stowaways are in the brig. A dubious Harpo is encouraged by Chico and Allan Jones (Riccardo Baroni) to escape by using the rope.

Looking just like three famous aviators: Chico, Allan Jones, and Harpo.

143

Groucho and three famous aviators are
watched with suspicion by Robert Emmet
O'Connor (Inspector Henderson).

Harpo has powdered his face with sugar and
dabbed his lips with ketchup at breakfast as
Groucho hides the three stowaways wanted for
impersonating the famous aviators.

President Coolidge greeting Lindbergh and
awarding the aviator a medal after his historic
flight in 1927, it more specifically draws on the
huge reception given to one General Italo Balbo
and his team of airmen from fascist Italy when
they arrived in Chicago in July 1933. This obscure event was recalled by a correspondent in
The Freedonia Gazette, which reproduced a newspaper picture of the bearded and uniformed Balbo
taking a drink of water at the official greeting. The
film was therefore taking a mild poke at Mussolini
and fascism.

The three stowaways hide in Groucho's hotel
room. Here the film revives Harpo's strange
appetite from *The Cocoanuts* (not surprisingly, as
it has the same writers, Kaufman and Ryskind).
Harpo breakfasts on a cigar sandwich and a tie
(snipped off Chico) placed between hotcakes.
There is a clever scene in which a suspicious
detective (Inspector Henderson by name—a vari-
ant on the Hennessy and Hennessey of the first
two Marx films) searches the apartment and is
driven mad as beds move and the rooms seem to
rearrange themselves behind his back, a sequence which culminates in a sublime glimpse of
Harpo, his face puffed out in a gookie and a doily
on his head, rocking in an armchair that is really
Chico covered with a sheet while Groucho sits
nearby reading a newspaper and wearing a false
beard—a sight that makes the man believe he has
wandered into the wrong room and retire hope-
lessly defeated.

As one of the stowaways, Allan Jones has
almost become one of the team, tagging along
much as Zeppo did. It seems a shame, in such
scenes, that Zeppo didn't play Riccardo but he
would not have registered as a convincing alternative opera star to Lassparri at the climax.

An indication of the "better" dramatic con-
struction favored by producer Irving G. Thalberg
is the way the Marxes, along with the two people
they care about, Rosa and Riccardo, are taken to
the depths of despair so that their ultimate triumph becomes the greater.

Gottlieb gains Mrs. Claypool's confidence and
has Groucho fired. Groucho learns about this in
an elaborately contrived sequence in which he

arrives at the New York Opera House, full of good will and at peace with the world, greeting everyone warmly, including the elevator man. Then Gottlieb reveals that he has taken over as Mrs. Claypool's business manager and she is there to confirm Groucho's dismissal (the first time Dumont has ever stood up to Groucho). Groucho makes a weak attempt to retrieve something from the wreckage before retreating empty-handed, only to be booted down four flights of stairs by the now unfriendly elevator man. Subsequently he is kicked out of his hotel room, nudged off his seat on a park bench, and—the final stroke—defeated by a drinking fountain that dries up on him.

Rosa also has been fired at Lassparri's instigation after she has again spurned his attentions. The Marx Brothers offer to give themselves up to the police for impersonating the aviators if Gottlieb will reinstate Rosa as the leading lady in that night's performance. He, of course, refuses. It is quite an extraordinary comedown for the team to be bargaining with the enemy. But Gottlieb's refusal of their offer is the final justification for the way they disrupt the evening's production of *Il Trovatore*. Gottlieb and Lassparri have asked for all that happens to them.

The climax is a brilliantly organized succession of incidents, setting Marxian aggressiveness against the Opera House establishment. The hallowed atmosphere is rent by Groucho yelling "Peanuts! Peanuts!" and by Chico and Harpo inserting "Take Me Out to the Ball Game" in the overture scores so that, after a carefully-timed buildup, all the pages turn and the orchestra launches into the populist number. Incongruities abound: the opera singers suddenly rendered ridiculous, performing in front of the wrong backcloths; Gottlieb and Inspector Henderson creeping on stage in ill-fitting gypsy costumes. The Marx Brothers are not only getting their own back, they are having a wonderful time, especially Harpo who makes faces, rips off the dress of a passing dancer and tickles an exposed belly, and clambers up the backcloth to escape the police in the wings.

Things grow more chaotic until the theater goes

Groucho begins to realize that he is on the way out when he finds Harry Tyler's workman removing his name from the office door.

The Marx Brothers and Allan Jones have made themselves at home in the office of Siegfried Rumann.

Siegfried Rumann tries to call the police but Harpo has rigged a weight to fall on his head.

Harpo and Chico fence the rest of the orchestra with violin bows before the performance of *Il Trovatore*.

Siegfried Rumann is about to be knocked out and pushed into a locker to put him out of the way while the Marxes continue to disrupt the opera.

In an outfit several sizes too small, Siegfried Rumann turns up in Margaret Dumont's box at the opera house as Groucho makes his escape. Dumont: "What are you doing?" Groucho: "It's all right. It's just the Tarzan in me."

pitch black and Lassparri's voice is choked off in mid-performance as the Marx Brothers kidnap him. When Riccardo takes over, and successfully insists Rosa be reinstated as leading lady oppo-

Harpo and Chico have donned gypsy costumes to disrupt the performance of *Il Trovatore*.

Harpo remains out of reach of Siegfried Rumann and Robert Emmet O'Connor.

The Marx Brothers are under arrest. Order is restored—but not for long.

site him, they perform so well that the audience obligingly refuses to have Lassparri back. Gottlieb is forced to negotiate a contract for Rosa and Riccardo's services with Groucho and Chico

147

Siegfried Rumann is forced to reason with Groucho to keep the services of Kitty Carlisle (Rosa, left) and Allan Jones.

while Harpo splits Gottlieb's evening coat up the back and cuddles close to him as he looks around, smiling up at him.

The Thalberg approach works. Put together with such care and imagination, it provides a highly acceptable substitute for the unrestrained nonconformity of the Paramount films. And yet, after a few viewings, *A Night at the Opera* begins to seem too pat, too rehearsed, too predictable, too comfortable. Everything goes too much to plan. It lacks the originality and nerve of their first two pictures. It lacks the freshness and spontaneity that makes each new viewing of the last three Paramount pictures come alive. Imposing form on the Marx Brothers is a contradiction: their humor should never seem reined in. But the trio was understandably interested in being as popular as possible, not least because Groucho, Chico, and Harpo had a share in the gross of *A Night at the Opera*. The softened approach to their characterizations made them accessible to a wider audience.

Groucho and Chico discuss a contract with Siegfried Rumann while Harpo makes some alterations to Rumann's jacket.

Groucho (Dr. Hugo Z. Hackenbush) has received a telegram reminding him of his former patient, Mrs. Upjohn: "Ah, Emily, she never forgot that hayride!"

A Day at the Races

1937

Dr. Hugo Z. Hackenbush: GROUCHO MARX. *Stuffy:* HARPO MARX. *Tony:* CHICO MARX. *Mrs. Emily Upjohn:* Margaret Dumont. *Dr. Leopold X. Steinberg:* Siegfried Rumann. *Gil Stewart:* Allan Jones. *Judy Standish:* Maureen O'Sullivan. *Morgan:* Douglas Dumbrille. *Whitmore:* Leonard Ceeley. *Flo Marlowe:* Esther Muir. *The Sheriff:* Robert Middlemass. *Solo dancer:* Vivien Fay. *Morgan's jockey:* Frankie Darro. *Doctor Wilmerding:* Charles Trowbridge. *Doctors:* Frank Dawson, Max Lucke, and Edward Le Saint. *Detective:* Pat Flaherty. *Messenger:* Si Jenks. *Race Judge:* Hooper Atchley. *Judges:* John Hyams, Wilbur Mack, Lee Murray. *Nurse:* Mary McLaren. *Drunk:* Jack Norton. *Telephone operator:* Jean Burt. *Singers:* Ivie Anderson and the Crinoline Choir. [Dorothy Dandridge and Carole Landis are reported to have appeared in bit roles.]

Director: Sam Wood. *Screenwriters:* Robert Pirosh, George Seaton, George Oppenheimer and *(uncredited) (additional material)* Al Boasberg. *Story by:* Robert Pirosh and George Seaton. *Cinematographer:* Joseph Ruttenberg. *Art directors:* Cedric Gibbons, Stan Rogers and *(set decorator)* Edwin B. Willis. *Editor:* Frank E. Hull. *Songs* "Blue Venetian Waters," "All God's Chillun Got Rhythm," "Tomorrow Is Another Day," "A Message From the Man in the Moon," *composers:* Bronislau Kaper and Walter Jurmann, *lyricist:* Gus Kahn. *Music director:* Franz Waxman. *Musical arranger:* Roger Edens. *Choral and orchestral arranger:* Leo Arnaud. *Orchestrators:* George Bassman and Paul Marquardt. *Choreographer:* Dave Gould. *Musical presentation:* Merrill Pye. *Wardrobe designer:* Dolly Tree. *Recording director:* Douglas Shearer. *Assistant directors:* Robert A. Golden, Al Shenberg. *Associate producer:* Max Siegel. *Producers (uncredited):* Irving G. Thalberg, Sam Wood, Lawrence Weingarten. *Production company/distributor:* Metro-Goldwyn-Mayer (Loew's Inc.). *Running time:* 109 minutes. *Release date:* June 11, 1937 (New York opening: June 17, 1937).

Robert Middlemass (the sheriff) demands payment for the feedbill. Chico (Tony) and Allan Jones (Gil Stewart) stall for time while Harpo (Stuffy) dips into the sheriff's pocket to recover the five dollar bill that Chico has handed over.

While it gives considerable satisfaction to most Marx devotees, *A Day at the Races* is a lesser achievement than *A Night at the Opera*. The film is again expertly cast and no expense has been spared to make it look good. Sam Wood was back in the director's chair. But new writers were assigned to the script and seem to have been intimidated by the responsibilities of creating a follow-up hit to *A Night at the Opera*.

The story is too closely constructed along the same principles as the earlier film; the humor is distinctly milder and the Marx Brothers are diminished in stature. They now seem comical misfits in a sane world instead of comical kings, no longer dominating their surroundings but on the defensive. They are courting popularity rather than dispensing their humor on the old take-it-or-leave-it basis.

The film is thirteen minutes longer than *Opera* but none the better for that; and, instead of being dispersed, the musical "relief" is bunched in two long sections which slow the proceedings down. The key scenes were again tested on the road and no doubt improved in the process; but they don't break much new ground. There are one or two worthwhile innovations (Harpo miming a message to Chico; Harpo and Chico rescuing Groucho from an amorous frame-up) but the film as a whole seems too unadventurous, the comedy is becoming more formularized. The Marx Brothers were on the decline.

"I'm going to someone who understands me. I'm going to Doctor Hackenbush! Why, I didn't know there was a thing the matter with me until I met him!" Thus cries Margaret Dumont as Mrs. Emily Upjohn, indignant at the sanitarium doctors' inability to find anything wrong with her. One doesn't need telling who this Doctor Hackenbush must be, and Margaret Dumont's blind faith in Groucho against all other medical opinion is all the richer when Groucho is revealed as being a veterinarian. But the film is making mistakes already: it shows Groucho working for a living, and in a skilled job at that, not doing well

Groucho finds that he needs to buy yet another book to decode the racing tip he has obtained from Chico.

Chico offers tootsie-frootsie ice-cream while Groucho waits patiently to hear what he's got to buy next to unravel Chico's racing tip.

and ready to abandon his vet's responsibilities at the drop of a telegram. It is clear that Groucho has caused Margaret Dumont totally unnecessary worry about her health, driving her into a sanitarium, in contrast to his usual harmless flirtations, this criticism being mitigated to some extent by her obvious pride in Groucho's diagnosis of double blood pressure: "Doctor Hackenbush tells me I am the only case in history. I have high blood pressure on my right side and low blood pressure on my left side."

When Groucho first arrives to head the medical staff at the sanitarium, Margaret Dumont cries "He's here! He's here!" in excitement and her touching faith in him doesn't waver when he goes on to treat her like any other of his former patients. He hands her a giant horse pill and reassures her: "You have nothing to worry about. The last patient I gave one of those to won the Kentucky Derby." However, he does try to conceal the pill from Whitmore, the sanitarium's business manager, so he is uncharacteristically on the defensive about it.

Groucho has to cope with several attempts to check on his credentials made by Whitmore. However, the man is not concerned with the patients' welfare but with discrediting Groucho in Mrs. Upjohn's eyes so that she will withdraw her promise of financial support for the sanitarium, enabling it to be turned into a gambling casino (Whitmore is in cahoots with Morgan, the local racetrack owner anxious to expand his business empire). Whitmore's questions about Groucho's medical past has him admitting that medically his experiences have been most unexciting, "except during the flu epidemic." Groucho waits for Whitmore to obligingly ask, "Ah, and what happened?" so that he can fire off the reply: "I got the flu."

When Whitmore tries to phone the Florida Medical Board to check up on Groucho's credentials, Groucho intercepts the call, pretending to be a somewhat deaf Colonel Hawkins of the records department talking during a hurricane. This causes Whitmore to shout down the phone, allowing Groucho as Hackenbush to buzz him on the intercom and berate him for making so much noise. Groucho is able to drive Whitmore into a frenzy of despair (much as Inspector Henderson was driven to distraction by the moving beds in *A Night at the Opera*). This is a splendid scene, quite in character for Groucho: instead of allaying Whitmore's suspicions by giving himself a glowing medical background, Groucho leaves him dissatisfied and even madder. Though Groucho has no reason to suspect Whitmore's motives, he knows a villain when he sees one, as his attitude to Trentino demonstrated in *Duck Soup*.

But Groucho thinks the game is up when Whitmore brings in an eminent specialist from Vienna, Doctor Leopold X. Steinberg, played by Siegfried Rumann, to examine Margaret Dumont. Groucho packs his suitcase and is almost out of the door before Chico persuades him to stay and bluff it out for the sake of the sanitarium's young owner, Judy Standish (Maureen O'Sullivan). Groucho has already shown some guilt over deceiving her (though not over deceiving Mrs. Upjohn), becoming distinctly embarrassed when Judy expresses her complete confidence in him and stops him confessing his veterinary past. He has even made use of Margaret Dumont's desire to please him, though not to his own advantage but to ask her to sign the notes that will save the sanitarium for Judy. All this concern for the heroine weakens Groucho.

Chico's Tony is even more consumed with concern for Judy. He is first shown trying to recruit new patients at the station. He is so loyal that he refuses to leave her even though she can't pay his wages. It is Chico's bright idea to make Mrs. Upjohn a partner in the sanitarium; to summon her favorite physician, Doctor Hackenbush; and to keep her from leaving by announcing Groucho's impending arrival. This is a new Chico, no longer moronic but quick-witted and practical.

In the contract scene between Groucho and Chico in *A Night at the Opera*, Chico was as dense as ever. In the equivalent sequence here, Chico is the smart one who makes a complete sucker out of Groucho, selling him in stages an elaborately coded racing tip. The seven-minute scene is wonderfully played, with Chico walking up and down with his "tootsie-frootsie" ice-cream cart waiting for Groucho to initiate the next stage of his fleecing. Groucho knows he is being taken for a ride but, having started, is helpless to do anything about it. The only odd thing about the scene is that the books do seem to contain genuine information, leading to a tip on a horse—but in a race that has just finished. The final twist is that Groucho had been intending to bet on the winner until Chico advised against it while Chico has invested the money from Groucho on that very same horse. However, Chico has not been conning Groucho to benefit himself: his winnings are to help Judy's boyfriend Gil Stewart (Allan Jones) keep his horse.

Harpo is once again a friend of Chico's. As in *A Night at the Opera*, he is first seen being maltreated by his employer: here, as Stuffy, a jockey for Morgan, he has won a race he was supposed to lose. With his past affection for horses, it is highly appropriate that he should be so closely associated with them. He even substitutes for a horse when the sheriff impounds Gil's nag, slipping into the bridle as the sheriff marches off.

Harpo and Chico are later spotted by the sheriff at the water carnival and take refuge with the orchestra. This provides an opportunity for Chico to play his piano piece before darting away. Harpo is left behind and he sits at the piano, starting to play and becoming so obstreperous that he destroys it. Such behavior seems rather too wanton for Harpo, without the usual mischievous edge, and its rather awkward point is to enable him to find a harp in the wreckage which he then plays seriously.

Harpo demonstrates his strange appetite in the scene where he is medically examined by Groucho, crunching up the thermometer and washing it down with a drink of poison. Groucho, having earlier demonstrated a lack of dedication (dashing off to the racetrack) as well as laziness (riding to his desk in a wheelchair), now displays his utter incompetence as a physician. He tries taking Harpo's pulse, looks at his watch, and

presents an entertaining alternative: "Either this man is dead or my watch has stopped." Chico points out that Groucho is using his auriscope the wrong way round and has read his own reflection in the mirror instead of looking at Harpo, whereupon Groucho prances around childishly pretending it was a joke on his part. Chico starts the scene with faith in Groucho's ability; he becomes very dubious and then discovers that Groucho is really a horse doctor (although the telltale inscription on the watch from a grateful horse owner suggests that he was a successful vet). Now Chico is horrified and disappointed because Judy is depending on Groucho.

Chico and Harpo collaborate to save Groucho from incurring Margaret Dumont's displeasure by being caught entertaining Flo Marlowe, a lanky blonde, in his room at midnight. Harpo overhears Whitmore describing the trap he has arranged and this leads to the first of his mimed message scenes, short and simple by later standards but one which makes Harpo collapse from sheer exhaustion when Chico has worked it out, including his hacking at a bush to convey Hackenbush and using the frame of a park sign to indicate that Groucho will be framed.

Groucho cuts a wonderfully absurd figure in his silk robe, preening himself in a mirror, spraying the air with perfume as he dances around to a Strauss waltz, tidying the flowers on a table set for two. But the extravagantly romantic mood is ruptured when Miss Marlowe arrives and they can't see each other past the flowers, when Groucho opens the tureen and takes out a can of soup—and when Chico and Harpo repeatedly enter in various guises to disrupt the proceedings. As Flo, Esther Muir proves a gallant foil, being sat on by Chico, covered in powder from her compact by Harpo's blowing, almost torn apart like her fur wrap, and covered by wallpaper when Chico and Harpo decide to redecorate the room. This last ploy enables Groucho to persuade Margaret Dumont, brought by Whitmore to witness his disgrace, that he is having the room redecorated for their honeymoon. Flo is nowhere to be seen—until she emerges from the depths of the

Harpo fools with the orchestra before Chico plays his solo at the Water Carnival.

couch like the crushed passenger in *Monkey Business*. As Flo storms out, Harpo slaps a piece of wallpaper to her rear so that she ends up like Ambassador Trentino in the reporting scene in *Duck Soup*. The three Marx Brothers have begun working together and they work as a team for the rest of the film.

First, there is the scene in the operating theater. Chico and Harpo burst in to help Groucho conduct his examination of Mrs. Upjohn under the eyes of Dr. Steinberg and Whitmore. The round of repeated introductions (copied from the opening scene of *A Night at the Opera*) and the constant washing of hands to delay the start become a little tiresome. But there are lots of inventive gags: Harpo, with "Joe's Service Station" printed on the back of his surgical gown, taking Mrs. Upjohn's purse in mistake for her pulse and pulling a nurse's uniform off her when she gives him a new gown. Margaret Dumont suffers some of her worse indignities here, having her face shaved, her legs flung up in the air on the examination table as Harpo cranks it up and down, and being drenched when Harpo turns on the overhead sprinklers. The scene suffers a little from following so closely on Harpo and Chico's similar disruption of Groucho's midnight tryst.

In the next scene, the three Marxes have taken

Chico and Harpo have burst in on Groucho's midnight date with Esther Muir (Flo). Chico checks with Harpo to confirm that this is the woman out to discredit Groucho.

refuge in a barn with Gil. This is the exact equivalent of the park scene in *A Night at the Opera* when everything seemed hopeless. Groucho tries to take all the blame and becomes indignant when Chico agrees to let him. Then

153

Chico sits on Esther Muir's lap and Harpo is about to follow as Groucho objects.

Harpo, Groucho, and Chico are about to pull Esther Muir apart.

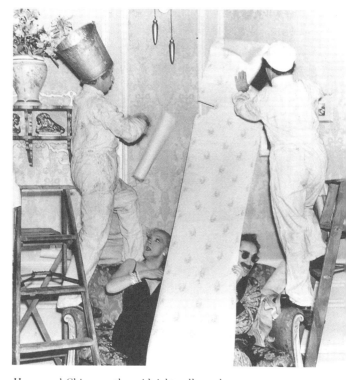

Harpo and Chico are the midnight callers who redecorate Groucho's room as he and Esther Muir try to ignore them. (Groucho has taken to dark glasses in one shot.)

154

Judy brings them blankets to make them more comfortable. She and Gil sing a number ("Tomorrow Is Another Day") and Harpo plays the flute and attracts the attention of some black children who think he's Gabriel. Harpo pops his head into various shacks and the adults come out to join them. Groucho and Chico eventually take part in the merrymaking which corresponds to the scene in steerage on the boat in *A Night at the Opera*, showing how well the team get on with the poor as contrasted with people in authority.

The music is presented as spontaneous and improvised, in contrast to the organization and ceremony of the water carnival (where Chico and Harpo only performed to gain time) or the opera in their previous film. The film now seems to present a patronizing, stereotyped image of happy, unsophisticated black folk, but it cannot be criticised for bad intentions. The mood is broken by a sharp hand-clap from Morgan, accompanied by his cronies, Whitmore and the sheriff, mean people who have no time for merriment. This leads to a mêlée directly comparable to the antics in the old barn in *Monkey Business*, but this is too well orchestrated and insufficiently idiosyncratic.

The climax of the film involves the Marxes and Gil delaying the big steeplechase race until Harpo can ride Gil's horse, Hi-Hat. It exactly corresponds to the disruption of the New York Opera House until Riccardo and Rosa were allowed to sing. Hi-Hat first has to be rescued from the sheriff's clutches and this is very unsatisfactorily arranged: Judy fakes being knocked unconscious in a car crash to fool the sheriff into releasing Hi-Hat so that he can transport her to the hospital. The sheriff is made to look good as he shows proper concern while Judy has been very underhanded. The sheriff is associated with Morgan and should have remained unsympathetic.

When Harpo is able to ride Hi-Hat, the Marxes allow the race to start, but Harpo does not display as much rapport with the animal as one would expect. The horse is known to react sharply to Morgan, who ill-treated him, so Harpo shows the

Fearing exposure, Groucho's instinct is to run—but Allan Jones, Harpo, and Chico persuade him to stay and bluff it out.

"This is absolutely insane!" cries Siegfried Rumann (Dr. Leopold X. Steinberg) as Harpo, Chico, and Groucho delay the examination of Margaret Dumont (Mrs. Upjohn). Leonard Ceeley (Whitmore) is at left.

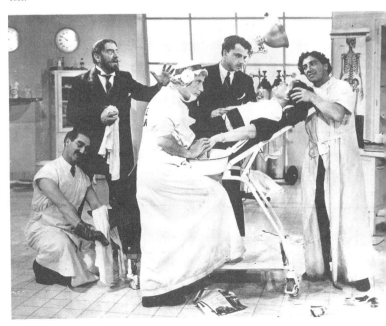

Chico attempts to shave Margaret Dumont while Harpo attends to her hand and Groucho gives her shoe a shine. Siegfried Rumann and Leonard Ceeley are suitably aghast.

Siegfried Rumann calls for an
X ray of Margaret Dumont
and Harpo responds with
newspaper extras.

horse Morgan's photograph (then loses it) for a
burst of speed, after which Groucho and Chico
keep managing to broadcast Morgan's voice over
the racetrack's speakers to spur Hi-Hat on. This
gives Hi-Hat an unfair advantage over the other
horses. Then there is the curious business by
which it is Morgan's jockey who rides Hi-Hat to
victory after Harpo and he inadvertently mount
the wrong horses following a spill at one of the
jumps. The delay before Hi-Hat is established as
the winner seems more than pointless: it deprives
Harpo of the glory of riding Hi-Hat over the final
stretch.

A Night at the Opera has much the stronger
climax because it is based on personalities—at
stake was a singing career and personal revenge.

Harpo plays the flute to the
black children who think he's
the angel Gabriel and follow
him in a song and dance.

Harpo encourages Ivie
Anderson to lead the singing
in the "All God's Chillun Got
Rhythm" number.

156

In *A Day at the Races*, the object is to gain money to save a business. Rosa was deprived of her rightful chance to sing by Lassparri's spitefulness, whereas Judy is merely having financial difficulties. She solves the problem from outside (with the prize money from the race) instead of on her home ground, by improving business at the sanitarium.

There is in any case a difference in atmosphere between racetrack and opera house. The latter is a much riper target with its associations with snobbery and elitism. The images of disruption are far more anarchic and incongruous. The conceit and pomposity of Gottlieb and Lassparri make them richer targets than a couple of greedy businessmen like Morgan and Whitmore. The climax to *A Night at the Opera* is that much better constructed and awe-inspiring. The climax to *A Day at the Races* could really have been played by any group of comedians.

Crash-landing into the enclosure of Douglass Dumbrille (Morgan), Groucho carries a microphone behind the flower in his lapel to pick up Morgan's voice and encourage Hi Hat to win the big race.

"What, running out again? You can't leave. You must stay. I've found a backer for you." Lucille Ball (Christine Marlowe) catches Groucho (Gordon Miller) and Chico (Harry Binelli) planning to skip the hotel.

Room Service

1938

Gordon Miller: GROUCHO MARX. *Faker Englund:* HARPO MARX. *Harry Binelli:* CHICO MARX. *Christine Marlowe:* Lucille Ball. *Hilda Manney:* Ann Miller. *Leo Davis:* Frank Albertson. *Gregory Wagner:* Donald MacBride. *Joseph Gribble:* Cliff Dunstan. *Timothy Hogarth:* Philip Loeb. *Sasha:* Alexander Asro. *Dr. Glass:* Charles Halton. *Simon Jenkins:* Philip Wood.

Director: William A. Seiter. *Screenwriter:* Morrie Ryskind. *From the play by:* John Murray and Allan [Allen] Boretz. *Cinematographer:* J. Roy Hunt. *Art directors:* Van Nest Polglase and Al Herman. *Set dresser:* Darrell Silvera. *Editor:* George Crone. *Music director:* Roy Webb. *Sound recordist:* John L. Cass. *Gowns designer:* Renié. *Assistant to the director:* Philip Loeb. *Assistant director:* James Anderson. *In charge of production:* Pandro S. Berman. *Production company/distributor:* RKO Radio. *Running time:* 78 minutes. *Release date:* September 30, 1938 (New York opening: September 21, 1938).

Room Service overlays a little of the established Marx Brothers humor on a hit Broadway farce. The result is neither a proper Marx Brothers picture nor a satisfying situational comedy. It is certainly not a good piece of filmmaking: having spent a record sum on buying the play, RKO Radio seems to have been reluctant to provide enough money to make a proper motion picture from it.

It is obvious from his past work for the Marxes that screenwriter Morrie Ryskind could have gone further than he did, but plainly RKO was intent on making sure that the play's plot and situations remained intact (one of the original cast, Philip Loeb, was made a special adviser, as well as playing a small part).

The play was staged on one set representing producer Gordon Miller's room in the White Way Hotel in New York. In the film, the opening scene is transferred to the hotel lobby (looking more fitted to the Alps than the Big Apple and strangely deserted). One scene is played out in the hotel manager's office. Briefly at the finale we see a first-night audience enjoying the play Miller is producing in the hotel's own theater. Otherwise, the film is almost entirely confined to two hotel rooms: just occasionally, the corridors and the view outside come into frame. Other hotel guests are hardly seen and, much more erroneously, the actors that Miller is so worried about are confined to a few shots of them performing on the stage at the very end of the film. Because the cast and the settings seem artificially restricted, the film of *Room Service* still looks like a play. The later *Love Happy* is much more successful in suggesting that there really is a show being put on.

The most persistent change in the original dialogue is the removal of the word "God," so that the play Miller is producing becomes *Hail and Farewell* instead of *Godspeed*, while expletives such as "God damn it!" and "What the hell!" are toned down to "Jumping butterballs!" and "What the blazes!" Even many of the bits of business that seem specially suited to one of the Marx Brothers prove to have been in the original play—such as Harpo arriving bare to the waist so that he can put on more clothes for his escape from the hotel, or Chico, referring to prisons, remarking "It's not so bad. If you behave, they make you a trustee."

The film suggests it will be a regular Marx Brothers picture by attiring Groucho and Chico in their familiar costumes and by keeping Harpo mute. And certainly there are lines and actions that seem well in character for all three of the Marxes. Helped by such moments, it is possible to visualize how in a freer adaptation *Room Service* could have approached a regular Marx Brothers comedy. For the Marx enthusiast, the routine farce situations are of little appeal. It is the flashes of true Marxian comedy that give *Room Service* some interest.

The central part of the producer Gordon Miller goes straight to Groucho. Miller is fast-talking and resourceful in all the tight corners that keep coming up, as well as being dishonest and unscrupulous. But his dialogue lacks the thrust and sparkle of a genuine Groucho character. In general, Miller is too rational in his methods, too concerned. The old Groucho enjoyed a showdown but Gordon Miller constantly fears one. The hotel manager is Groucho's brother-in-law, which explains how much credit he has been given but which raises the odd specter of Groucho having a sister (and one called Flossie at that). There are times, too, when Groucho is unnaturally silent, as when he and Chico are pulling on clothes to leave the hotel or they are all eating the food which Groucho has browbeaten the waiter Sasha into bringing them. "I don't care about food for myself, Sash," he tells the man, "but if you let a great American author starve to death, his blood will be on your hands. Do you know what the penalty is for murder in this country?" Fine stuff, but his manner of delivery lacks the old ferocity and bite, and again when Groucho tries to obtain food by telephoning down and speaking with a dialect, it is very halfhearted—he starts with the Colonel Hawkins voice from *A Day at the Races* but it quickly slips and fools no one.

Yet there are a few flashes of the traditional Groucho. Trying to get rid of the bothersome playwright, he pictures the man's mother sitting by the fireside all alone without her son. "We have no fireside," objects the playwright. "Then how do you listen to the President's speeches?" retorts Groucho, with a line not found in the play. Later he threatens to see that the obstructive figure of the hotel chief is reduced to a bellboy, then reflects, "No, that's too good for him. I'll make him a guest." This could be Groucho's hotel managers of *The Cocoanuts* or the later *A Night in Casablanca* speaking. Groucho slips in a splendid loping walk across the hotel lobby, and there is a sublime glimpse of his furtively cheating himself at solitaire. A nice moment occurs when

Chico tries telling Donald MacBride (Wagner, the hotel chief) that he and Frank Albertson (author Leo Davis) are not packing to leave but unpacking to stay.

"I'm going now and I'll brain any man who tries to stop me," cries Frank Albertson as he leaves the hotel room to meet his girl despite the protests of Groucho and Chico.

he introduces his general assistant Harpo as "the brains of the organization." Harpo is standing there, mouth agape, looking as moronic as possible, and Groucho adds tartly, "That'll give you some idea of the organization."

Chico appears as Harry Binelli, originally Harry Binion. It is not at all clear what Chico's character does—but presumably, like Binion, he is the director of the play. Miller in the stage production of *Room Service* calls Binion "Harry" but Groucho calls Chico "Binelli," signifying the less cordial relationship that usually exists between Groucho and Chico. The idea of Chico doing something as elaborate as directing a play is innovative but we never see any rehearsals taking place. We do at least have Chico's report on progress, which is splendidly in character: "The rehearsal, she's-a wonderful. Yes sirree, it's-a wonderful. I still think it's a terrible play but it makes a wonderful rehearsal." (The play certainly seems to be every bit as bad as he suggests.) Chico's remarks are also nicely ill-timed, coming when Groucho is trying to keep the author happy for fear of losing the play. "If you don't mind, I'd like to wash up," says the newly arrived young man, unaware of the desperate situation, prompting Chico to remark with characteristic bluntness, "The rest of us are washed up already." Chico is just as direct when Groucho gets the notion that the waiter Sasha could supply them with food—he looks the waiter over and declares: "He looks just right to me. I could eat him raw." Similarly, when a financial backer protests that he has a weak heart as they pressure him into signing a contract, Chico's response is: "Then you'd better hurry—here's the pen."

Harpo assumes the part of a third character, Faker Englund, who was not as important as Miller or Binion in the original play. Most of Faker's lines are given to Chico, either directly or by Chico explaining Faker's actions when in the play he spoke for himself (this interpretative function of Chico's, of course, being consistent with other Marx films). Harpo is left with little to do (including no harp sequence), but he still manages some felicitous moments. His ravenous appetite leads to the engaging spectacle of his stuffing away like an automaton the dinner brought by Sasha. He conveys it to his mouth with no apparent pause for chewing and swallowing,

"Hail and farewell!" Groucho, Chico, and Lucille Ball dispatch Philip Loeb (debt collector Timothy Hogarth), watched by Donald MacBride (Wagner, left).

Chico, Frank Albertson, Lucille Ball, and Harpo (Faker Englund) look on as Groucho examines the contract with their newfound backer and is dismayed to find that his lawyer has departed without signing it.

and he doesn't stop when his arm gets caught up with Chico's. Nor does he waste a thing: when Chico throws salt over his shoulder, Harpo's hand is there to snatch at it and he licks it up. Earlier, when a turkey he has brought with him escapes, there is the glorious sight of him pursuing it around a bedroom with a cudgel, contriving to smash all the most vulnerable objects in range, such as vases and the head of the play's prospective backer.

From Harpo comes another coy confession about his love life but, instead of producing a photograph of a horse, he brings out a miniature doll. This is useful when he plays sick and the hotel doctor wants him to say "Ah" as he is able to respond with a high-tooting squeak from the toy under the bedclothes. And there is an endearingly childlike literalness about him when, hearing the playwright declare that he has burned his bridges behind him, Harpo lifts up the back of the man's coat and inspects his pants. Equally childlike, but in traditional character, is the way he keeps drinking the glasses of medicine the hotel chief pours out for the playwright when the latter is feigning a suicide attempt to delay the closing

of his play in mid-performance in the hotel's theater. A flash of the genuine, playful Harpo also surfaces when he and Groucho doff their hats, bow, and straighten up with the wrong ones, Harpo having deftly switched them over. And Harpo's chewing a sandwich with the cellophane wrapper on recalls his bizarre sandwich in *A Night at the Opera* or his snack during *The Cocoanuts*.

As a whole, the film (like the play) shows a refreshingly scant regard for decency and sensitive feelings. Neither Groucho nor Chico have any scruples about hocking their author's typewriter, and when the debt collector (finely played as a slow-witted, timid individual by Philip Loeb) comes for some back payments, they tell him the typewriter's owner is in an insane asylum. Unfortunately, he took the machine with him. As Chico puts it, "He likes to hear the little bell ring." The hotel doctor is labeled a quack by Chico, posing briefly as a rival doctor, and is tied up in the bathroom. Even in farce, it is quite unbelievable that the doctor should later come out on the Marxes' side against his own boss, the hotel chief, after the indignity he has suffered. When the

161

"Well, brother Wagner, let's start the champagne flowing," says Groucho before the play's opening night performance, not knowing that Donald MacBride has learned that the backer's check is no good, as Chico mulls over the situation.

Frank Albertson asks Groucho and Chico about the great big surprise that hotel chief Wagner has promised them on the opening night of the play.

Imprisoned in the hotel room on opening night, Harpo checks the window for escape possibilities and Chico asks how high up they are.

162

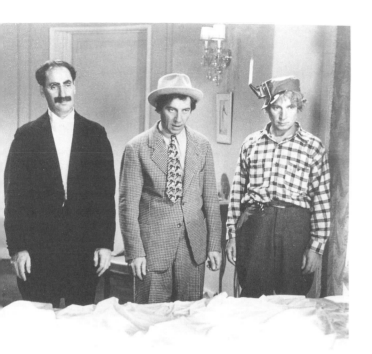

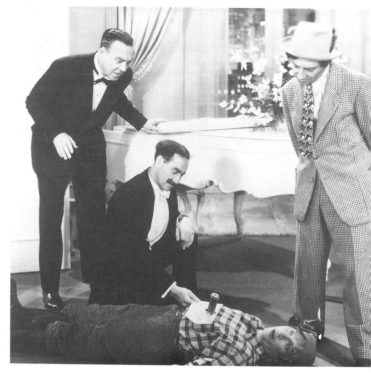

With Harpo soon joining in on the harmonica, Groucho and Chico line up to sing "one last sweet cheerio" to Frank Albertson who has pretended to die from poison.

mock suicide of the author is staged, the executive regrets his attempts to halt the play as he looks at the body and Groucho and Chico sing "One last sweet cheerio" while Harpo brings in a wreath to lay on the corpse. Were it not a ruse, it would be quite a touching moment.

At an earlier point when everything seems hopeless, Groucho looks at Harpo, Chico and the playwright, saying, "Well, the quartet is complete. What shall we do? Sing 'Sweet Adeline'?" The suggestion immediately evokes memories of the four stowaways in *Monkey Business* doing precisely that. Sadly, this is worlds apart.

The gap might have been narrower. Zeppo could have played the author and given the other three's scenes with the character the extra fillip of a family reunion. The play might have been a musical, providing Chico and Harpo with an excuse to perform their solos. Siegfried Rumann should have played the irate hotel chief and rescued the part from the tiresome level of continual bluster it has in the hands of Donald MacBride (retained from the Broadway cast, he has failed to modify his performance for the closer inspection of the camera). And Margaret Dumont could have been a gullible and long-suffering potential backer—Groucho is handicapped by having no suitable females to insult (Lucille Ball

Harpo fakes his death as Donald MacBride, looks horrified while Groucho reads the note blaming him, and Chico suggests giving the body to a medical student.

While dumping the body of Harpo in the alley outside the hotel, Groucho and Donald MacBride have attracted the attention of a policeman.

and Ann Miller, in small parts, do not engage his attention).

Richard Rowland, an early Marxian commentator, summed up the experiment: "No ordinary farce hotel room can hold the Marx Brothers: infinity can scarcely hold them. The well-made play—and *Room Service* was such—with its many doors, all carefully planned to supply comic entrances and exits, is too restrictive. The Brothers need Casablanca, where various worlds meet, or the backstage of a theater, which is whole worlds in itself, or the limitless background of a battlefield or the whole Atlantic Ocean, for their comedy, opening as it does on vast vistas of eternity."

Harpo swells up his chest to impress Chico
with his qualifications to succeed Goliath as
the circus strongman.

At the Circus

1939

J. Cheever Loophole: GROUCHO MARX. *Punchy:*
HARPO MARX. *Antonio Pirelli:* CHICO MARX.
Mrs. Suzanna Dukesbury: Margaret Dumont. *Jeff Wilson:* Kenny Baker. *Julie Randall:* Florence Rice.
Peerless Pauline: Eve Arden. *Goliath:* Nat Pendleton.
Jardinet: Fritz Feld. *John Carter:* James Burke. *Little Professor Atom:* Jerry Marenghi. *Whitcomb:* Barnett
Parker. *Chef in diner:* Frank Orth. *Ringmaster:* Emory
Parnell. *Telegraph office clerk:* Irving Bacon. *Cab
driver:* Matt McHugh. *Redcap:* Willie Best. *Gibraltar:*
Charles Gemora. *Taxi driver:* Matt McHugh. *Checker
player:* Buck Mack. *Telegrapher:* Frank Darien.

Director: Edward Buzzell. *Screenwriter:* Irving
Brecher. *Cinematographer:* Leonard M. Smith. *Art
directors:* Cedric Gibbons and Stan Rogers. *Set decorator:* Edwin B. Willis. *Editor:* William H. Terhune.
Music director: Franz Waxman. *Songs "Lydia, the
Tattooed Lady," "Two Blind Loves," "Step Up and
Take a Bow," "Swingali," composer:* Harold Arlen,
lyricist: E. Y. Harburg. *Vocal and orchestral arrangers:* Murray Cutter, George Bassmann, Ken Darby.
Dance director: Bobby Connolly. *Costume designers:
(women)* Dolly Tree, *(men)* Valles. *Recording director:* Douglas Shearer. *Assistant director:* Sandy Roth.
Producer: Mervyn LeRoy. *Production company/
distributor:* Metro-Goldwyn-Mayer (Loew's Inc.).
Running time: 87 minutes. *Release date:* October 20,
1939 (New York opening: November 16, 1939).

Placing the Marxes against a circus background
was a promising idea; but also a demanding one.
In previous films, the brothers had rarely fitted in
with their surroundings, being unsympathetic to
their values. The circus is a different matter, at
least for Chico and Harpo. As British critic
William Whitebait observed in a contemporary
review: "The circus ring is where by tradition the

165

Groucho (J. Cheever
Loophole), the missing
attorney for the plaintiff,
is found catnapping in the
jury box. Cut sequence
with Byron Foulger (at
desk, in front of Groucho)
as the defendant.

Groucho with Irene Colman (his client) in the cut courtroom
sequence.

Marx Brothers belong, with the Fratellinis and
the world's best clowns, and to see them swinging
on a trapeze, running with the clowns, and firing
Margaret Dumont from a cannon, reminds us of
the real origins of their humor, which is by no
means specifically modern as the surrealist interpreters of it would like to suggest."

Unfortunately, there is no real sawdust atmosphere. It seems to have been beyond the writer,
Irving Brecher, and director, Edward Buzzell, to
develop the background or subsidary characters
effectively. The opera house, the ocean liner, the
sanitarium, and the racetrack were all much more
convincingly established in the Marxes' preced-
ing MGM films. To judge by the number of extras
in some of the scenes, *At the Circus* was quite
highly budgeted. It is simply a fault of approach
that Harpo and Chico do not spring more naturally from this environment. One difficulty is the
number of crooks that are operating in the circus—some of them fellow performers who ought
to be better behaved if the supposed camaraderie
of the traveling circus means anything.

The film introduces a young circus operator,
Jeff Wilson, about to meet the deadline on a final
payment on a loan. Jeff also doubles as the film's
romantic and singing lead: as played by Kenny
Baker, he is a sorry successor to Allan Jones,

As Groucho tries to board the circus train without a badge, Harpo (Punchy) and the seal come along with theirs and are passed by Chico (Antonio).

rivaled only by Oscar Shaw for insufferability. Florence Rice is the pallid heroine.

The script requires Chico to be Jeff's devoted friend, Antonio, as he was Judy's in *A Day at the Races*. "I ain't got nothing but you can always have half," he tells Jeff and, scenting trouble, he consults his notebook to see who can help out. Just as he conjured up Groucho to keep Mrs. Upjohn from leaving the Standish Sanitarium, so here Chico summons Groucho, as lawyer J. Cheever Loophole, into this film by another telegram.

Groucho was provided with an establishing scene in a courtroom before the telegram arrived. It was filmed but understandably deleted in editing. The script shows it to have been very feeble material, making Groucho look ridiculous. It opens well enough with Groucho, as the missing attorney for a glamorous brunette bringing a breach of promise suit, being spotted asleep in the jury box. The defendant's attorney protests to the judge that all Groucho has introduced in evidence is an affidavit with half the pages missing. "Well, affa-davit is better than none,"

Groucho assures Kenny Baker (Jeff Wilson), being tended to by Florence Rice (Julie Randall), that, with him on the case, the stolen circus money is practically back in his pocket.

says Groucho, stealing Chico's line of humor. It is, by Groucho's admission, his first case in nine years and it misfires when he himself, rather than the meek defendant, is identified as having been with the woman on the night in question (this twist having been used earlier in a court case scene in the first episode of the *Flywheel, Shyster, and Flywheel* radio series). Groucho makes a beeline for the nearest exit, only to be stopped by a quartet of messenger boys who sing Chico's telegram to him: "Happy birthday to you, happy birthday to you, come quickly to Luxton, or the circus is through." (The full script for this sequence will be found in *The Freedonia Gazette* 13, Winter 1984.)

Without this scene, it is still apparent that Groucho answers Chico's call because he has nothing better to do. In *A Day at the Races*, he was tempted to leave his veterinary practice for another crack at Margaret Dumont, but here he doesn't learn of her existence until much later on. He merely arrives in response to Chico's unspecific offer of work for the circus.

Chico introduces Groucho to his friend Punchy (Harpo). Groucho mistakes Harpo for Jeff Wilson when they are introduced—for one look at Harpo's most hideously blank expression leads Groucho to assess him as "the executive type." This is comparable to his being described as "the brains of the organization" in *Room Service*, only there Groucho was kidding while here he seems serious, which makes him unusually stupid.

When Jeff is robbed of the vital takings, the attempt to recover it provides a more mundane basis for a plot than the clash of personalities on which the best scenes in *A Night at the Opera* were based. Groucho, styling himself "the legal eagle," steps in to investigate the robbery. "Now watch the eagle swoop down!" he cries, but at the first sight of the gigantic suspect, Goliath the Strongman, he quickly backs away, apologizing for disturbing him, and soon wants to quit. (This wall of muscle is played by Nat Pendleton, one of the star football players in *Horse Feathers*.) Not only is Groucho alarmed by Goliath but he is even taken aback by the sharp sound of a train whistle and by a flower (the prop of a magician) that opens unexpectedly as he hands it to the heroine while he is, somewhat sickeningly, promising his help in any way.

At a later stage, Groucho visits another performer, Peerless Pauline (Eve Arden), whose act includes walking upside down in suction boots. He notices her slipping the stolen money into her bosom. "There must be some way of getting that money without getting in trouble with the Hays Office," he remarks in an aside. A quick cut to a close-up on Groucho for that line would have let this seem more of a spontaneous ad-lib but instead the camera tracks ponderously in to hear him say it. To dislodge the money, he suggests she take a walk on the ceiling but he has to do it as well before she will agree. Groucho reluctantly puts on a rather demeaning costume, and then gets stuck when the money drops and she swings

down to reclaim it. To see him so obviously and predictably outwitted marks quite a decline. He may possibly become more sympathetic but the resourcefulness of the old Groucho was more valuable. Making matters worse, Groucho threatens her with the law. This might just be taken as his threatening her with his legal skill, but it seems to suggest calling in the police as though Groucho were an ordinary citizen instead of, as previously, someone who took matters into his own hands. In this new role, the least he could do is eventually recover the money but that job falls to the circus gorilla. However, Groucho does a splendid job of handling Margaret Dumont as the film's rich Mrs. Dukesbury.

In *At the Circus*, Chico becomes a particularly stupid character again, lacking the guile of *A Day at the Races*. He guards the circus train with the precious money aboard (an index of how much he is trusted by Jeff) and, when Groucho arrives in the pouring rain, won't allow him on board without a pass badge, despite the fact that he summoned Groucho and Groucho couldn't possibly have one. Harpo comes along and has hundreds of the right badge inside his coat (as he had police badges in *The Cocoanuts* and *Horse Feathers*); even the seal he is escorting under an umbrella (demonstrating his kindness to animals) proves to have a badge. Eventually Chico relents and gives Groucho a badge, but he still can't go on board because it's last year's one and he is rudely pushed back into a puddle. The basic inspiration for the scene is obviously the one at the speakeasy door in *Horse Feathers* but there Chico didn't know Groucho and had no reason to let him in, whereas here it seems nonsensical for Chico to obstruct the ally he summoned so urgently. (Soon after, Groucho is found comfortably aboard the train anyway—how he managed this is never explained.)

There is even a second scene of this type when Chico blocks Groucho's every attempt to obtain a cigar from the midget to compare with the butt found at the scene of the robbery. Each time Groucho asks for one of the midget's cigars, Chico asininely offers one of his own. When Chico

Margaret Dumont (Mrs. Dukesbury) being serenaded by Groucho: "Oh, Suzanna, won't you fly with me, for I need ten thousand dollars, 'cause the sheriff's after me . . ."

Groucho announces himself as Mr. Dukesbury to Barnett Parker (Whitcomb, Mrs. Dukesbury's butler) and asks her room number.

Groucho walks on the ceiling with Eve Arden (Peerless Pauline) in the hope of dislodging the stolen money from her chest.

sabotages Groucho's auction in *The Cocoanuts* with the same persistence, it is funny because Groucho has only himself to blame as he arranged for Chico to do it—the humor lies not so much in Chico's stupidity as in the way Groucho's underhand scheming rebounds on him. The cigar scene is moronic and pointless, for both Groucho and Chico want to solve the crime. It is also unpleasant to see the pair of them attempting to harass a midget, even if he is one of the villains and well able to take care of himself.

Harpo is, on the whole, better served. Again he works for a bad guy, Goliath, as the strongman's assistant, and is roughly treated, being blamed

169

Chico and Groucho grill Jerry Marenghi (Little Professor Atom) about the missing money.

Chico and Harpo consider how to search Nat Pendleton (Goliath) for the missing money.

for a mishap during a performance. He gets on well with animals, playing checkers with a seal, riding an ostrich, and pacifying the lions with a trombone, showing a power of communion with dumb animals (the dumb speaking to the dumb). This gift is equated by some susceptible black circus hands with mesmerism and Harpo is likened to Svengali. This leads into another song and dance session, one that is less elaborate and artistic than that of *A Day at the Races*, highly patronizing by today's standards but again showing Harpo's rapport with the underprivileged, who pay rapt attention to his harp solo.

There is a good scene for Harpo when Chico decides to "re-destruct" the crime and gives Harpo the role of the crook. Harpo doesn't want to be a crook, even though he later provides evidence of a criminal past in the form of a wanted notice, "Fifty Cents Reward for Jaywalking" (recalling an earlier poster in *The Cocoanuts*). To Chico, this only proves that crime doesn't pay: you don't get enough for jaywalking. Chico explains to Harpo that he merely has to act the crook: Harpo's childish notion of acting leads him to kiss his way up Chico's arm, getting so carried away that he has Chico flat out on his back. As they reenact the crime, Harpo plays enthusiastically and whacks Chico over the head. When Chico decides it would be safer to reverse the roles and be the crook, Harpo takes him at his word and whacks him again. (The word "crook" had an equally emotive effect on Harpo in *A Day at the Races:* he started after Whitmore the moment Chico declared he was a crook, and Chico had to hold him back.)

Perhaps the finest example of Harpo's physical humor occurs in his rescue of Groucho from his predicament in Peerless Pauline's tent, hanging upside down. Harpo speedily solves the problem by undoing Groucho's bootlaces, letting him fall to the floor even more painfully than when he missed the net in *Horse Feathers*. Harpo's responses are often immediate—as when he sticks dynamite into the vase on Groucho's head in *Duck Soup*—without taking the consequences into account.

Disturbed by the noise that Harpo and Chico have been making searching his compartment on the train, Nat Pendleton has switched on the light. As he settles back, Harpo switches it off.

Chico tries to rouse Harpo
after he has swallowed the
sleeping pills intended to
keep Goliath quiet.

Groucho gives Margaret Dumont
a hand in getting ready for the
banquet: "I used to be a riveter
on the Golden Gate Bridge."

One of the film's best scenes concerns Chico
and Harpo's search of Goliath's compartment on
the circus train while the strongman is asleep in
the lower bunk. Chico reckons that, if he becomes restless, they will soothe him back to sleep
like a baby. Harpo helpfully produces a baby's
bottle full of milk. Chico decides they will work in
the dark. Harpo puts on dark glasses. They make
a noise at which Goliath stirs. Chico snaps out the
light and Goliath flips it back on. Harpo, occupying a coat hanging from a hook (as he did in *Horse
Feathers*), turns it out. When everything is quiet,
Harpo switches the light on again, falls out of the
coat, and goes across to join Chico who is hiding
in the upper bunk. Chico starts down and
crunches Harpo's hand. Harpo grasps it in agony
and rushes to the cabinet over the wash basin,
pours iodine on it, and rubs his hand up and down
on the floor like a paint brush (his hands took on
this limp, lifeless quality in *A Night at the Opera*
when he pretended to have crushed them in a
piano lid).

They start to search Goliath himself who has,
uncooperatively, gone to sleep grasping the top of

the blanket with his hands while the lower end is
wrapped tightly around his feet. Harpo scissors
across the blanket just short of the hands and feet,
and looks around. Chico pulls out a pillow and
Harpo cuts it open, letting fluff drift all over the
room. Harpo picks up a wad of cotton wool and
attaches it to his face like a beard, pads his
stomach, rings a bell, and waves a spittoon like

Santa Claus collecting for charity amidst the swirling snow of fluff. It is an instant, magical, and hilarious transformation, all the funnier because this distraction has occurred at such an unsuitable time and place. Chico helps it along by singing "Jingle Bells" and dropping a coin in the spittoon. Like the burglary in *Duck Soup* or the switching of paintings in *Animal Crackers*, it shows that Harpo and Chico are incapable of operating discreetly. Goliath is shifting uneasily, so Chico concocts a sleeping potion. Harpo promptly swallows it (like the medicine in *Room Service*) and passes out. Chico tries slapping his face and telling him to wake up, alternating this with snatches of a lullaby to soothe the restless giant.

Harpo comes round and slits open Goliath's mattress, clambering inside to search it. Goliath sits up as Harpo tunnels underneath him. A horn sounds, as it does beneath the lemonade vendor in *Duck Soup*. Goliath decides he would be better off in the top bunk and swings his mattress up there on top of Chico. He settles down on top of both of them—another human sandwich like that of *Monkey Business*. After Goliath has given up trying to sleep and departed, Chico slaps Harpo vigorously and a long stream of compressed fluff issues from his mouth.

Groucho's songs are always a highlight and the one he performs here, "Lydia, the Tattooed Lady," is among the best he ever had. All about Lydia, whose epidermis was an education in itself, the song's lyrics by E. Y. Harburg include a reference to her body featuring Captain Spaulding exploring the Amazon as well as Godiva "but with her pajamas on." (The reference to a picture of "Washington crossing the Delaware" actually has its origin in episode fifteen of *Flywheel, Shyster, and Flywheel* in which Groucho refers to it being tattooed on his chest.) Groucho sings and dances "Lydia" on the train, the same setting being used for Chico's piano playing. Regrettably, the other songs in the film by Harburg and composer Harold Arlen are only mediocre.

There can be no doubt that the scenes which reunite Groucho with Margaret Dumont give him his most effective moments, but it is some fifty-two minutes into the picture before she is first seen. There's his storming of Dukesbury Manor after learning that Jeff has an aunt, America's wealthiest widow, who could save the circus. Groucho races around Whitcomb, the butler, and the camera follows him, reinforcing this charge through the portals of snobbery. After likening the place to a hotel (as he did Rittenhouse Manor in *Animal Crackers*), he ascends the stairs and bellows down the corridors: "Oh, larooo! Mrs. Dukesbury! Yahoo!" "What in the world . . . " remarks Margaret Dumont as Groucho sweeps into her boudoir. "Keep your shirt on," he tells her, "I'm looking for old lady Dukesbury." She identifies herself. "Snookums!" he cries, rushing to her side and clasping her hand as he kneels. She doesn't know him. "You mean you've forgotten. I know, you have forgotten! Those June nights on the Riviera when we sat beneath those shimmering skies moonlight bathing in the Mediterranean. We were young, gay, reckless! That night I drank champagne from your slipper. Two quarts. It would have held more but you were wearing inner soles." Groucho's romantic outpourings come to a characteristically crude finish.

Whitcomb and Mrs. Dukesbury are the first two people over whom he has been able to assert himself. But, after this splendid beginning, the scene degenerates rapidly. Groucho's dialogue, as when explaining fluctuation in a French accent, is feeble and forced (while his pocketing of all her cigars is too petty a touch). From this scene it emerges that Mrs. Dukesbury is holding a big soirée to which the select Four Hundred of Newport are being invited. Jardinet and his entire symphony orchestra have been hired to come all the way from Paris to perform. Groucho may have been inept in trying to recover Jeff's missing money, but he is quick-witted enough to think of substituting a performance by the circus to earn the required amount. Groucho tries to stop Jardinet ever landing but his "FBI message" to the boat is not very inspired—the moment he mentions a dope ring, the jokes using the word "dope"

At the banquet. Groucho: "I love you feverishly."
Margaret Dumont: "Oh, not here, m'sieur, not here!"

are depressingly predictable as Groucho describes Jardinet as the "head dope" and offer the "full dope" on him. Groucho's jokes should never be obvious (such lines are Chico's specialty) but from this film onwards they too often are.

In the climax, Jardinet and his musicians are set adrift on their specially built floating orchestral platform and play the Prelude to Act 3 of Wagner's *Lohengrin* to an audience of seagulls. Jeff Wilson gets to work setting up his circus on the front lawn of Dukesbury Manor while Groucho looks after things on the inside, counting heads as the Four Hundred arrive (it emphasizes them as mere numbers, not individual people), making introductions for Margaret Dumont as he did when she was Mrs. Claypool, and holding the guests there until Jeff is ready. He wields the weight of decorum to his advantage by calling for further cups of coffee after all the other guests have finished, which is more than enough to keep them seated and waiting, making them not only nameless but sheeplike in their adherence to the laws of social etiquette. Groucho also fills in time

Fritz Feld (Jardinet) arrives at the banquet and tells Margaret Dumont: "When I get here what do I find? Animals!" Groucho: "Animals! Mrs. Dukesbury's friends are my friends. I'll take care of him!"

by declaring to Dumont how feverishly he loves her just as a giraffe puts its head through the window and licks her exposed shoulder, giving her the greatest sensual thrill of her entire relationship with him.

173

Getting the high sign while confronting Fritz Feld that the circus is now ready to perform in place of him, Groucho tells Chico: "Take this bearded symphony down to the bandstand and see that he gets a good send-off."

Groucho: "And since Mrs. Dukesbury and her check book are entirely responsible for this magnificent shindig, I suggest we give the kid a great big hand."

Groucho and Margaret Dumont relax at the circus show.

The film assumes that the guests, although they have dutifully assembled to hear highbrow music, would much rather taste the simple, undemanding pleasures of the circus. Given the opportunity, they are quite happy to be ushered into their seats without any protest while Jardinet and his orchestra play on, drifting forgotten along Atlantic shipping lanes. Margaret Dumont unbends enough to share a cola with Groucho, each with different straws in the happiest-ever image of the two of them together. However, there is a more spectacular entertainment than planned for, and Margaret Dumont being dispatched by cannon to cling as part of a human chain swinging above ground is quite something, even if (of necessity) marred by the use of back projection and doubles (on the ground, Groucho rises to the occasion with another ringside commentary). The stolen money is recovered, the villains are rounded up, and Mrs. Dukesbury, back on terra firma, is delighted with the success of her evening. Indeed, all the people other than the bad guys have thoroughly enjoyed themselves—a mass conversion to the Marx philosophy of taking life as it comes, unwinding and having fun.

Harpo and Chico greet Walter Woolf King (Beecher, left).

Go West

1940

S. Quentin Quale: GROUCHO MARX. *Rusty Pan-ello:* HARPO MARX. *Joe Panello:* CHICO MARX. *Terry Turner:* John Carroll. *Eve Wilson:* Diana Lewis. *Red Baxter:* Robert Barrat. *John Beecher:* Walter Woolf King. *Lulubelle:* June MacCloy. *Railroad President:* George Lessey. *Halfbreed ("Indian Pete"):* Mitchell Lewis. *Dan Wilson:* Tully Marshall. *Railroad ticket clerk:* Edward Gargan. *Drunk in saloon:* Arthur Housman. *Telegraph clerk:* Harry Tyler. *Mary Lou, first saloon girl:* Iris Adrian. *Melody, second saloon girl:* Joan Woodbury. With Joe Jule, Harry Wilson.

Director: Edward Buzzell. *Screenwriter:* Irving Brecher. *Cinematographer:* Leonard Smith. *Art directors:* Cedric Gibbons and Stan Rogers. *Set decorator:* Edwin B. Willis. *Music director:* Georgie Stoll. *Orchestrator:* George Bassman. *Song "Ridin' the Range,"* composer: Roger Edens, *lyricist:* Gus Kahn. *Songs "As If I Didn't Know" and "You Can't Argue With Love,"* composer: Bronislau Kaper, *lyricist:* Gus

Kahn. *Harpo's solo "From the Land of the Sky Blue Water,"* composer: Charles Wakefield Cadman. *Editor:* Blanche Sewell. *Recording director:* Douglas Shearer. *Costume designers:* (men) Gile Steele, (women) Dolly Tree. *Assistant director:* Sandy Roth. *Producer:* Jack Cummings. *Production company/distributor:* Metro-Goldwyn-Mayer (Loew's Inc.). *Running time:* 80 minutes. *Release date:* December 6, 1940 (New York opening: February 20, 1941).

Go West was the work of the same writer and director as *At the Circus*. It puts the Marx Brothers in a period setting and takes away their familiar outfits. Groucho plays S. Quentin Quale, a name somewhat crudely derived from the term "San Quentin quail"—sexually attractive underage women that can put a man inside. Chico and Harpo play brothers—Joe and Rusty Panello.

The film begins rather promisingly in a railroad station in the East. Groucho makes an imposing entry loping into the booking hall followed by a long line of porters. They come to a halt. "Any of you boys got change of ten cents?" he asks. They haven't. "Well . . . keep the baggage!" It turns out he is ten dollars short for a ticket to the West. Harpo arrives with Chico. Harpo is also heading West, but he has only ten dollars of his fare left. Explaining what he did with the rest, he outlines a wavy shape, which Chico interprets as a snake before realizing he means a dame (he made the same mistake when Harpo tried to describe Flo Marlowe in *A Day at the Races*). Groucho needs Harpo's ten dollars; Harpo needs sixty dollars from Groucho. From this unequal base, Groucho sets out to fleece Harpo, but Chico and Harpo take advantage of him at every turn.

Chico explains that his brother Harpo is going West to pick the gold right off the street. Harpo produces a shovel and practices scooping it up. Groucho, confident that he faces a pair of absolute simpletons, warns them that out West they shoot at anything that looks Eastern. "Why, they'd blow his head off if he was out West with that flea incubator," warns Groucho, referring to Harpo's hat, and offers him a beaverskin one for ten dollars. Chico offers one dollar. "Well, I'll take it," says Groucho, and Harpo hauls out his purse which is hidden in his pants on the far end of a length of thread. He hands over a ten dollar bill which Groucho quickly pockets. Chico has to remind him about the change, and Groucho reluctantly counts out nine dollars while Harpo retrieves his ten spot by pulling on the thread which is attached to it.

Groucho then ridicules the coat Harpo is wearing (all the funnier as his own outfit is quite preposterous) and goes on to sell him a coat. By various means, Chico persuades Groucho to keep taking the same note and dispense more change. When the suspicious Groucho keeps his hand in his pocket with the ten spot, Harpo merely opens up his pants with some scissors and snips at the pocket to regain the money. When Groucho tucks his remaining money in his hat for safekeeping,

Harpo switches hats on him, leaving him to stride off in the beaverskin one.

It is very satisfying to see Groucho so expertly outwitted by his brothers, and the Marxes extract full value from the scene. It gives them a lot to work with; if it covers familiar ground, at least the ground has been well chosen. The inspiration is obviously the Groucho/Chico racing tip scene from *A Day at the Races* (especially when Chico brings up sales tax), combined with that film's sequence in which the same note is used and reused to give the sheriff part of the feedbill (except that now the note is on a thread).

Unfortunately, this is the only memorable scene in the entire picture. Once the Marxes actually arrive in the West, they prove to be no match at all for the inhabitants until the climax. One doesn't expect to find Chico confiding nervously to Harpo, "Rusty, I no like-a the West," the moment they arrive in town and witness a gunfight.

Chico and Harpo become kind and considerate characters, befriending an old prospector and immediately advancing him ten dollars for a grubstake. In a crowded stagecoach a mother has only to say that her baby can't stand the jerks for Chico and Harpo to rise and make for the door. When a fellow traveler, John Beecher, offers them a contract for a valuable land deed, he instructs Harpo to stamp it on the bottom and Harpo almost stamps the rear end of the infant instead. So much of the material is this feeble, in sad contrast to comparable moments in the past, as when Harpo produced a real seal for a contract in *Horse Feathers* (at least he might have actually stamped the infant's bottom).

All three Marxes become a laughing stock in the Crystal Palace Saloon. Harpo and Chico hand over to the bartender an I.O.U. for drinks, which is considered hilariously funny, and are chased off the premises. Groucho makes an imposing-enough entry to the sound of gunfire, twirling his six-shooters and announcing "Nobody can outshoot Two-Gun Quale. Boys, sweep out the gutter." "Why, there's nobody out there," somebody reports. "Well, sweep out the gutter," is all that

Groucho has produced the kind of hat he says Harpo should wear out West and has left the tail hanging in front of Harpo's face. "Isn't that tail supposed to be in the back?" asks Chico. Groucho lifts the tail and looks at Harpo's face. "Not on him," he declares.

Any of you boys got change of ten cents? Well . . . keep the baggage." Groucho (S. Quentin Quale) arrives at the railroad station, headed for the West.

Harpo (Rusty) demonstrates to Chico (Joe) and Groucho how he expects to find gold lying all over the street when he arrives out West.

Groucho can muster as a comeback, and everybody understandably loses interest in him.

Just as anticlimactic is an exchange which follows a scene in which Groucho sets out to sell the land deed to villain Red Baxter and his cohort, Beecher, and has the deed taken from him. Already, on the stagecoach, he has backed down from a fight with Beecher after the latter merely pointed out he was bigger than Groucho. Now he is reduced to threatening the law (just as he did in *At the Circus*) and Baxter indulges in some fancy shooting to advise him against it. When Groucho picks out an exact target as though he were about to reply with some even

Walter Woolf King tries to make Chico sign a contract giving him a valuable land deed but Groucho keeps bidding more.

Harpo and Chico are thirsty and penniless. (Harpo proves to be so dry that he can strike a match on his tongue.)

fancier shooting, hopes are raised. Baxter peers hard and can just about discern the target. "What good eyesight you've got!" comments Groucho and lets it go at that. This comic letdown works for a comedian like Bob Hope specializing in cowardice but is not Groucho's style at all. (There is one exception, Groucho fainting at the mention of a wild caterpillar in *Animal Crackers*, which worked as he was stressing his bravery and the contrast was so farcical.)

The scene is followed by Groucho being tripped and falling down the stairs in full view of the townsfolk. When Chico and Harpo revive him, he says, "I was going to thrash them within an inch of their lives but I didn't have a tape measure." This is merely a variation on the more succinct "I'd horsewhip you if I had a horse" in *Horse Feathers* where Groucho idly used it to browbeat Zeppo. Here he has real reason to thrash somebody but is sadly incapable of dealing with him physically or verbally. True, he was kicked down a longer flight of stairs in *A Night at the Opera*, but there it spurred him to a magnificent revenge. Harpo at least is not afraid of Red Baxter and prepares to draw on him. But his gun becomes a clothes brush, though redeemingly the brush then turns out to be a gun after all. However, Harpo seems as

surprised as anyone, and all three Marxes beat a hasty retreat.

There is another lamentable scene in which the trio apologize to the film's leading lady, Eve Wilson (Diana Lewis), for losing her father's deed to Baxter. The Marxes decide to break into the saloon at night and recover the deed from the safe. (By coincidence, in Laurel and Hardy's *Way Out West*, released by MGM in 1937, Stan and Ollie lost a valuable land deed, looked up the late owner's daughter, and broke into a saloon at night to recover it.)

When the saloon singer Lulubelle and another girl hear the noise the Marxes are making, Groucho and Chico decide to keep the two occupied while Harpo gets the deed. The girls bring in some bottles and Groucho and Chico soon lose control (June MacCloy's Lulubelle is reminiscent of *Way Out West*'s Lola who dealt just as effectively with Laurel and Hardy, though she is also comparable to Peerless Pauline in *At the Circus* who turned the tables on Groucho.) At least Harpo, busily blowing the safe in the next room, has the respect of the girls: "That redhead, he's a demon!" one of them remarks. He is clever enough to let one of the girls pour away her drink into his hat so that he can have it and he also

178

Robert Barrat (Red Baxter) asks June
MacCloy (Lulubelle) to look after Groucho, as
Walter Woolf King watches.

Groucho helps June MacCloy finish her
number "You Can't Argue With Love."

Groucho has been pushed down some stairs with an empty bag
after trying to sell the land deed to Robert Barrat. "Brandy!
Brandy! Pour brandy down my throat," he cries as Chico and
Harpo look on, disappointed.

Marx Brothers alternate with villains in taking control of the
situation until John Carroll (Terry Turner), seen with Diana
Lewis (Eve Wilson), gains the upper hand for good.

Harpo comes a-gunning for Robert
Barrat after the latter has stolen the
valuable land deed from Groucho.

John Carroll, guitar-strumming Groucho, and Chico sing "Ridin' the Range," accompanied by Harpo o harmonica with Diana Lewis tagging along.

As Chico tries to talk Indian to the chief, Groucho translates: "He wants to know if you want starch in your shirts."

removes a girl's tiara from her head with a magnet. He has a lot of fun opening the safe, as when using a stick of dynamite that turns out to be a Christmas cracker (like the gun becoming a brush) which then explodes (like the brush going off). Harpo is again surprised, as he is by a curious bit in which the drawers of a desk open of their own accord. The scene ends amiably enough in a pastiche of traditional Western twists as Marxes and villains alternately burst in and gain control of the situation, but it takes the arrival of Eve's boyfriend, Terry Turner (John Carroll), to conclusively gain the upper hand from Red Baxter and his men.

The Marxes celebrate with Carroll by singing "Ridin' the Range," one of the most pleasant numbers in all their work. But then they stop at an Indian village, and the film reaches its absolute nadir. Chico and Groucho are so bad that they seem like feeble imitations of themselves. Chico claims he can speak Indian because he was born in Indianapolis and all three jump into the arms of Indian braves with fright at the sight of a medicine man. Marx devotees rightly lament some of the cuts made to their pictures, but this is one cut that cries out to have been made . . . excepting only that the scene leads Harpo to a makeshift harp for an agreeable solo.

The climax, with the Marxes racing the villains and battling with them on a train, is moderately amusing. The railroad isn't as deserving a target for the disruption the Marxes cause as the opera house or racetrack were: while Beecher is acting for the railroad, the bosses back East have shown themselves in a sympathetic light; and it is a mistake to have the train demolish the house of an innocent farmer. But the main drawback to the scene is that it isn't really tailored to the particular talents of the Marx Brothers. It would be just as amusing if it featured Abbott and Costello or Martin and Lewis, whereas Buster Keaton showed in *The General* (1926) how to make a railroad chase work more distinctively. It is possible that Keaton did suggest some gags here (as he worked in a similar capacity on *At the Circus*): there is one moment, in which Harpo, standing at the side of the track, escapes injury by being in line with the doors of the farmhouse as it is pushed along by the train, that recalls the house falling on Buster in *Steamboat Bill Jr.* (1928). The idea of breaking up the carriages to fuel the boiler is a good one but again hardly original: a boat is similarly treated in the climactic race of the Will Rogers comedy *Steamboat Round the Bend* (1935).

Scenes need to be stamped with the distinctive personalities of the Marxes to work, but too many of the jokes are mechanical, with speeded up footage and doubles. Others are simply too fee-ble: "Brake! The brake!" yells Groucho as the train hurtles on with Harpo in control, and Harpo obligingly breaks the brake and throws it away. This is a joke that Harpo can get away with better than most comedians but it is very feeble compared to the "Tie on-a the bed, throw the rope out of the window" misunderstanding in *Horse Feathers*, which wasn't the brightest gag in that picture anyway. At one point, Harpo lies straddled between two carriages holding the train together: he slowly stretches as the gap widens and a good idea (better suited to animation) is marred in the execution as it is too obvious where Harpo's legs really end and the extension begins. Earlier tricks with Harpo's anatomy like the leg-pulling and handwringing of *Monkey Business* were less elaborate and much more effective. The same kind of fault occurs at the close of *Go West*, at the ceremonial opening of a new section of railroad as Harpo, invited to drive in the golden spike, knocks a railroad president into the ground. (The gag was suggested by the bungling that attended the real spike-driving at the historic meeting of the Union Pacific and Central Pacific railroads.)

Groucho's trip out West was a mistake, as there was no scope for Margaret Dumont or a pompous figure in the Siegfried Rumann mould to engage his attention. At one point in the climactic train ride, Groucho lifts the gag off the mouth of the train engineer to ask him something and comments to the audience, "You know, this is the best gag in the picture." He isn't far wrong.

Harpo charms a snake during the "Sing While You Sell" number, watched by Groucho.

The Big Store

1941

Wolf J. Flywheel: GROUCHO MARX. *Wacky:* HARPO MARX. *Ravelli:* CHICO MARX. *Martha Phelps:* Margaret Dumont. *Mr. Grover:* Douglass Dumbrille. *Tommy Rogers:* Tony Martin. *Joan Sutton:* Virginia Grey. *Fred Sutton:* William Tannen. *Peggy Arden:* Marion Martin. *Kitty:* Virginia O'Brien. *Giuseppi:* Henry Armetta. *Maria, Giuseppi's wife:* Anna Demetrio. *George Hastings:* Paul Stanton. *Arthur Hastings:* Russell Hicks. *Duke:* Bradley Page. *Finance company man:* Charles Lane. *Detective:* Dewey Robinson. *Piano mover:* Adrian Morris. *Store commissionaire:* Edgar Dearing. *Customer seeking record:* Clara Blandick. *Bedding Department manager:* Pierre Watkin. *Gangsters:* Al Hill and George Lloyd. *Press photographers:* William Newell and Milton Kibbee. With Six Hits and a Miss.

Director: Charles Riesner. *Screen writers:* Sid Kuller, Hal Fimberg, and Ray Golden. *Story by:* Nat Perrin. *Cinematographer:* Charles Lawton. *Art directors:* Ced-ric Gibbons and Stan Rogers. *Set decorator:* Edwin B. Willis. *Editor:* Conrad A. Nervig. *Music director:* Georgie Stoll. *Songs "Sing While You Sell," "Tenement Symphony," composer:* Hal Borne, *lyricists:* Sid Kuller and Hal Fimberg. *Song "If It's You," composer:* Ben Oakland, *lyricists:* Milton Drake and Artie Shaw. *Music adaptor:* Earl Brent. *Vocal and orchestrations:* Leo Arnaud, George Bassman, Herb Taylor, and Robert Van Eps. *Dance director:* Arthur Appell. *Recording director:* Douglas Shearer. *Assistant director:* Sandy Roth. *Producer:* Louis K. Sidney. *Production company/distributor:* Metro-Goldwyn-Mayer (Loew's Inc.). *Running time:* 83 minutes. *Release date:* June 20, 1941 (New York opening: June 26, 1941).

The Big Store had the right kind of setting for a Marx Brothers picture, it had new writers and a new director, and it brought on Margaret Dumont early (rather than belatedly, as in *At the Circus*). But the result is a flat little picture, with dull material performed for much more than its worth by Groucho, Harpo, and Chico.

The Marxes now have jobs—just. Chico runs a music conservatory and narrowly avoids having his piano repossessed. Groucho waits for clients as head of a detective agency, with Harpo as his assistant, and ends up having his car repossessed. The three are linked by Harpo and Chico being brothers again. Chico's Ravelli is the best friend of singing star Tommy Rogers, a former pupil played by Tony Martin. Martin and Margaret Dumont, as his aunt, Martha Phelps, have inherited a department store. (Martha Phelps is nowhere near grand enough a name for Dumont.)

Villainy is dispensed by Douglass Dumbrille (who, since playing Morgan in *A Day at the Races*, has grown an extra "s" on his first name): as Grover, manager of the department store, he has been cooking the books and faces exposure. He is remarkably unscrupulous: he wants to kill Tommy, then marry Margaret Dumont and bump her off in an accident to become owner of the store; he doesn't hesitate to kidnap Tommy's girl to further his plans. He has many people involved in his nefarious schemes: Tommy's girl's brother, an assistant manager, and two hoods.

There's far too much plot and a lot of Tony Martin singing (only to be expected as he does share equal billing with the Marx Brothers, the first time they'd needed a costar since *The Cocoanuts*). In a shortish picture, this doesn't leave a lot of time for the Marx Brothers to perform, which is probably to the good considering the weakness of much of what they are given.

There's a particularly dismal sequence in the bedding department where (an unlikely story) Groucho is sleeping off an all-night session as Tommy Rogers's bodyguard while Tommy has been going over the books with Grover. Grover arranges for an immediate half-price sale in the bedding department to draw crowds and drive Groucho out (for improbable plot reasons). And a fat Italian with a wife and twelve children comes

along and turns out to be an old acquaintance of Chico's and Harpo's; they all trod grapes together back in Naples. First, the Italian, Giuseppi, becomes angry, thinking that Chico, by the way he is talking, is making fun of his accent—i.e. Giuseppi finds Chico's accent phony, as it obviously is. But then Chico turns out to actually come from Italy—making him a real Italian after all. Very confusing. Then there's all kinds of concealed beds into which the Italian kids plus newly arrived Indian and Oriental children can disappear in a scene that took a lot of time and trouble but just never gets anywhere.

Groucho and Margaret Dumont have one fairly good five-minute scene near the start, with Harpo contributing. In a complete reversal of past practice, it is Dumont who seeks out Groucho's Wolf J. Flywheel, having selected him from a list of private eyes, and a new desperation is evident in Groucho by the preparations he has made to impress any potential client who should cross his threshold. The old indifference and incompetence assert themselves in time but he tries hard to gain work from her.

As for Harpo, called Wacky this time, he takes on the innovatory role of assistant to Groucho besides being Chico's brother. This makes the strongest link between the three since *Monkey Business* (excluding the special case of *Room Service*).

As Groucho's factotum, Harpo prepares his breakfast while he finishes perusing *The Wall Street Journal*. Groucho then tells Harpo to go out and sell it—a sad indication of enforced thriftiness from a man who once threw away cigarette lighters. But he immediately changes his mind and tells Harpo not to bother—clearly, the scriptwriters wanted to register the idea but didn't want Harpo to go off and hold up the scene. But the result is to make Groucho seem indecisive, which is quite wrong.

Margaret Dumont arrives and wipes her feet on a rug that will turn out to be Groucho's coat when they leave (only, in a continuity error, it is by then on the back of the door). The place has been transformed into a hive of contrived activity for

Harpo has driven Groucho and Margaret Dumont to the Phelps Department Store.

Groucho (Wolf J. Flywheel) studies a fake telgram delivered by his assistant, Harpo (Wacky), seeking to impress his new client, Margaret Dumont (Mrs. Phelps), with how busy he is.

Tony Martin (Tommy Rogers), to please his aunt, Margaret Dumont, accepts Groucho as his bodyguard, much to the annoyance of Douglass Dumbrille (Grover).

Groucho works on Margaret Dumont.

her benefit. Harpo dutifully makes a record of her remarks on his typewriter but it operates at the decibel level of a road-drill and she can't make herself heard. They struggle on against the clatter of the machine which at one point looks as though it also empties toast when the toaster next to it

Groucho has returned Margaret Dumont's missing purse to her while Harpo holds some of the money he removed, as Chico (Ravelli) and Tony Martin look on.

"I'm fed up with the three of you," Douglass Dumbrille tells Groucho, Harpo, and Chico.

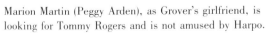

Marion Martin (Peggy Arden), as Grover's girlfriend, is looking for Tommy Rogers and is not amused by Harpo.

Henry Armetta (Giuseppi, right) has finally remembered his old friend Chico from the days they pressed grapes together back in Italy. Watching are Anna Demetrio (Maria, Giuseppi's wife) and some of their kids.

Harpo fools around with Chico during their piano duet, as store customers watch on.

Chico has taken a flash photograph that will reveal who kidnapped the girlfriend of Tony Martin during a blackout. As Harpo casts a sly grin, Groucho tells him to develop the film.

Groucho examines the negative with Harpo and Chico: "This thing looks like Grover, is built like Grover, and is dressed like Grover. Who do you think it is?"

goes off. It does, however, disgorge its carriage which flies over to land on Groucho's desk. Harpo rushes across, not wasting a second as his super-efficient secretary, but seizes a phone instead of the carriage. There is a surreal absurdity about the situation. Groucho could order Harpo to stop making the noise and Harpo cannot possibly hear what is being said to take it down anyway. But the kind of rules the Marxes follow preclude any sensible solution. Groucho and Margaret Dumont struggle on, trying to make each other heard by getting close together at the corner of his desk as Harpo resumes his thunderous typing. By now the coffee in Groucho's desk is boiling over and Groucho tells her he's "dripping with offers" as it spurts over his pinstripes. Harpo further reveals the extent of the preplanned impression of activity as he takes in a telegram from a fake hand attached to the back of a door and industriously dashes across to bring it to Groucho's attention. Groucho turns its offer down in favor of working for Dumont, suggesting a fee of a mere six thousand dollars but readily backing down to five hundred with a five dollar advance (the old flitting between extremes).

As in *Duck Soup*, Harpo is also Groucho's chauffeur. But here, Marxian comedy now being tamer, he does his job properly apart from a fit of the giggles at the prospect of driving Dumont in their ramshackle jalopy. When he gets the vehicle moving, Dumont's seat collapses, Groucho quickwittedly assuring her that it's protection against flying bullets. When they arrive at the store, Harpo opens the door only to have it come off completely. Left alone, he starts clearing out the vehicle until he comes under the surveillance of a cop. In the same way that Chico and the playwright reversed their packing under scrutiny in *Room Service*, so Harpo neatly reverses himself and throws all the junk back in. Later he makes an unusual appeal to authority by having the cop shift a car that has parked by a fireplug. When the cop has moved on, Harpo drives his car into the space and throws the fireplug (a lightweight dummy) into the back. This exhibits the same cunning as his set of portable lampposts for dog-catching in *Horse Feathers*.

Inside the store, Groucho is taken by Dumont to Grover's office. He instinctively senses that Grover is really a nasty piece of work and the scene provides a brisk display of Groucho's rudeness and incompetence. Grover has merely to ask "How do you do?" for Groucho to take umbrage and declare, "That's rather a personal question, isn't it?" Dumont introduces Groucho as a new floorwalker, a job that will let him keep an eye on Tommy. Grover eyes him with a suspicion akin to Whitmore looking at the new doctor in *A Day at the Races*. Again his credentials are questioned. Groucho considers himself highly qualified for the job: "I was a shoplifter for three years" (paralleling Groucho's medical experience, catching the flu, in *Races*). When he stupidly lets slip that he is really a detective, Grover understandably finds this even more improbable than his being a floorwalker. "If he's a detective, I'm a monkey's uncle," declares Grover, inviting an appropriate comeback from Groucho, as did Jennings in *Horse Feathers* ("If this is a singing lesson, I'm a ring-tailed monkey") but such openings make it too easy for Groucho.

In his music conservatory, Chico is teaching children to play the piano and when his back is turned they imitate his shooting-the-keys technique with their index fingers. One can envision the Chico style spreading worldwide from this modest base to the horror of the music world. The place has a friendly atmosphere and Chico largely abandons the crooked, stupid outlook of past films.

Chico and Harpo perform a piano duet, the first time they have ever properly collaborated musically in their films, during which they also do a form of conga, circling round, over, and under each other while keeping up their playing—ostensibly to draw a large crowd that might include two killers loose in the store (as if they would be distracted from their work).

Harpo's harp solo is inventive, a fantasy sequence in which he eyes a store mannequin dressed in a dandy's costume and the next moment is wearing its wig and costume and playing some Mozart in a period setting (much more appropriate to his instrument than the usual

Harpo, Chico (holding the incriminating print), and Groucho charge Douglass Dumbrille when he tries to take the evidence at gunpoint. They escape into the store, leading to a big chase.

Holding the photograph that proves Grover's guilt, Harpo has slid down the wires onto the counter and is temporarily halted during the climactic chase.

contemporary one, though he did play in period costume on stage). He is backed by two reflections of himself in mirrors. After a while the mirror images become independent-minded and break off keeping in time with him and even take up different instruments, confounding Harpo at first—but then, as he warms to the idea, he nods cheerfully and carries on with his own playing. One of his reflections plays a lively bass and the other hot jazz on the violin. It is a felicitous sequence and one that stirs up in the gentlest way the confusion over identity that is a recurring feature of the Marx pictures. As Grouchos proliferated in *Duck Soup*, so Harpos proliferate here, but this time they are part of Harpo.

The scene has a lightness of touch that is in complete contrast to Tony Martin's heavily overproduced and overextended big production number, "The Tenement Symphony," or Virginia O'Brien's peculiar frozen-faced rendition of a swingtime "Rock-a-Bye Baby." Groucho himself sings and dances but not in a specialty number of his own, merely contributing to the elaborate but dull "Sing While You Sell" number.

In *The Big Store*, Groucho woos Margaret Dumont with some occasionally effective banter. When she recognizes his poetic utterings as the work of Byron, Groucho assures her, "He was thinking of you when he wrote it." Contemplating their future together, Dumont wonders, "Tell me, Wolfie dear, will we have a beautiful home?" He answers: "Of course. You're not planning on moving, are you?" "No," she replies, "but I'm afraid that after we've married a while, a beautiful young girl will come along and you'll forget all about me." "Don't be silly," responds Groucho, "I'll write you twice a week."

Although Groucho and Chico are purported to have never met before the film starts, when Chico says, "Look at me and laugh," while taking his photograph, Groucho slips in a fraternal jest: "I've been doing that for twenty years."

A photograph brings about the climax of the film, after a flash exposure catches Grover in the act of abducting Tommy Rogers's fiancée in the darkness of a prearranged power cut. Grover manages to destroy the negative, but the Marxes have a print taken from it and are chased all over the big store, swinging on lamps, jumping over rolls of linoleum, and skating along counters, being very obviously impersonated by stunt doubles much of the time. The sequence has the same drawback as the hectic train ride of *Go West:* the ending would suit any team of comedians and is not tailored for the Marxes. It has a bad lapse when the Marxes want to surrender to the villains after falling light bulbs in a storeroom make them think they are under fire. The scene should have been played the other way round, with the Marxes subduing the villains with the light bulbs.

The Big Store had to be the Marx Brothers' farewell picture—at least from MGM. It was all too apparent that the studio had run completely out of good ideas.

In fiddling with his vacuum cleaner, Harpo (Rusty) accidentally sucks up the toupee of Sig Ruman (Heinrich Stubel). (This posed still wrongly suggests he does it out of mischief.)

A Night in Casablanca

1946

Ronald Kornblow: GROUCHO MARX. *Rusty:* HARPO MARX. *Corbaccio:* CHICO MARX. *Count Pfefferman, alias Heinrich Stubel:* Sig Ruman. *Beatrice Rheiner:* Lisette Verea. *Lt. Pierre Delmar:* Charles Drake. *Annette:* Lois Collier. *Captain Brizzard:* Dan Seymour. *Galoux:* Lewis Russell. *Kurt:* Frederick Giermann. *Emile:* Harro Mellor. *Spy:* David Hoffman. *Smythe:* Paul Harvey. *Maître d':* Philip van Zandt. *Military man in restaurant:* Arthur Torey. [Ruth Roman worked on the film as an extra.]

Director: Archie L. Mayo. *Screenwriters:* Joseph Fields, Roland Kibbee and *(additional material) (uncredited)* Frank Tashlin. *Cinematographer:* James Van Trees. *Production designer:* Duncan Cramer. *Set decorator:* Edward Boyle. *Editorial supervisor:* Gregg G. Tallas. *Film cutter:* Grace Baughman. *Music composer:* Werner Janssen. *Song "Who's Sorry Now,"* composer: Ted Snyder, *lyricists:* Bert Kalmar and Harry Ruby. *Sound:* Frank Webster. *Makeup artist:* Otis Malcom. *Hair stylist:* Scotty Rackin. *Executive production manager:* Joe C. Gilpin. *Assistant director:* Jack Sullivan. *Producer:* David L. Loew. *Production company:* Loma Vista. *Distributor:* United Artists. *Running time:* 85 minutes. *Release date:* May 10, 1946 (New York opening: August 11, 1946).

Making a comeback after five years, the Marx Brothers were now looking old. And they were old. In fact, Chico was in his late fifties, Groucho in his mid-fifties, and Harpo in between. Harpo suffers particularly, lacking his usual abundant wig—apparently he just dyed and curled his own hair—so that his face is more exposed and it is looking lined and worn. It seems a contradiction for so magical a clown to be unable to resist the inroads of age. Harpo's kind of mischief is essen-

189

Sig Ruman is enraged after Groucho (Ronald Kornblow) has tipped soup down his front.

Lisette Verea (Beatrice Rheiner) takes Groucho onto the dance floor for a rumba.

tially youthful, and at times he looks like a man unable to accept his years, although physically he is as limber as ever and technically his performance is just as assured. Aging has made no readily discernible difference to Chico; and Groucho, if no longer the young wolf, is no less effective as an elderly roué, his bent-over walk perhaps now symptomatic of physical decline although it is as swift as ever.

New ideas and new directions might have countered the team's tired look, but the main trouble with *A Night in Casablanca* is a lack of originality. Whereas the best Marx Brothers films were ahead of their time, this one leans on their familiar routines, attempting to freshen them with a topical plot about an escaped Nazi and a few references to *Casablanca* and *To Have and Have Not*. The police are seen rounding up "all likely suspects" when a murder is committed as they did in *Casablanca*. There one suspect runs away and is shot down; here a cop picks on Harpo leaning against a wall, asking him sarcastically if he's holding it up and soon finding that Harpo is telling the truth when he nods in agreement. And when the vamp Beatrice Rheiner says to Groucho that she will be singing just for him at the cabaret, Groucho replies in a husky voice, recalling Lauren Bacall in *To Have and Have Not*: "You don't have to sing for me—just whistle."

Films such as *Casablanca* and *To Have and Have Not* could have been effectively parodied in detail but this isn't the picture to do it. *A Night in Casablanca* has a feeble plot of its own to follow, is not so well cast nor so effectively made as they were, lacking their sense of atmosphere and detail. At least Siegfried Rumann, now plain Sig Ruman, makes a welcome reappearance in a Marx movie as the intemperate Nazi villain, Heinrich Stubel.

The wheel turns full circle and here is Groucho, formerly Mr. Hammer of *The Cocoanuts*, again a hotel manager with an uninspired name: Ronald Kornblow. Many of his lines could come from Mr. Hammer (but would have been funnier in 1929), as when the staff is assembled to meet him. "Never mind the staff!" he cries. "Assemble the

Groucho staggers back to the hotel after surviving attempts to run him down and is introduced by Lois Collier (Annette) to Charles Drake (her fiancé, Pierre Delmar). Groucho asks why they haven't married. Drake: "Marriage is impossible." Groucho: "Only after you're married."

Encouraged by Chico (Corbaccio), a hungry Harpo tests the lung brought in for Groucho to see if it's poisoned.

guests. I'll tell them what I expect of them." It means first of all: "Courtesy towards the employees: They must learn that a kind word will get them further with a bellboy or a chambermaid than a couple of drinks. Of course, a kind word and a couple of drinks will get them still further . . . and if it gets them any further than that, it will get them thrown out of the hotel." These lines capture Groucho's old sense of mischief as does his proposal to change all the numbers on all the rooms. "But the guests!" splutters one of his employers, "They will go into the wrong rooms. Think of the confusion!" "Yeah," retorts Groucho, "but think of the fun!"

Time has passed and no longer can Groucho's eccentricities be accepted with just a bewildered shrug. Here he is regarded as an incompetent fool by his superiors and only keeps his job because, unknown to him, all the previous managers have met sudden deaths and no one else will take it. Even so, there is a limit to his employers' tolerance and he is jailed on suspicion of having fixed

Groucho agrees to visit Lisette Verea in her room in half an hour.

191

the gambling tables. This marks a further stage in the reduction of Groucho. In the early films he was fully accepted for what he was; with the MGM period he starts to be questioned about his qualifications and is often made to look small; now, instead of doing the deceiving, it is he who is being duped (although he does ask some questions about his predecessors). This is fine for a comedian like Bob Hope but it is not suited to Groucho.

As in *The Cocoanuts*, Groucho proves adept at handling the guests over the phone. "You've been up in your room three and a half hours and your trunks haven't arrived? Well, put your pants on. Nobody will know the difference." A would-be guest by the name of Smythe, who invites trouble by imperiously ordering Harpo out of his way, rapping on the reception desk with his cane for attention and calling Groucho a clerk, is enraged to a state of apoplexy when Groucho sees the spelling of Smith with a "y" as sheer affectation and goes on to assume evrything else about him, like his claim to be married to the woman standing with him, to be equally suspect. "You'll hear from me!" bellows Smythe as he withdraws. "Do—if it's only a postcard," replies Groucho sweetly.

And no sooner has Groucho set eyes on the police chief's beard than he reacts with a customary derogatory comment: "I've seen five o'clock shadow but this is ridiculous!" (The part is played by Dan Seymour, the Vichy police chief in *To Have and Have Not*, providing another link to that film.)

Chico, called here Corbaccio, plays a fairly straightforward role in *A Night in Casablanca*. But he is back to crooked ways, rigging prices on his camel taxis. When Groucho wants to hire one, it looks as though he will be taken for another ride by Chico. But the scene never develops that far. (In the original script, Groucho queried the rates as he boards a camel. "Don't worry, boss. Whatever you got I take," replied Chico.)

Once again Chico is the devoted friend of Pierre, the romantic lead, and once again it's hard to see the attraction as he is colorlessly played by newcomer Charles Drake. His girl-friend (Lois Collier) is no better, but at least they don't sing. As a Frenchman wanted on charges of collaborating with the enemy, he is offered information that would help clear his name but can't afford to pay the informer. He almost takes it by force and the watching Chico comments, "He'll never get anything from that rat without money. That rat is just-a like me." Harpo applauds the truth of this so enthusiastically that Chico is put out: "Hey, what am I saying?" Harpo wants to pick pockets to raise the money but Chico surprisingly stops him. (Chico's close friendship with Harpo is eloquently stated in their elaborate back-to-back, through-the-legs handshake when they meet). Chico has little to do on his own. He gets in a piano piece, of course, which he introduces as "a little classy number—the second movement from the 'Beer Barrel Polka.' "

Chico does have an unexpected amorous triumph with the vamp Beatrice. As the Nazi's valet, Rusty, Harpo learns that Ruman plans to shoot Groucho so that he can succeed him as manager and have a free hand to look for treasure that is hidden in the hotel. He arranges for Beatrice to lure Groucho to her room so that he can burst in playing the enraged fiancé. This leads to Harpo miming a message to Chico as he did in similar circumstances in *A Day at the Races*—the sequence here, with Harpo outlining Beatrice's curves and Chico first reading it as a snake, is ingenious and enjoyable. Although Chico can read Harpo's mime, it baffles Groucho—Harpo is as usual beyond Groucho's understanding. Chico sets out to save Groucho, offering his services as a bodyguard. Groucho asks about his camel business. "In the daytime I'm in the camel business, at night I'm a bodyguard." As in other Groucho-Chico conversations, Groucho acts as the obliging feed: "What happens if I get shot during the day?" "I give you a free ride on my camel!" replies Chico, never lost for an answer. "If I'm your bodyguard, I'll watch you like a mother watches a baby," he further assures Groucho. "Is the mother pretty?" asks Groucho, suddenly interested.

Groucho won't abandon his rendezvous with Beatrice. He arrives at her door with all the prerequisites for a wildly romantic evening: a big bunch of hired roses, champagne, champagne glasses stuffed in his pockets. The curtains are drawn, Strauss is on the turntable. The mood is more that of Mata Hari and World War I while the setup is reminiscent of Groucho's date with Miss Marlowe in *A Day at the Races*, especially when Chico knocks to ask, "Hey, boss, you got a woman in there?" Groucho decides on a move to his room but Beatrice is unwilling to leave her dog, telling him in a babyish voice: "You wouldn't want me to leave my little poochie-goochie." "I'll meet you halfway," says Groucho. "Bring the poochie and leave the goochie here." They do move there and back, keeping one jump ahead of Ruman's sudden appearances brandishing his revolver, and in the process Chico gets the jump on Groucho and ends up alone with Beatrice, not only enhancing his own image but putting a big dent in Groucho's great lover reputation at the same time. (Offscreen, Chico was a notable ladies' man but this is the most tangible evidence of it in the team's work.)

Harpo has nothing else to equal the sight gag with the falling building at the start of the film, but manages many appealing moments. He displays some of his old interest in women. But when he gives his leg to a girl and she runs off scared, he no longer pursues her. And the leg now has to be explained as a harmless gesture. Harpo has a hinged sole on his shoe for snapping up litter. All he was interested in was collecting her cigarette butt. Whatever became of the satyr of *Monkey Business?*

Another old trait that is revived more whole-heartedly is the *recherché* appetite. Chico uses Harpo to test Groucho's food for poison. Harpo is first thrown bits of food to catch in his mouth like a performing seal. He silences Groucho's protests at losing a meal by pretending to writhe in agony for a moment. Eating like a maniac, he moves on to a lighted candle, transferring the flame to the end of a finger, chewing off some wax and then replacing the flame. He offers the inkwell to Groucho, then downs the ink himself; takes a cup of coffee from Groucho's hands, swallows the coffee and nibbles at the china, and starts on a stick of celery with Chico eating from the other end. A hungry Groucho asks us, "Wouldn't it be great if they ate each other?"

Harpo becomes the reluctant "volunteer" when the hotel elevator stalls between floors and Chico and Groucho push him out through the roof to bring assistance. (Harpo was previously forced into volunteering in *Duck Soup* and *A Night at the Opera*.) He stumbles into the secret room containing the missing treasure that happens to include a harp. A hideous portrait on a Rembrandt prompts him into making a gookie for comparison (like the imitative face he makes at a performer on stage in *A Night at the Opera*), and he is more attracted to the beautiful woman in another Rembrandt who inspires him to perform the Second Hungarian Rhapsody on the harp, after which he folds up the painting and stuffs it inside his shirt (like the Beaugard in *Animal Crackers*) to bring it out later as a pinup (shades of the calendar girl in *Horse Feathers*).

In his job as Ruman's valet, Harpo is treated as badly as he was by Lassparri or Morgan in earlier films. Although he is not above a bit of tomfoolery, he is picked on when he is doing his best, as with his device for cleaning several shoes at once or his attempt to replace a missing toupée with a mop head. Harpo has unwittingly sucked up the German's hairpiece into his vacuum cleaner and Ruman can't be seen without it as a scar on his forehead identifies him as a wanted Nazi. Harpo's offer of a mop head earns him the attentions of Kurt, one of the Nazi's henchmen, who describes himself as the finest swordsman in all Bavaria. Ruman feels a little bloodletting would be soothing, so swords are produced and Harpo has first choice: being no fool, he takes both. But the duel gets underway and Harpo parries every move, leaning against a wall and yawning as Kurt exhausts himself. It is a fine demonstration of his effortless command over a situation. The score is kept by the rings on a curtain rod, as it was during the battle in *Duck Soup*.

In the hotel's casino, Harpo seems to remain the favored child of the gods when, naïvely persisting with the same number at the gambling tables, he breaks the bank. But this leads to him

"These roses, I shall keep them forever," says Lisette Verea as Groucho settles down for their date. "That's what you think," he replies. "I only rented them for an hour."

With Chico's encouragement, Harpo insists on betting the same number for a third time and breaks the bank after Groucho spins the wheel.

Harpo produces a pinup he has taken from the hidden Nazi treasure, and Chico and Groucho find it to be Rembrandt.

194

being put in jail, charged with having rigged the game with Groucho. Chico and Pierre are also in jail. This is again the point of despair reached so clearly in *A Night at the Opera* and *A Day at the Races* but it is much less convincingly arranged and therefore much weaker. Ruman and his gang are loose, able to search the hotel while the Marx Brothers sit around in jail apportioning the blame. Chico and Groucho decide it rests with Harpo, who isn't at all pleased at being picked on. They break out of jail and the relatively routine means compared with the similar sequence in *The Cocoanuts* emphasizes the loss of imagination over the intervening years.

The following scene is a good one: the Marxes drive Ruman out of his mind as he is packing in his hotel room by unpacking his clothes behind his back. They dart to and from their hiding places in a display of almost balletic precision backed by split-second timing and complete silence by which they are never quite seen by Ruman. At the start, just before Ruman enters his hotel room, they hear him coming and look around for hiding places, and it is Groucho, as usual when competing with Chico and Harpo, who comes off worst—he keeps getting shouldered out and rushes around helplessly, only diving into a closet in the nick of time. But their subsequent cooperation shows a pleasant sense of team unity, even if they take their work more seriously than they would have in the past, Groucho declaring, "We can't keep this up much longer," when of course the Marxes in their prime would never have given it a thought.

The scene provokes a mental disarray comparable to that induced in Inspector Henderson in *A Day at the Races*. But while Henderson was on his guard, the Nazi here thinks he is safe and alone in his own room and has no reason to suspect anyone else's presence. And when he is joined by Kurt and without looking hands him a fountain pen that Harpo intercepts, causing an argument between the two men, Harpo goes a stage further than the friction he caused between the captain and the first officer in the Punch and Judy scene in *Monkey Business*. There the first officer knows

Harpo is at work and it is just a matter of proving it. Here, quite invisible to the two men, he is able to make them both satisfied the other is playing him up.

The climax occurs on an airplane intended to take Ruman and his gang out of the country. A reformed Beatrice helps the Marx Brothers aboard and Harpo soon knocks out the pilot and settles down hopefully at the controls, pulling and pushing levers at random so that the plane bounces, slows down, accelerates, and generally alarms everyone. Beatrice hastily revives the pilot but Harpo, as sensitive to crooks as he was in *At the Circus*, firmly hits the half-dazed man on the head again. Perhaps he has complete faith in his own ability to fly the plane. As one critic said: "You want everything for him, his delights are so simple. I thought it monstrous to let the aeroplane crash when he flew it. The director seems to me to show no understanding of Marxian magic. A plane flown by mad Harpo should have the happiest landing." Quite right. (Harpo's ineptness at the controls of a train in *Go West* was another scripting error.) At least, if Harpo has to crash the plane, he chooses police headquarters so that Ruman, left behind on the ground, can arrive in hot pursuit minus his toupée and be promptly arrested.

The romantic leads then contribute something useful by kissing—stimulating Beatrice to rashly lament, "If a thing like that could only happen to me . . . " Trying to escape the fate of Thelma Todd at the end of *Horse Feathers*, Beatrice flees in panic from a lustful Groucho, Chico, and Harpo , . . a pleasing image with which to end the last full-fledged Marx picture.

Chico and Harpo drive Sig Ruman to drink by disrupting his packing behind his back.

"Mr. Grunion, I want you to help me," says Marilyn Monroe to Groucho. "Some men are following me."

Love Happy

1940 / Released 3/3/50)

Harpo: HARPO MARX. *Faustino:* CHICO MARX. *Sam Grunion:* GROUCHO MARX. *Maggie Phillips:* Vera-Ellen. *Madame Egelichi:* Ilona Massey. *Bunny Dolan:* Marion Hutton. *Alphonse Zoto:* Raymond Burr. *Throckmorton:* Melville Cooper. *Mike Johnson:* Paul Valentine. *Mr. Lyons:* Leon Belasco. *Mackinaw:* Eric Blore. *Hannibal Zoto:* Bruce Gordon. *Grunion's client:* Marilyn Monroe. *Cop delivering Harpo:* Edward Gargan. *Assassin in Grunion's office:* Otto Waldis. *Clergyman in "Sadie Thompson" number:* House Peters Jr.

Director: David Miller. *Screenwriters:* Frank Tashlin, Mac Benoff, and *(uncredited)* Ben Hecht. *Original story by:* Harpo Marx. *Cinematographer:* William C. Mellor. *Production designer:* Gabriel Scognamillo. *Set decorator:* Casey Roberts. *Editors:* Basil Wrangell and Al Joseph. *Music score and songs "Love Happy" and "Willow Weep for Me" by:* Ann Ronell. *Orchestra conductor:* Paul Smith. *Orchestral arranger:* Harry Geller. *Production numbers staged by:* Billy Daniel. *Special effects:* Howard A. Anderson. *Wardrobe designers:* Grace Houston, Norma, and *(men)* Richard Bachler. *Makeup artist:* Fred Phillips. *Hair stylist:* Scotty Racking. *Production manager:* Ray Heinze. *Presented by:* Mary Pickford. *Producer:* Lester Cowan. *Production company:* Artists' Alliance. *Distributor:* United Artists. *Running time:* 85 minutes. *Release date:* March 3, 1950 (New York opening: April 7, 1950).

In *Love Happy*, Harpo appears as a solitary tramp helping out an impoverished stage company which believes it will have the greatest smash hit since *Show Boat*. He is the one who brings the group food and it practically buries him in the rush. However, it is enough for him to receive a smile of gratitude from Maggie, the leading lady (played by Vera-Ellen), whom he secretly loves.

This is a very different Harpo from the lustful fellow of past acquaintance. The character is even called Harpo and the real Harpo, who provided the film's story, has softened him to become a sentimental "little fellow." He makes a point of comforting Maggie when she's in distress, doing little tricks, bringing out his harp to stop her sobbing (playing "Swanee River" with strains of the *Love Happy* theme tune, although she's gone before he's finished). Harpo lives in what is apparently a disused hut in Central Park, although one enhanced by a fancy chandelier. These humble conditions add to the pathos of his hopeless affection for Maggie.

Chico appears as Faustino the Great. "Somebody told me you're putting on a show with unknowns," he tells the young producer (Paul Valentine). "You're hiring-a peoples a-never been heard of. Well, I'm the most unknown and unheard of actors who's never been on Broadway." It's a nice piece of argument and on a younger Chico it would be fine but here it makes him seem rather pathetic to be pursuing a stage career so late in life and to be so brusquely rejected (although he wangles a job later, offering to work for no pay). It turns out the thing he's most unknown for is mind reading. After this, Chico has little to do worth remembering, though he does read Harpo's mind over the telephone (as well as one of his mimes). He makes a considerable effort to stop the show's scenery being reclaimed by amusing its owner at the piano but fails to persuade him (making the scene very anticlimactic). There are one or two nostalgic references to the past—to tootsie-frootsie ice cream (*A Day at the Races*) and a few words of mumbled (mock?) Italian (*Horse Feathers*, etc.) but this is a diminished Chico.

Groucho appears without his painted mustache and frock coat but with his cigar, looking much older than in *A Night in Casablanca*. His work in *Love Happy* is confined to appearances at the start and finish, and a linking narration. In the latter capacity, he tells how, as private detective Sam Grunion, he has been tracking down the royal Romanoff diamonds. "For eleven years I trailed them . . . through the Khyber Pass, over the Pyrenees, round the Cape of Good Hope, and in the Gimbel's basement." One of his later scenes involves him fleetingly with Marilyn Monroe in one of her minor early roles. "Is there anything I can do for you?" asks Groucho, then turns to the audience and notes: "What a ridiculous statement." "Mr. Grunion," she murmurs, "I want you to help me . . . some men are following me." Can Groucho drop everything to oblige? He tries, but a hired killer won't let him.

He sports a Sherlock Holmes hat that likens him to some bird of prey as he stalks the rooftops at the end, accompanied by irritatingly obtrusive and mimicking music (the film as a whole is badly overscored). Here he meets up with Harpo and the supposedly seductive Madame Egelichi (Ilona Massey), who heads the gang seeking the valuable diamond necklace. When she declares within Harpo's hearing that she would kill anyone with the necklace, Harpo engagingly reverts to his old, selfish character by planting it on Groucho, knowing full well he can retrieve it at a more opportune moment. Groucho remains no match for Harpo.

Groucho has problems trying to search Madame Egelichi for the necklace, much as he had with Peerless Pauline in *At the Circus*. "If this were a French picture, I could do it," he leers but the effect is tame. He hasn't a good quip in the entire picture. There is something rather seedy about Groucho's manner and appearance in *Love Happy*, as there was in his previous appearance as a private detective in *The Big Store*, but there it was only apparent in one scene.

Chico also falls under the spell of Madame Egelichi at one point. He promises to do anything for her and she sends him out for sardine tins, hoping that he will return with one that contains the hidden necklace. Chico wholeheartedly declares that if she likes sardines that much he'll cover her in sardines, giving it the sound of a rather lewd proposition (better than anything Groucho manages in the film). Chico returns, pleased at having served her better than she can

Harpo emerges from the basement of the store, laden with goodies, and sneaks off past the cop on the sidewalk.

Starved and tortured for three days to make him reveal the whereabouts of the missing sardine can, the ravenous Harpo threatens to shoot himself unless they let him eat the apple they perched on his head for a William Tell ordeal. Watching are Bruce Gordon (Hannibal Zoto), Raymond Burr (Alphonse Zoto), Ilona Massey (Madame Egelichi), and Melville Cooper (Throckmorton).

Marion Martin (Bunny Dolan) interrogates the dolls in the brutal "Who Stole That Jam?" number before turning on Harpo.

Chico (Faustino) tries to prevent Leon Belasco (Mr. Lyons) from removing the scenery and costumes from the production by playing a duet with him on the stage.

imagine. He unloads tins of anchovy and can't understand her short-tempered reaction.

It is essentially Harpo's film. He is on-screen the most and his talent still shines through at times. His manner retains a youthful gaiety and jauntiness about it. His features have become perhaps even more flexible and rubbery with the creases of age and his expressions still make a fascinating study, like the childish scowl on his face when he's pushed around as part of an oddly brutal stage number. But the moments of intended pathos are unsuccessful because we feel no concern for Maggie. We cared far more for Rosa in *A Night at the Opera* or Judy in *A Day at the Races*, who really had something to worry about and who put a brave face on things (better-written parts played by better actresses). Harpo's big sequences suffer from too many effects with speeded film and other obvious trick work.

He's first seen on the sidewalk outside a delicatessen, helping customers as they leave, carrying their baskets or lighting a cigarette with a blowtorch attachment that works through the flower in his buttonhole (reminiscent of the actual blowtorch he had in *Duck Soup*). He is also quickly passing foodstuffs into his raincoat pocket for the starving actors. Only a small dog is smart enough to see what he is up to and, maintaining the traditional antipathy between dogs and Harpo, tries to give Harpo away by yapping. Harpo gets his revenge by showing it a gookie through the car window, making it scuttle with terror under a rug.

In the basement of the delicatessen, Harpo makes a quick foray and unknowingly removes the sardine can in which the Romanoff diamonds are being delivered to Madame Egelichi. Eventually, Harpo is caught by the villains and searched for the tin. Madame Egelichi literally entrances him with her physical charms—his face sets in suspended dubiousness, mouth half-open, eyes fixed on her. One would like to think he is only play-acting but he has really succumbed to her allure. The pockets of his old raincoat yield a mountain of junk that includes a welcome mat, a pair of legs from a shop-window mannequin, a barber's pole, a block of ice (from *Horse Feathers*, perhaps), a mailbox marked "Moss Kaufman" (i.e. George S. Kaufman and Moss Hart), a live dog, and so on. Unfortunately, the joke is flattened by its excessive length, making it glaringly obvious as he stands pressed up against the wall that the items are being pulled through a hole behind him. Harpo's sleeve yielded a continuing array of silver in *Animal Crackers* but in dribs and drabs, not the steady progression here, and had a

"I'm going to cover you with sardines. That's how much I love you," Chico tells Ilona Massey after he declares his adoration and she asks him to bring all the sardine cans in the theater.

Groucho (Sam Grunion) with Otto Waldis (an assassin) who is preparing to kill him for failing to recover the Romanoff diamonds.

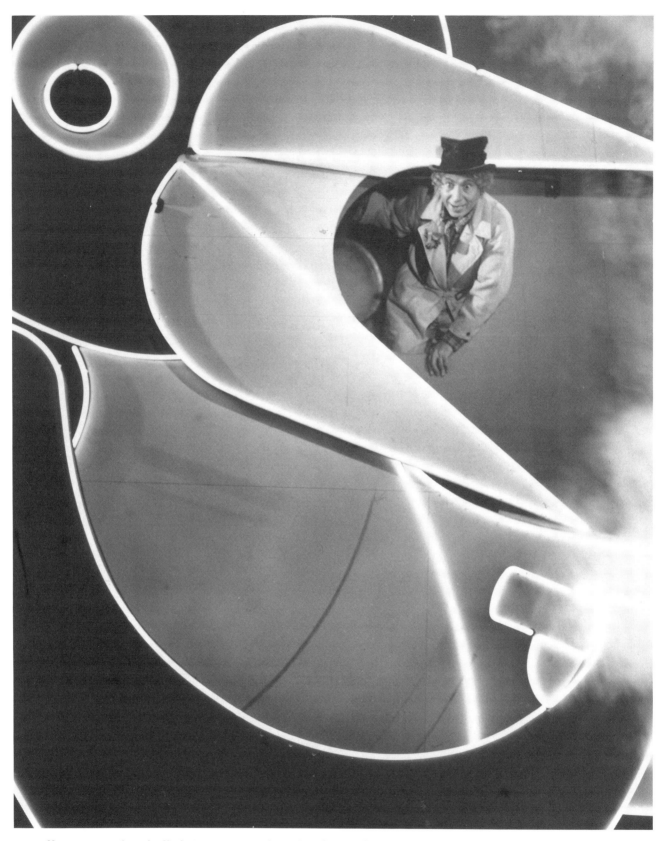

Harpo emerges from the Kool cigarette sign in the rooftop chase finale.

buildup to the arrival of a coffee pot. And showing the sheer volume of Harpo's possessions is the unimaginative way of doing it. The range was much better established in earlier films when he produced a candle lit at both ends or a steaming cup of coffee. The man who has these has everything, whereas in *Love Happy* a definite limit is reached when Harpo has nothing more on his person.

When the gang set about torturing Harpo, one feels that he might have disconcerted them by enjoying their attentions, but he comes to look rather upset (even so, his miserable expression has something witty about it, like every Harpo face). Harpo spends days being tortured (what, no fanciful escape?) and is facing an ordeal on William Tell lines when there is a delightful moment as he snatches the apple off his head and ravenously bites into it. He grabs a gun and, instead of pointing it at the villains, threatens to shoot himself if they don't let him finish eating the fruit. He pulls the trigger a couple of times to show he means it. But like the gun in the clothes brush in *Go West* that was first empty, then loaded, this eventually proves to have real ammunition.

Later, Maggie is grabbed by the gang in her dressing room. Harpo realizes what is going on and rushes off to get help. This leads to a good message scene with Chico, Harpo doing his quick charades and Chico some inspired guessing, egged on by whistles of encouragement, at last recognizing Harpo's outline of a woman's shape instead of mistaking it for a snake.

The climax of the film is the chase over the rooftops and up and down the neon signs of Times Square. The amount of advertising (apparently paid for by the companies concerned) makes the product placement rows of recent years look insignificant. The sequence is moderately but not memorably amusing. A couple of Harpo's old tricks emerge: the habit of giving his leg (Groucho receiving it) and the appearance of one of the mannequin's legs, adding one more to the collection of false limbs that have been featured in Harpo's career. Here, too, we find Harpo riding a

Harpo blows smoke from a cigarette sign into the face of Melville Cooper who has punched him in the stomach during the climactic rooftop chase. Bruce Gordon (Hannibal Zoto) is behind.

In the rooftop climax, Chico, held by Melville Cooper, willingly gives Ilona Massey the diamonds and she gives him a jab from her gun in return.

201

horse once more: it is the winged horse of the Mobilgas neon sign and Harpo rides it to get away from the gangsters below.

The parts of Harpo's performance in *Love Happy* that linger most vividly are several sight gags that have a cartoon quality. Told by Chico, who is trying to read his mind, that he should clear his head, Harpo inserts a handkerchief in one ear and pulls it out of the other, then runs it back and forth. He staggers out of a neon sign that puffs smoke to promote Kool cigarettes and the smoke comes out of his ears as well as his mouth. He brushes his hair in a mirror which turns over to reveal the back of his head. (These gags were probably contributed by co-scenarist Frank Tashlin, with his animation background.) In contrast to the emptying of his coat, these are quite convincingly executed. There is another gag that would have worked better in a cartoon: Harpo whisks out a tablecloth with all the plates and cutlery laid out on it, but the cloth crumples under the weight of the attached props.

How, then, do the Marxes finish their joint big screen career? Chico very surprisingly ends up working for Groucho instead of joining up with Harpo, playing cards with a large dog and losing his jacket to the animal. This is too obvious and wrong—Chico should beat the dog. He is allowed a streak of his old stubbornness when he won't answer Groucho's telephone for him.

Groucho becomes the latest husband of Madame Egelichi, and it is sad to watch him being henpecked over the telephone. Marilyn Monroe should have wandered back in around here.

Harpo at least—and it is his film—departs in a fitting manner. He doesn't get the girl, but it was obvious that he never would as she is in love with someone younger. He does, however, carry off the royal Romanoff diamonds as a souvenir of his adventures (unaware they have any real value). The show is a success, Maggie is happy, and he can move on. Throwing aside the humble abode which had been his home, he makes off into the darkness beyond the neon signs, dancing a little jig, a Puck-like "merry wanderer of the night."

THE MARX BROTHERS'
OTHER
FILM APPEARANCES

HUMORISK

(uncompleted? unreleased) (circa 1920/21)

Watson: HARPO MARX. (*Villain*): GROUCHO MARX. (?): CHICO MARX. (*Heroine*): Mildred Davis.

Director: Dick Smith. *Screenwriter:* Jo Swerling.

TOO MANY KISSES

(1925)

Richard Gaylord Jr.: Richard Dix. *Yvonne Hurja:* Frances Howard. *Julio:* William Powell. *Richard Gaylord Sr.:* Frank Currier. *Simmons:* Joseph Burke. *Manuel Hurja:* Albert Tavernier. *Miguel:* Arthur Ludwig. *Flapper:* Alyce Mills. *Pedro:* Paul Panzer. *The Village Peter Pan:* HARPO MARX.

Director: Paul Sloane. *Screenwriter:* Gerald Duffy. *From the story "A Maker of Gestures" by:* John Monk Saunders. *Cinematographer:* Hal Rosson. *Presenters:* Adolph Zukor, Jesse L. Lasky. *Production company:* Famous Players-Lasky. *Distributor:* Paramount. *Length:* 5,759 ft. (6 reels).

THE HOUSE THAT SHADOWS BUILT

(1931)

GROUCHO MARX. HARPO MARX. CHICO MARX. ZEPPO MARX.

Production company/distributor: Paramount.

HOLLYWOOD ON PARADE

(part of series) (1932)

GROUCHO MARX. HARPO MARX. CHICO MARX. Skeets Gallagher. Eddie Lambert and his Orchestra. Ivan Lebedeff. Lois Wilson. Fifi D'Orsay. Claire Windsor. Vivian Duncan.

Production company/distributor: Paramount. *Length:* 1 reel.

HOLLYWOOD ON PARADE

(part of series) (1933)

CHICO MARX. W. C. Fields. Buster Crabbe. Earl Carroll Girls.

Production company/distributor: Paramount. *Length:* 1 reel.

LA FIESTA DE SANTA BARBARA

(1935)

Entertainers: The Gumm Sisters [Judy Garland], Maria Gambarelli, Eduardo Durant's Spanish Orchestra, The Spanish Troubadors, The Dude Ranch Wranglers, Steffi Duna, Paul Porcasi. *Master of ceremonies:* Leo Carrillo. *Spectators:* Adrienne Ames, Binnie Barnes, Warner Baxter, Mary Carlisle, Irvin S. Cobb, Chester Conklin, Gary Cooper, Andy Devine, Ralph Forbes, Rosalind Keith, Ida Lupino, Buster Keaton, Edmund Lowe, HARPO MARX, Joe Morrison, Cecelia Parker, Gilbert Roland, Shirley Ross, Robert Taylor, Toby Wing. *Narrator:* Pete Smith.

Producer: Louis Lewyn. Technicolor. *Production company/distributor:* Metro-Goldwyn-Mayer (Loew's Inc.). *Running time:* 19 minutes. *Release date:* December 7, 1935.

YOURS FOR THE ASKING

(1936)

Johnny Lamb: George Raft. *Lucille Sutton:* Dolores Costello Barrymore. *Gert Malloy:* Ida Lupino. *Dictionary McKinney/Colonel Evelyn Carstairs:* Reginald Owen. *Saratoga:* James Gleason. *Bicarbonate:* Edgar Kennedy. *Honeysuckle:* Lynne Overman. *Perry Barnes:* Skeets Gallagher. *May:* Betty Blythe. *Extras:* GROUCHO MARX, Charles Ruggles.

Director: Alexander Hall. *Screenwriters:* Eve Greene, Harlan Ware, and Philip MacDonald. *From a story by:* William R. Lipman, William H. Wright. *Cinematographer:* Theodor Sparkuhl. *Art directors:* Hans Dreier, Roland Anderson. *Producer:* Lewis E. Gensler. *Production company/distributor:* Paramount. *Running time:* 68 minutes. *Release date:* July 24, 1936.

HOLLYWOOD—THE SECOND STEP

(An MGM Miniature) (1936)

Himself: CHICO MARX. Maureen O'Sullivan. *Narrator:* Carey Wilson.

Director: Felix E. Feist. *Screenwriter:* Mauri Grashin. *Production company/distributor:* Metro-Goldwyn-Mayer (Loew's Inc.). *Length:* 10 minutes. *Release date:* December 5, 1936.

SUNDAY NIGHT AT THE TROCADERO
(1937)

Reginald Denny. George Hamilton's Music Box Music. Louis and Celeste. Madina and Mimosa. [Peter] Lind Hayes. Gaylord Carter. Connee Boswell. *Guest stars:* Robert Benchley, Sally Blane, Eric Blore, June Collyer, Stuart Erwin, Glenda Farrell, Dick Foran, Norman Foster, Russell Gleason, John Howard, Arthur Lake, Mr. and Mrs. GROUCHO MARX, Frank McHugh, Frank Morgan, Chester Morris, Benny Rubin, Margaret Vail, Bert Wheeler, Toby Wing.

Director: George Sidney. *Dialogue writer:* John Kraft. *Producer:* Louis Lewyn. *Production company/distributor:* Metro-Goldwyn-Mayer (Loew's Inc.). *Length:* 20 minutes. *Release date:* October 2, 1937.

SCREEN SNAPSHOTS No. 2
(1943)

GROUCHO MARX. Carole Landis.

Director: Ralph Staub. *Production company/distributor:* Columbia. *Length:* 1 reel. *Release date:* circa September 1943.

Footage of Groucho reused in later number of *Screen Snapshots Hollywood's Great Comedians* (1953).

STAGE DOOR CANTEEN
(1943)

Eileen: Cheryl Walker. *"Dakota" Ed Smith:* William Terry. *Jean:* Marjorie Riordan. *"California":* Lon McCallister. *Ella Sue:* Margaret Early. *"Texas":* Michael Harrison [Sunset Carson]. *Mamie:* Dorothea Kent. *"Jersey":* Fred Brady. *Lillian:* Marion Shockley. *The Australian:* Patrick O'Moore. *Stars at the Stage Door Canteen:* Judith Anderson, Henry Armetta, Benny Baker, Tallulah Bankhead, Ralph Bellamy, Edgar Bergen and Charlie McCarthy, Ray Bolger, Helen Broderick, Ina Claire, Katharine Cornell, Lloyd Corrigan, Jane Cowl, Jane Darwell, William Demarest, Virginia Field, Dorothy Fields, Gracie Fields, Lynn Fontanne, Arlene Francis, Vinton Freedley, Billy Gilbert, Lucile Gleason, Vera Gordon, Virginia Grey, Helen Hayes, Katharine Hepburn, Hugh Herbert, Jean Hersholt, Sam Jaffe, Allen Jenkins, George Jessel, Roscoe Karns, Virginia Kaye, Tom Kennedy, Otto Kruger, June Lang, Betty

Lawford, Gertrude Lawrence, Gypsy Rose Lee, Alfred Lunt, Bert Lytell, Aline MacMahon, HARPO MARX, Elsa Maxwell, Helen Menken, Yehudi Menuhin, Ethel Merman, Ralph Morgan, Alan Mowbray, Paul Muni, Elliott Nugent, Merle Oberon, Franklin Pangborn, Helen Parrish, Brock Pemberton, George Raft, Lanny Ross, Selena Royle, Martha Scott, Cornelia Otis Skinner, Ned Sparks, Bill Stern, Ethel Waters, Johnny Weissmuller, Arleen Whelan, Dame May Whitty, Ed Wynn. *Bands:* Count Basie, Benny Goodman, Guy Lombardo, Xavier Cugat, Kay Kyser, Freddy Martin.

Director: Frank Borzage. *Screenwriter:* Delmer Daves. *Cinematographer:* Harry Wild. *Production designer:* Harry Horner. *Art director:* Hans Peters. *Editor:* Hal Kern. *Music composer:* Harry Rich. *Music director:* C. Bakaleinikoff. *Producer/production company:* Sol Lesser. *Distributor:* United Artists. *Running time:* 132 minutes. *Release date:* May 12, 1943 (New York opening: June 24, 1943).

SCREEN SNAPSHOTS No. 8
(1943)

GROUCHO MARX. HARPO MARX. CHICO MARX. Gene Autry. Tyrone Power. Lou Holtz. Ritz Brothers. Annabella. Kay Kyser. Alan Mowbray.

Director: Ralph Staub. *Production company/distributor:* Columbia. *Running time:* 10 minutes.

THE ALL-STAR BOND RALLY
(1945)

Jeanne Crain. Bing Crosby. Linda Darnell. Betty Grable. Bob Hope. Harry James Band. Glenn Langan. Frank Latimore. Fay Marlowe. HARPO MARX. Fibber McGee and Molly. Carmen Miranda. Frank Sinatra.

Director: Michael Audley. *Distributor:* 20th Century-Fox. *Length:* 2 reels.

COPACABANA
(1947)

Lionel Q. Devereaux: GROUCHO MARX. *Carmen Novarro:* Carmen Miranda. *Steve Hunt:* Steve Cochran. *Anne:* Gloria Jean. *Liggett:* Ralph Sanford. *Himself:* Andy Russell. *Murphy:* Andrew Toombes. *Cop:* Edgar Dearing. *Bouncer:* Dewey Robinson. *Them-*

selves: Louis Sobel, Earl Wilson, Abel Green. De Castro Sisters. Raul and Eva Reyes. Igor Dega. Kay Gorcey. Merle McHugh. Dee Turnell. Maxine Fife. Toni Kelly. Chili Williams. Abigail Adams. Jill Meredith.

Director: Alfred E. Green. *Screenwriters:* Laslo Vadnay, Alan [Allen] Boretz, Howard Harris, and (*additional dialogue*) Sydney R. Zelinka. *Cinematographer:* Bert Glennon. *Production designer:* Duncan Cramer. *Set decorator:* Julia Heron. *Music director and composer of incidental music:* Edward Ward. *Songs:* Sam Coslow. *Song "Go West, Young Man" by:* Bert Kalmar and Harry Ruby. *Musical numbers staged by:* Larry Ceballos. *Musical arrangers:* Jack Mason, Howard Zweifel, Bob Gordon. *Musical advisor:* Eddie Durant. *Editor:* Philip Cahn. *Sound recordist:* Fred Lau. *Music editor:* Weldon Hancock. *Costume designer:* Barjansky. *Makeup supervisor:* Bob Stephanoff. *Hair stylist:* Marie Clark. *Special photographic effects:* John Fulton. *Assistant director:* Harold Godsoe. *Dialogue director:* Irvin Berwick. *Production assistant:* Sid Ross. *Assistant to producer:* Dave Sebastian. *Production manager:* Raoul Pagel. *Associate producer:* Walter Bachelor. *Producer:* Sam Coslow. *Presented by:* David L. Hersh. *Production company:* Beacon. *Distributor:* United Artists. *Running time:* 90 minutes. *Release date:* May 30, 1947 (New York opening: July 12, 1947).

MR. MUSIC
(1950)

Paul Merrick: Bing Crosby. *Katherine Holbrook:* Nancy Olson. *Alex Conway:* Charles Coburn. *Lorna Marvis:* Ruth Hussey. *Jefferson Blake:* Robert Stack. *Haggerty:* Tom Ewell. *Aunt Amy:* Ida Moore. *Danforth:* Charles Kemper. *Tippy Carpenter:* Donald Woods. *Jerome Thisby:* Claud Curdle [Richard Haydn]. *Themselves:* Gower Champion, Marge Champion. *Guest artists:* GROUCHO MARX, Dorothy Kirsten, Peggy Lee, The Merry Macs.

Director: Richard Haydn. *Screenwriter:* Arthur Sheekman. *Suggested by the play* Accent on Youth *by:* Samson Raphaelson. *Cinematographer:* George Barnes. *Art directors:* Hans Dreier and Earl Hedrick. *Editorial supervisor:* Doane Harrison. *Editor:* Everett Douglas. *Songs:* "Life Is So Peculiar," "High on the List," "Wouldn't It Be Funny," "Wasn't I There?," "Mr. Music," "Once More the Blue and White," "Milady," and "Then You'll Be Home." *New songs by:*

James Van Heusen and Johnny Burke. *Music director:* Van Cleave. *Music associate:* Troy Sanders. *Special vocal arranger:* Joseph J. Lilley. *Dance director:* Gower Champion. *Sound recordists:* Harry Lindgren and John Cope. *Set decorators:* Sam Comer and Ray Moyer. *Process cinematographer:* Farciot Edouart. *Gowns designer:* Edith Head. *Makeup supervisor:* Wally Westmore. *Assistant director:* Harry Caplan. *Producer:* Robert L. Welch. *Production company/ distributor:* Paramount. *Running time:* 113 minutes. *Release date:* December 28, 1950 (New York opening: December 28, 1950).

DOUBLE DYNAMITE
(1951)

Mildred Goodhue: Jane Russell. *Emil J. Keck:* GROUCHO MARX. *Johnny Dalton:* Frank Sinatra. *Bob Pulsifer:* Don McGuire. *R. B. Pulsifer Sr.:* Howard Freeman. *Man with sunglasses:* Nestor Paiva. *Mr. Kofer:* Frank Orth. *J. L. McKissack:* Harry Hayden. *Baganucci:* William Edmunds. *Tailman:* Russ Thorson. *Frankie Boy:* Joe Devlin. *Max:* Lou Nova. *Waiter:* Benny Burt. *Wire-service man:* Bill Snyder. *Hatchet-faced lady:* Claire Du Brey. *Santa Clauses:* Charles Coleman, Virgil Johansen. *Little old lady:* Ida Moore. *Goons:* Harry Kingston, Kermit Kegley. *Maitre d':* Jean De Briac. *Messenger:* George Chandler. *Mr. Hartman:* Hal K. Dawson. *Bank guard:* William Bailey. *Chef:* Jack Chefe. *Waiter:* Al Murphy. *Detectives:* Jim Nolan, Lee Phelps. *Hotel maid:* Lillian West. *Boy:* Dickie Derrel. *Sergeant:* Charles Sullivan. *Lieutenant:* Harold Goodwin. Bill Erwin. Charles Regan. Dick Gordon. Mike Lally. Jack Jahries. Gil Perkins. Jack Gargan.

Director: Irving Cummings. *Screenwriters:* Melville Shavelson and (*additional dialogue*) Harry Crane. *From a story by:* Leo Rosten. *Based on a character created by:* Mannie Manheim. *Cinematographer:* Robert De Grasse. *Art directors:* Albert S. D'Agostino and Feild M. Gray. *Music composer:* Leigh Harline. *Songs "It's Only Money" and "Kisses and Tears" by:* Sammy Cahn and Jule Styne. *Music conductor:* C. Bakaleinikoff. *Editor:* Harry Marker. *Sound recordists:* Phil Brigandi and Clem Portman. *Set decorators:* Darrell Silvera and Harley Miller. *Makeup supervisor:* Gordon Bau. *Assistant director:* James Lane. *Producer:* Irving Cummings Jr. *Production company/distributor:* RKO Radio. *Running time:* 80 minutes. *Release date:*

December 1951 (New York opening: December 25, 1951).

A GIRL IN EVERY PORT
(1952)

Benny Linn: GROUCHO MARX. *Jane Sweet:* Marie Wilson. *Tim Dunnevan:* William Bendix. *Bert Sedgwick:* Don DeFore. *Garvey:* Gene Lockhart. *Millicent:* Dee Hartford. *Navy Lieutenant:* Hanley Stafford. *"High-Life":* Teddy Hart. *Drive-In manager:* Percy Helton. *Skeezer:* George E. Stone.

Director: Chester Erskine. *Screenwriter:* Chester Erskine. *From the story "They Sell Sailors Elephants" by:* Frederick Hazlitt Brennan. *Cinematographer:* Nicholas Musuraca. *Art directors:* Albert S. D'Agostino and Walter E. Keller. *Editor:* Ralph Dawson. *Music composer:* Roy Webb. *Music director:* C. Bakaleinikoff. *Set decorators:* Darrell Silvera and Harley Miller. *Sound recordists:* Philip Brigandi and Clem Portman. *Special effects:* Harold Stine. *Gowns:* Michael Woulfe. *Makeup artist:* Mel Berns. *Hair stylist:* Larry Germain. *Producers:* Irving Allen, Irving Cummings Jr. *Production company/distributor:* RKO Radio. *Running time:* 87 mins. *Release date:* January 1952 (New York opening: February 13, 1952).

SPORTS ANTICS
(date unknown—1950s)

Guest star: CHICO MARX.

WILL SUCCESS SPOIL ROCK HUNTER?
(1957)

Rockwell Hunter: Tony Randall. *Rita Marlowe:* Jayne Mansfield. *Jenny:* Betsy Drake. *Violet:* Joan Blondell. *Le Salle Junior:* John Williams. *Henry Rufus:* Henry Jones. *April:* Lili Gentle. *Bobo Branigansky:* Mickey Hargitay. *Georgie Schmidlapp:* GROUCHO MARX. *Calypso singer:* Georgia Carr. *TV interviewer:* Dick Whittinghill. *Gladys:* Ann McCrea. *Junior's secretary:* Lida Piazza. *Mailmen:* Bob Adler, Phil Chambers. *Mr. Ezarus:* Larry Kerr. *Annie:* Sherrill Terry. *Hotel doorman:* Mack Williams. *Receptionist:* Patrick Powell. *Breakfast food demonstrator:* Carmen Nisbit. *Razor demonstrator:* Richard Deems. *Theatre manager:* Benny Rubin. *Scrubwomen:* Minta Durfee, Edith Russell. *Voice of Ed Sullivan:* Don Corey. *Frenchmen:* Alberto Morin and Louis Mercier. *Secretary:* Stella Stevens.

Director: Frank Tashlin. *Screenwriter:* Frank Tashlin. *From the 1955 stage play by:* George Axelrod. *Cinematographer (in* CinemaScope *and* Color by De Luxe*):* Joe MacDonald. *Art directors:* Lyle R. Wheeler, Leland Fuller. *Editor:* Hugh S. Fowler. *Music composer:* Cyril J. Mockridge. *Music director:* Lionel Newman. *Vocal supervisor:* Ken Darby. *Song "You Got It Made":* Bobby Troup. *Orchestrator:* Edward B. Powell. *Sound:* E. Clayton Ward and Frank Moran. *Set decorators:* Walter M. Scott and Bertram Granger. *Executive wardrobe designer:* Charles Le Maire. *Special camera effects:* L. B. Abbott. *Assistant director:* Joseph E. Rickards. *Producer:* Frank Tashlin. *Production company/distributor:* 20th Century-Fox. *Running time:* 94 minutes. *Release date:* August 1957.

THE STORY OF MANKIND
(1957)

The Spirit of Man: Ronald Colman. *The Devil:* Vincent Price. *High Judge:* Sir Cedric Hardwicke. *Joan of Arc:* Hedy Lamarr. *Peter Minuit:* GROUCHO MARX. *Isaac Newton:* HARPO MARX. *Monk:* CHICO MARX. *Cleopatra:* Virginia Mayo. *Queen Elizabeth:* Agnes Moorehead. *Nero:* Peter Lorre. *Hippocrates:* Charles Coburn. *Spanish envoy:* Cesar Romero. *Khufu:* John Carradine. *Napoleon:* Dennis Hopper. *Marie Antoinette:* Marie Wilson. *Mark Antony:* Helmut Dantine. *Sir Walter Raleigh:* Edward Everett Horton. *Shakespeare:* Reginald Gardiner. *Josephine:* Marie Windsor. *Waiter:* George E. Stone. *Early Christian woman:* Cathy O'Donnell. *Early Christian child:* Melinda Marx. *Major domo:* Melville Cooper. *Bishop of Beauvais:* Henry Daniell. *Moses:* Francis X. Bushman. *Alexander Graham Bell:* Jim Ameche. *Adolf Hitler:* Bobby Watson. *Columbus:* Anthony Dexter. *Cleopatra's brother:* Bart Mattson. *Helen of Troy:* Dani Crayne. *Laughing Water:* Eden Hartford. *Marquis de Varennes:* Franklin Pangborn. *Apprentice:* Nick Cravat. *Concubine:* Ziva Rodann. *Abraham Lincoln:* Austin Green. *Indian brave:* Harry Ruby. *Julius Caesar:* Reginald Schallert. *Indian chief:* Abraham Sofaer. *Armana:* Marvin Miller. *Court clerk:* Tudor Owen.

Director: Irwin Allen. *Screenwriters:* Irwin Allen and Charles Bennett. *From the book by:* Hendrik Willem van Loon. *Cinematographer (in* Technicolor*):* Nicholas Musuraca. *Art director:* Art Loel. *Supervising film editor:* Roland Gross. *Editor:* Gene Palmer. *Music composer and conductor:* Paul Sawtell. *Sound record-*

ist: Stanley Jones. *Associate producer:* George E. Swink. *Producer:* Irwin Allen. *Production company:* Cambridge. *Distributor:* Warner Bros. *Running time:* 100 minutes. *Release date:* November 8, 1957.

SHOWDOWN AT ULCER GULCH
(1958)

GROUCHO MARX. CHICO MARX. Ernie Kovacs. Edie Adams. Bob Hope. Bing Crosby. Salome Jens. Orson Bean.

Production company: Shamus Culhane. *For:* The Saturday Evening Post.

GOT IT MADE
(1961)

HARPO MARX.

Director: Ira Marvin. *For:* Ford Motors.

SKIDOO
(1968)

Tony Banks: Jackie Gleason. *Flo Banks:* Carol Channing. *Angie:* Frankie Avalon. *A tower guard:* Fred Clark. *Leech:* Michael Constantine. *The Man:* Frank Gorshin. *Stash:* John Phillip Law. *The Senator:* Peter Lawford. *The Warden:* Burgess Meredith. *Captain Garbaldo:* George Raft. *Hechy:* Cesar Romero. *"Blue Chips" Packard:* Mickey Rooney. *"God":* GROUCHO MARX. *The Professor (Fred):* Austin Pendleton. *Darlene Banks:* Alexandra Hay. *"God"'s mistress:* Luna [Donyale Luna]. *Harry:* Arnold Stang. *The Mayor:* Doro Merande. *Mayor's husband:* Phil Arnold. *Switchboard operators:* Slim Pickens and Robert Donner. *Beany:* Richard Kiel. *Geronimo:* Tom Law. *"Eggs" Benedict:* Jaik Rosenstein. *The Amazon:* Stacy King. *Prison guards:* Renny Roker and Roman Gabriel. *Tower guard:* Harry Nilsson. *Convict:* William Cannon. *Themselves:* Stone Country. *Green Bay Packers:* Orange County Ramblers.

Director: Otto Preminger. *Screenwriter:* Doran William Cannon. *From a story by:* Erik Kirkland. *Cinematographer (in* Panavision *and* Technicolor*):* Leon Shamroy. *Art director:* Robert E. Smith. *Set decorator:* Fred Price. *Editor:* George Rohrs. *Music and lyrics:* Harry Nilsson. *Music arranger and conductor:* George Tipton. *Sound:* Glenn Anderson, Franklin Milton, and Lloyd Hanks. *Costume designer:* Rudi Gernreich. *Makeup:* Web Overlander. *Hairdressing:* Vivian Thompson. *Special effects:* Charles Spurgeon. *Producer:* Otto Preminger. *Production company:* Sigma. *Distributor:* Paramount. *Running time:* 98 minutes. *Release date:* December 19, 1968 (Miami premiere).

SCREENPLAY BY A MARX BROTHER

THE KING AND THE CHORUS GIRL (1937)

Alfred: Fernand Gravet. *Dorothy:* Joan Blondell. *Count Humber:* Edward Everett Horton. *Don Ald:* Alan Mowbray. *Duchess Anne:* Mary Nash. *Babette:* Jane Wyman. *Gaston:* Luis Alberni. *Singer:* Kenny Baker. *Specialty:* Shaw and Lee. *Waiter:* Ben Welden.

Concierge: Adrian Resley. *Professor Kornish:* Lionel Pape. *Footman:* Leonard Mudie. *Chauffeur:* Ferdinand Schumann-Heink. *Eric:* Torben Meyer. *Theatre manager:* Armand Kaliz. *Hatcheck girl:* Georgette Rhodes. *Servants:* George Sorel, Alphonse Martel. *Violinists:* Sam Ash, Lee Kohlmar. *Policeman:* Carlos San Martin. *Junior officer:* Gaston Glass. *Waiter:*

Jacques Lory. *Captain of ocean liner:* Robert Graves. *Stewardess:* Adele St. Maur. *Yacht captain:* Georges Renavent.

Director: Mervyn LeRoy. *Screenwriters:* Norman Krasna and GROUCHO MARX, (*additional dialogue and contribution to treatment*) Arthur Sheekman, (*additional dialogue*) Julius J. Epstein, (*contribution to screenplay*) Sherman Rogers. *Cinematographer:* Tony Gaudio. *Editor:* Thomas Richards. *Songs:* Werner Richard Heymann and Ted Koehler. *Music director:* Leo F. Forbstein. *Dance director:* Bobby Connolly. *Producer:* Mervyn LeRoy. *Production company/ distributor:* Warner Bros. *Running time:* 94 minutes. *Release date:* March 27, 1937.

THE MARX BROTHERS ON TELEVISION

This list excludes the Marx Brothers' guest appearances as themselves on talk shows and some variety shows. Lengths include commercial breaks.

PAPA ROMANI

(episode of *Silver Theatre*) (1950)

CHICO MARX. William Frawley. Margaret Hamilton.

Broadcast: January 19, 1950 (CBS) (repeated May 15, 1950).

YOU BET YOUR LIFE

(weekly quiz show) (1950–61)

Host: GROUCHO MARX. *Announcer:* George Fenneman. *Secret word girl:* Marilyn Burtis.
Director: Bernie Smith, John Guedel. *Producer:* John Guedel. *Length:* 30 minutes.

Broadcast (with seasonal breaks): September 5, 1950 to September 21, 1961 (NBC).

THE COLLEGE BOWL

(weekly series) (1950–51)

Host: CHICO MARX. Andy Williams. Barbara Ruick. Vickie Barrett. Jimmy Brock. Kenny Buffert. Joan Holloway. Paula Huston. Lee Lindsey. Tommy Morton. Stanley Prager. Evelyn Ward.

Director: Marshall Diskin. *Writers:* Howard Harris, Sydney Zelinka. *Producer:* Martin Gosch. *Length:* 30 minutes.

Broadcast: October 2, 1950 to March 26, 1951 (ABC).

I LOVE LUCY

(episode)

Lucy: Lucille Ball. *Himself:* HARPO MARX. Doris Singleton.

Length: 30 minutes.

Broadcast: May 9, 1955 (CBS).

SNOW SHOES

(episode of *Playhouse 90*) (1957)

Hard-Boiled Harry: Barry Sullivan. *Dolly:* Marilyn Maxwell. *Sentimental Mousie:* Stuart Erwin. *Rebel:* Wallace Ford. *Felix the Great:* John Carradine. *Parker:* Kenny Delmar. *Harpo:* HARPO MARX. *Jamieson:* Addison Richards. *Carruthers:* Thomas Palmer. *Cop:* Frank Sully. *Bellboy and Announcer:* Jason Wingreen. *Reporter:* James McCallion. *Snow Shoes:* Tony, the Wonder Horse.

Director: Ralph Nelson. *Writer:* Bob Barbash. *Additional dialogue:* George Bruce. *Art Director:* Al Heschong. *Producer:* Martin Manulis. *Length:* 90 minutes.

Broadcast: January 3, 1957 (CBS).

NO TIME AT ALL

(episode of *Playhouse 90*) (1958)

Ben Gammon: William Lundigan. *Emmy Verdon:* Betsy Palmer. *Karen:* Jane Greer. *Marshall Keats:* Keenan Wynn. *Allardyce:* Reginald Gardiner. *Grimes:* James Gleason. *Stanley Leeds:* Jack Haley. *Mrs. Leeds:* Mary Beth Hughes. *Manager:* Cliff Edwards. *Mr. Kramer:* CHICO MARX. Buster Keaton. Sylvia Sidney. Harry Einstein. Jay C. Flippen. Florence Halop. Shepperd Strudwick. Regis Toomey.

Director: David Swift. *Writers:* David Swift, Charles Einstein. *From the novel by:* Charles Einstein. *Cinematographer:* Hal Mohr. *Editor:* Samuel Gold. *Producer:* Jaime Del Valle. *Length:* 90 minutes.

Broadcast: February 13, 1958 (CBS).

THE RED MILL

(Du Pont Show of the Month) (1958)

Johnny Shaw: Donald O'Connor. *Gretchen Van Damm:* Shirley Jones. *Aunt Bertha:* Elaine Stritch. *Mayor Jan Van Borkern:* Edward Andrews. *Rod Carter:* Mike Nichols. *Candy Carter:* Elaine May. *Narrators: (words)* Evelyn Rudie, *(music)* HARPO MARX.

Director: Delbert Mann. *Writer:* Robert Alan Aurthur. *From the operetta* The Red Mill *by:* Victor Herbert. *Lyricist:* Henry Blossom. *Choreographer:* Eugene Loring. *Music director:* Don Walker. *Producer:* Fred Coe. Color. *Length:* 90 minutes.

Broadcast: April 19, 1958 (CBS).

THE INCREDIBLE JEWEL ROBBERY

(episode of *G.E. Theater*) (1959)

Nick: HARPO MARX. *Harry:* CHICO MARX. *Jewelry store manager:* Benny Rubin. *Woman:* Joy Rogers. *(Uncredited cameo):* GROUCHO MARX. *Series host:* Ronald Reagan.

Director: Mitchell Leisen. *Writers:* Dallas Gaultois and James Edmiston. *Cinematographer:* William A. Sickner. *Editor:* Michael R. McAdam. *Art director:* John Meehan. *Music composer:* Elmer Bernstein. *Producer:* Harry Tugend. *Production company:* Revue. *Length:* 30 minutes.

Broadcast: March 8, 1959 (CBS).

THE MIKADO

(Bell Telephone Hour) (1960)

KoKo: GROUCHO MARX. *Katisha:* Helen Traubel. *Mikado:* Dennis King. *Pooh-Bah:* Stanley Holloway. *Nanki-Poo:* Robert Rounseville. *Yum-Yum:* Barbara Meister. *Peep-Bo:* Melinda Marx. *Pitti-Sing:* Sharon Randall. *Chorus:* Norman Luboff Choir.

Director: Norman Campbell. *Adapter:* Martyn Green. *From the musical play by:* Gilbert and Sullivan. Color. *Scenic designer:* Paul Barnes. *Costume designer:* Ray Aghayan. *Choreographer:* Jack Regas. *Music director:* Donald Voorhees. *Producer:* Martyn Green. *Executive producer:* Barry Wood. *Production company:* Henry

Jaffe Enterprises. *Length:* 60 minutes. *Broadcast:* April 29, 1960 (NBC).

SILENT PANIC

(episode of *The June Allyson Show*) (1960)

Dummy: HARPO MARX. *Daniels:* Ernest Truex. *Lieutenant:* Bert Freed. *Popper:* John Banner. *Young stranger:* Bill Marx. *Series host:* June Allyson. *Director:* Arthur Hiller. *Writer:* Arthur Dales. *Producer:* Peter Kortner. *Length:* 30 minutes. *Broadcast:* December 22, 1960 (CBS).

MERRILY WE ROLL ALONG

(Du Pont Show of the Week)

Narrator: GROUCHO MARX. *In clips:* Keystone Kops, Will Rogers, Ben Turpin.
Writer: Phil Reisman Jr. *Music composers:* Robert Russell Bennett, Skitch Henderson. *Producer:* Bob Bendick. *Length:* 60 minutes.
Broadcast: October 22, 1961 (NBC).

THE WONDERFUL WORLD OF TOYS

(Du Pont Show of the Week) (1961)

HARPO MARX. Carol Burnett. Edie Adams. Merv Griffin. *Guests:* Mitch Miller, Milton Berle, Rube Goldberg, Eva Gabor, Elsa Maxwell, Audrey Meadows.
Length: 60 minutes.
Broadcast: November 12, 1961 (CBS).

TELL IT TO GROUCHO

(weekly TV quiz show) (1962)

GROUCHO MARX. *Announcer:* George Fenneman. *Assistants:* Jack Wheeler, Patty Harmon.
Director: Robert Dwan. *Music director:* Jerry Fielding. *Producer:* Bernie Smith. *Executive producer:* John Guedel. *Length:* 30 minutes.
Broadcast: January 11 to May 31, 1962 (CBS).

THE HOLDOUT

(episode of *G.E. Theater*)

John Graham: GROUCHO MARX. *Fred Judson:* Dennis Hopper. *Margie Graham:* Brooke Hayward. *Charles Judson:* Fred Clark. *Ellen Graham:* Dorothy Green. *Series host:* Ronald Reagan.
Director: Charles Haas. *Writer:* Max Ehrlich. *Pro-*

ducer: Stanley Rubin. *Length:* 30 minutes. *Broadcast:* January 14, 1962 (CBS).

THE MUSICALE

(episode of *Mr. Smith Goes to Washington*) (1962)

Smith: Fess Parker. *Pat:* Sandra Warner. *Cooter:* Red Foley. *Arnie:* Stan Irwin. *Pierre LeGrand:* Emil Genest. *Headwaiter:* Ben Wright. *Frank:* Lee Krieger. *Himself:* HARPO MARX.
Length: 30 minutes.
Broadcast: October 20, 1962 (ABC).

TIME FOR ELIZABETH

(episode of *Bob Hope Chrysler Theater*) (1964)

Ed Davis: GROUCHO MARX. *Kay Davis:* Kathryn Eames. *Vivian Morgan:* Eden Marx. *Amie:* Carole Wells. *Richard Coburn:* John Considine. *Walter Schaeffer:* Roland Winters.
Director: Ezra Stone. *Writer:* Alex Gottlieb. *From the stage play by:* GROUCHO MARX and Norman Krasna. *Length:* 60 minutes.
Broadcast: April 24, 1964 (NBC).

GROUCHO

(weekly TV quiz show in Great Britain) (1965)

GROUCHO MARX. *Compere:* Keith Fordyce.
Director: Ronald Marriott. *Devisers:* Robert Dwan, Bernie Smith. *Production company:* Rediffusion. *Length:* 30 minutes.
Broadcast: June 17 to July 15, 1965 (ITV).

THE GREATEST INVENTION IN THE WORLD

(episode of I Dream of Jeannie) (1967)

Jeannie: Barbara Eden. *Tony:* Larry Hagman. *Dr. Bellows:* Hayden Rorke. *Roger:* Bill Daily. *Peterson:* Barton MacLane. *Himself (cameo):* GROUCHO MARX.
Producer: Sidney Sheldon. Color. *Length:* 30 minutes.
Broadcast: January 9, 1967 (NBC).

JULIA

(episode) (1968)

Julia: Diahann Carroll. *Dr. Chegley:* Lloyd Nolan. *Hannah:* Lurene Tuttle. *Eddie:* Eddie Quillan. *Corey:* Marc Copage. *Himself (cameo):* GROUCHO MARX.

Color. *Length:* 30 minutes.
Broadcast: December 3, 1968 (NBC).

JOYS

(special) (1976)

Bob Hope. Don Adams. Jack Albertson. Marty Allen. Steve Allen. Desi Arnaz. Bill Barty. Rona Barrett. Milton Berle. Foster Brooks. Les Brown. George Burns. Red Buttons. Pat Buttram. John Byner. Sid Caesar. Sammy Cahn. Glen Campbell. Jack Carter. Charo. Jerry Colonna. Mike Connors. Scatman Crothers. Bill Dana. Angie Dickinson. Phyllis Diller. Jamie Farr. George Gobel. Jim Hutton. David Jans-sen. Alan King. George Kirby. Don Knotts. Fred MacMurray. Dean Martin. GROUCHO MARX. Jan Murray. Wayne Newton. Vincent Price. Freddie Prinze. Don Rickles. Harry Ritz. Telly Savalas. Phil Silvers. Larry Storch. Abe Vigoda. Jimmie Walker. Flip Wilson.

Director: Dick McDonough. *Writers:* Ben Starr, Charles Lee, Gig Henry, Paul Pumpian, Harvey Weitzman, Ruth Batchelor, Jeffrey Barron. *Producer:* Hal Kanter. *Executive producer:* Bob Hope. *Production company:* Bob Hope Enterprises. *Length:* 90 minutes.
Broadcast: March 5, 1976 (NBC).

APPENDIX: MARGARET DUMONT

She was born Marguerite Baker on October 20, 1889, in Brooklyn, New York. Her mother was French and her father Irish. A "delicate" child, she was brought up for the most part in Europe where she was educated by a private tutor. Her mother wanted her to be an opera singer. She took singing lessons and adopted her mother's maiden name of Dumont for professional purposes, appearing in revues in London, Paris, Vienna, and Berlin. While playing at the Casino de Paris, in Paris, she was spotted by J. J. Shubert, who signed her to appear in New York opposite Lew Fields as a replacement for Louise Dresser in the 1907 musical *The Girl Behind the Counter*. Her association with Fields was renewed with *The Belle of Brittany* (1909) and *Summer Widowers* (1910).

Following marriage to wealthy John Moller, Jr., heir to a sugar fortune, she retired from the stage and divided her time between Palm Springs, Paris, and New York, becoming the kind of society leader she so often played on screen, until Moller's death eight years later. She then returned to the boards (according to Groucho, her husband had left her little money, so she may not have had much choice). She appeared on Broadway with George M. Cohan in *Mary* (1920), which had a long run of 219 performances. She played Madame Ovieda in *The Fan*, which ran for thirty-two performances beginning October 3, 1921. The following May 8, she opened in the musical *Go Easy, Mabel*, which lasted sixteen performances. On Christmas Day 1923, she reappeared with George M. Cohan in *The Rise of Rosie O'Reilly*, which racked up ninety-seven performances.

In 1925, while performing at the Apollo in New York in *The Four-Flusher*, she was spotted by George S. Kaufman at one of the play's sixty-five performances. "I was playing a small-town social climber when George S. Kaufman saw me and asked if I'd be the society leader who had the part opposite Groucho Marx in *The Cocoanuts*. I was amused and said yes.

"I was told that the Marx Brothers needed an actress with dignity and poise, to lend legitimate dramatic balance to their comedy. At the opening rehearsal, I wore a chiffon dress with long sleeves. My introduction to Harpo was when I found his foot in my sleeve," she later reminisced. "After three weeks as Groucho's leading lady, I nearly had a nervous breakdown. He pushed me about, pulled chairs from under me, broiled steaks in the fireplace of my apartment, put frogs in my bath, and made my life miserable on the stage and off. But I don't regret a minute of it. I just love those boys."

She further recalled: "I almost went crazy. During rehearsals they never gave me any lines to learn and when it came down to two days before the opening in Boston, I couldn't stand it any longer. I went to Groucho and complained. 'Don't you worry about the lines,' he said. 'You just go on and we'll get along all right.' " She waited in vain for a cue to join Groucho on stage. He had wandered in front of the curtain, so she stepped forward and hoped for the best. "Won't you lie down?" he asked, pointing to a park bench on the stage.

In *The Cocoanuts*, she wore a dress with a long train and Harpo made a habit of following her off stage leaping from one side to the other of the trailing cloth. One evening, he landed on the train, pulling off her dress and leaving her exposed to the audience in her underwear.

But not even her underwear was safe. In *The Marx Brothers Scrapbook*, Harry Ruby recalled an occasion during the stage run of *Animal Crackers*:

> One night just before the curtain went up she told me, "Harry, I bought the most beautiful petticoat today and I'm wearing it tonight." So just before the curtain went up I told Harpo about her petticoat, which was a crazy thing to do. After the curtain went up Harpo comes out while she was on the stage, raises his hand under her dress and pulls off the petticoat. Well, Dumont nearly passed out. Only the Marx Bros. could do something like that.

She soon regarded a whalebone corset as essential protection for working around the Marxes. And she dressed more sensibly. As she recalled while making *A Day at the Races:* "Chiffons and laces are out. I usually have my dresses made of velvets and gold cloth. They are both very strong as they have to be when you play one of those love scenes with Groucho."

She had soon learned that her role in *The Cocoanuts* was strictly that of a straight woman. "I thought the society leader funny, but whenever I tried to clown her, Groucho would say, 'I like you dignified.' "

Of her time with *The Cocoanuts*, she declared, "Chico is the one who always saved my life. He kept Groucho from climbing all over me and

216

always stopped Harpo when he began hooking legs with that cane of his." But it was Chico who teamed up with Harpo to hide five alarm clocks in her berth on tour, timed to go off at hourly intervals. Actress Margaret Irving (who toured with her in *Animal Crackers*) has gone on record with the story of how Dumont retired early one night on a train and the Marxes stripped a conductor down to his underwear and flung him into her compartment. If Groucho is to be believed, things got even worse:

Once we were traveling on a train from New York to California and she had a drawing room. We had then been working together, say, for about eight years. One night, we went to the drawing room and took off all her clothes. That's all that happened . . . there were many other girls on the show and we had other plans. We took all her clothes off and left. You could hear her screaming all the way from the drawing room where she was to where the engineer was blowing the train's whistle.

After playing in the stage and film versions of *The Cocoanuts* and *Animal Crackers* and joining the Marxes for their London appearance in early 1931, she tried to resume a separate stage career in a musical version of the celebrated farce *Nothing But the Truth*, which opened on October 28, 1932, as *Tell Her the Truth*. She appeared with John Sheehan, Jr., Lillian Emerson, Andrew Tombes, William Frawley, Raymond Walburn, and Hobart Cavanaugh. It closed after just eleven performances and marked her last Broadway appearance.

She went to Hollywood to rejoin the Marx Brothers in *Duck Soup* and stayed there, pursuing a movie career with and without the team. But she did get to appear before live audiences again. Although it was Dorothy Christie who played Mrs. Claypool on the tour prior to filming *A Night at the Opera*, Margaret went out to help test the script of *A Day at the Races* with the three Marxes. "They'd change the act every day and never tell me," she recalled to Kyle Crichton of *Collier's* at the time of the film's release. "Out front were three writers,

checking the laughs and determining what should be tried next. The secret of working with Groucho is to be alert every minute and never get fussed. When he starts talking something never heard before on land or sea, it is up to me to go right along with him. It's hard work but nobody could ask for a more interesting job."

She paid high tribute to Groucho. "He has the most inventive mind I've ever met. He keeps gnawing at a bit of funny business, changing it, working it backwards, skipping lines, altering it every time we try it—and finally it becomes something immense. If he's afraid of anything at all, it's a matinee audience. The women often don't get his style of humor. It's too fast for them. But Harpo and Chico always save the matinees. The women have a motherly feeling for Harpo . . ."

She rarely saw the Marx Brothers outside of work. By the time of *A Day at the Races*, she had a three-room apartment in the middle of Hollywood, where she liked to cook her own meals. Her idea of relaxation was to go to a movie: she had no interest in racetracks, opera houses, or nightclubs.

Her ambition was to progress from being a foil to comedians to more demanding character roles, although she insisted the former was a challenge in itself. "The only thing that ever hurt me about my job was being called a stooge. I resent that. Playing comedy in the movies is a hard job. You can't just stand still and wait for the laughs, but they do have to be timed so that the laughter won't wash out the next lines. When that wait comes it is necessary to be doing something the whole time and not just something haphazard. That's what is called acting." She worked on Irving Thalberg and believed she had persuaded him to give her meatier parts, but he died before she had any chance to find out.

Sadly, when she did gain a role in a top-flight picture, *The Women*, it was her misfortune to be edited out. But she was stretched more than usual back again with the Marx Brothers in *At the Circus*. As she told the press at the time, "For the benefit of those who wonder if I actually did perform on a trapeze, the answer is yes. Most people suspect me of using a stand-in. But I hung head down while the Marx boys clutched my legs. I had to see it through." This, she said, was the last time she prepared to work for the team.

But there was not that much work available. Around the time Groucho was making *Go West* without her, he referred to her in a letter to writer friend Arthur Sheekman: "She's at liberty, not an unusual condition for her, and I imagine she'd be very appreciative of anything that fitted her, and wouldn't expect too much of a salary." She seemed at times to blame the Marx Brothers for stifling her career. In *Living With Chico*, Maxine Marx recalls having lunch with her.

> She arrived at the restaurant wearing white gloves up to the elbow and carrying a lorgnette. During the meal, Miss Dumont talked about how the Marx Brothers had affected her career. "The boys r-r-r-ruined my car-r-r-r-eee-r," she trilled. "How, Miss Dumont?" "Oh, my dear. Nobody took me seriously as a dramatic actress. People always thought they saw Groucho peeking out from behind my skirt."

She may never have really appreciated the humor to which she contributed so much. Groucho liked to relate that she was as dumb as her screen image, and gave some illustrations of this. He remarked in 1965,

> You know, the curious thing about Margaret, in all the years we played together she never seemed to vary. She was always the austere, dignified dowager that we presented in the pictures. She was the same off the stage as she was on. That was part of her charm. She actually didn't understand any of the jokes. I'm serious—she really didn't understand the jokes. Very seldom. I know there was a joke in *Duck Soup* which was at the finish of the picture. It was a kind of a war and we were in a small cottage—Margaret and myself. She said to me, "What are you doing, Rufus?" I said, "I'm fighting for your honor which is more than you ever did." And later she asked me what did I mean by that.

And in an interview:

> She had no idea what I was talking about, at any time. Frequently she would ask me, "Why are they laughing now?" I tried to explain to her. There was a line when Harpo and Chico were stealing a painting, in *Animal Crackers*, and Margaret Dumont and I came in the room, and it was pitch dark. She said, "My, it's so dark in here you can't see your hand in front of your face." And I said, "Well, you wouldn't get much enjoyment out of *that*." And the audience laughed like hell, and she came to me after the scene and said, "Julie, why did they laugh there? What was funny about that? It *was* dark, and I *couldn't* see my hand."

Harry Ruby has corroborated Groucho. "She was great, but she used to come up to me and say, 'Harry, I love the boys, but I don't know what they're talking about!" When Groucho received his special Academy Award in 1974, he was mostly serious, wishing that his deceased brothers and Margaret Dumont could have been there to share the honor: "She was a great straight lady even though she never got any of my jokes." The audience laughed.

In the 1950s, when film parts were fewer and further between, she began doing television work. She played a recurring role in the 1952–53 season of Marie Wilson's comedy series *My Friend Irma* on CBS. Her part was that of Mrs. Rhinelander, socialite mother of Brooks West's Richard Rhinelander III, who was the millionaire employer and boyfriend of Marie Wilson's Manhattan roommate.

But she was more often engaged for single episodes of series, as when she appeared with Estelle Winwood in the episode (circa 1959) "Mrs. Lovelace Comes to Tea" of *The Donna Reed Show*.

When she gained a role in the big screen, big budget Rosalind Russell vehicle, *Auntie Mame*, in May 1958, her casting made a news item in *The Hollywood Reporter* but, apart from a fleeting glimpse, she ended up on the cutting room floor.

Despite failing health, she never stopped

working and appeared on television with Bob Hope, Dean Martin, and others. Just a few days before her death, aged seventy-five, on March 6, 1965, from a heart attack in her Hollywood home, she was reunited with Groucho in a television sketch recreating the arrival of Captain Spaulding in *Animal Crackers* for *The Hollywood Palace*. When it was shown on Saturday April 17, 1965, no mention was made of her recent demise.

Though she worked with so many of the great comedians, she is indelibly associated with Groucho and the Marx Brothers. There was something extra in her performances with them—they brought out the best in her. She seemed to find the Marxes interesting, fascinating, inexplicable—never ridiculous or disgusting. In their films, she was not just a prim, proper, dull figure. She seemed to have a sense of humor along with a faith in courtesy, good manners, reason, and that kind of thing which enabled her to accept the Marx Brothers. There was a real rapport. One likes to think this was the real Margaret Dumont.

What she did and the way that she did it were inimitable. There can be few character players of so limited a range who have made such a lasting impression or aroused so much sympathetic affection in audiences. She won at least one award, being named Best Supporting Actress by the Screen Actors Guild in 1937 for *A Day at the Races*. It was then that she had her only major magazine interview, with Kyle Crichton in *Collier's*.

It was in that year that Cecilia Ager commented: "There ought to be a statue erected, or a Congressional Medal awarded, or a national holiday proclaimed, to honor that great woman, Margaret Dumont, the dame who takes the raps from the Marx Brothers . . . a lady of epic ability to take it . . . her fortitude is nothing human. It's godlike."

"Don't call me a stooge," Margaret Dumont said. "I think it's terrible and I'll resent it. I'm not a stooge. I'm the best straight woman in Hollywood. There's an art to playing straight. You must build up your man, but never top him, never steal the laughs from him."

Straight woman or stooge—she was one of a kind.

THE FILMS

Several of Margaret Dumont's appearances were in uncredited bit parts, and she may well have made more than are recorded here. Published cast lists indicate that she played a Mrs. Wagstaff in George Cukor's *The Women* (1939), but she is not credited on the film itself and there was no sign of her in a recent check of a complete print, so it is clear that she was edited out. An illustrated filmography in *The Freedonia Gazette*, No. 9, Winter 1982, provided some of the following role descriptions.

A TALE OF TWO CITIES

(1917, Fox)

Director: Frank Lloyd.
Star: William Farnum.
According to the British *Monthly Film Bulletin* (August 1971, p. 173), she appeared as a prisoner in the Bastille. [But is this being confused with the 1935 MGM version, which seems the more likely as it was being made at a period when she was doing some uncredited bits for that studio?)

THE COCOANUTS

(1929, Paramount)

Directors: Robert Florey, Joseph Santley.
Stars: Four Marx Bros.
Comedy; as Mrs. Potter.

ANIMAL CRACKERS

(1930, Paramount)

Director: Victor Heerman.
Stars: Four Marx Bros.
Comedy; as Mrs. Rittenhouse.

THE GIRL HABIT

(1931, Paramount)

Director: Edward Cline.
Stars: Charles Ruggles, Sue Conroy, Tamara Geva.
Comedy; as Mrs. Ledyard, strict mother of the heroine (Conroy).

DUCK SOUP

(1933, Paramount)

Director: Leo McCarey.
Stars: Four Marx Bros.
Comedy; as Mrs. Teasdale.

GRIDIRON FLASH

(1934, RKO Radio)

Director: Glenn Tryon.
Stars: Eddie Quillan, Betty Furness.
Football drama; as Mrs. Fields, wife of character played by Lucien Littlefield.

FIFTEEN WIVES

(1934, Invincible)

Director: Frank R. Strayer.
Stars: Conway Tearle, Natalie Moorhead, Raymond Hatton, Noel Francis.
Murder mystery; as Sybilla Crum.

KENTUCKY KERNELS

(1934, RKO Radio)

Director: George Stevens.
Stars: Wheeler and Woolsey.
Comedy; as the monocled Mrs. Baxter, the good-natured head of the Children's Welfare League who supplies the glass-breaking Spanky McFarland for adoption to W. & W.

AFTER OFFICE HOURS

(1935, MGM)

Director: Robert Z. Leonard.
Stars: Constance Bennett, Clark Gable.
Comedy; as Mrs. Murchison, early arrival at swish nightclub.

RECKLESS

(1935, MGM)

Director: Victor Fleming.
Stars: Jean Harlow, William Powell, Franchot Tone.
Drama; as theatergoer yelling at Mona (Harlow), "Get off the stage, vermin!"

RENDEZVOUS

(1935, MGM)

Director: William K. Howard.
Stars: William Powell, Rosalind Russell.
Drama; as Mrs. Hendricks.

A NIGHT AT THE OPERA

(1935, MGM)

Director: Sam Wood.
Stars: Three Marx Bros.
Comedy; as Mrs. Claypool.

ORCHIDS TO YOU

(1935, Fox)

Director: William A. Seiter.
Stars: John Boles, Jean Muir.
Comedy-drama; (role untraced).

ANYTHING GOES

(1936, Paramount)

Director: Lewis Milestone.
Stars: Bing Crosby, Ethel Merman.
Musical comedy; as Mrs. Wentworth, passenger on an ocean liner who almost has her dog stolen by Crosby.

THE SONG AND DANCE MAN

(1936, 20th Century-Fox)

Director: Allan Dwan.
Stars: Claire Trevor, Paul Kelly, Michael Whalen.
Drama of the theater; as Mrs. Whitney.

A DAY AT THE RACES

(1937, MGM)

Director: Sam Wood.
Stars: Three Marx Bros.
Comedy; as Mrs. Emily Upjohn.

THE LIFE OF THE PARTY

(1937, RKO Radio)

Director: William A. Seiter.
Stars: Joe Penner, Parkyakarkus.
Comedy; as Mrs. Penner, lead's mother.

YOUTH ON PAROLE

(1937, Republic)

Director: Phil Rosen.
Stars: Marian Marsh, Gordon Oliver.

Drama; as The Landlady. [On this film, she achieved third billing, her best ever.]

HIGH FLYERS
(1937, RKO Radio)

Director: Edward Cline.
Stars: Wheeler and Woolsey.
Comedy; as Mrs. Arlington, wife of character played by Paul Harvey.

WISE GIRL
(1937, RKO Radio)

Director: Leigh Jason.
Stars: Miriam Hopkins, Ray Milland.
Comedy; as Mrs. Bell-Rivington.

DRAMATIC SCHOOL
(1938, MGM)

Director: Robert B. Sinclair.
Stars: Luise Rainer, Paulette Goddard.
Drama; as The Pantomime Teacher.

AT THE CIRCUS
(1939, MGM)

Director: Edward Buzzell.
Stars: Three Marx Bros.
Comedy; as Mrs. Suzanna Dukesbury.

FOR BEAUTY'S SAKE
(1940, 20th Century-Fox)

Director: Shepard Traube.
Stars: Ted North, Marjorie Weaver.
Comedy mystery; literally letting her hair down, as Mrs. Franklin Evans, who suffers some inexpert attention in a beauty salon.

THE BIG STORE
(1941, MGM)

Director: Charles Riesner.
Stars: Three Marx Bros.
Comedy; as Martha Phelps.

NEVER GIVE A SUCKER AN EVEN BREAK
(1941, Universal)

Director: Edward Cline.
Star: W. C. Fields.
Comedy; in the film-within-the-film, as Mrs. Hemogloben, wealthy and eccentric man-hating owner of a mountaintop retreat where she lives with her lovely, innocent daughter Ouliotta (Susan Miller), guarded by a gorilla and mastiff. When Fields literally drops in on her from the sky, she is easily flattered by his attentions despite her past experience of men. [With heavy eyebrows, hair piled up, and little to say, she is particularly stiff and unattractive here.]

SING YOUR WORRIES AWAY
(1942, RKO Radio)

Director: A. Edward Sutherland.
Stars: Bert Lahr, Buddy Ebsen.
Musical comedy; as Flo Faulkener.

BORN TO SING
(1942, MGM)

Director: Edward Ludwig.
Stars: Virginia Weidler, Ray McDonald.
Musical drama; as Mrs. E. V. Lawson.

TALES OF MANHATTAN
(1942, 20th Century-Fox)

Director: Julien Duvivier.
Star (episode): W. C. Fields.
Comedy sequence; as do-gooder Mrs. Mangerhankie (or Langerhankie), who hosts a meeting of the Uptown Association for the Downfall of Alcohol which is sabotaged by her wealthy husband (Chester Clute) who spikes the cocoanut milk refreshment, inducing merriment and delight among all present, including the lecturer (Fields) and the lady herself. [Originally deleted from this all-star production, the episode has survived and been shown occasionally as a separate item for its obvious historic interest.]

ABOUT FACE
(1942, Hal Roach/United Artists)

Director: Kurt Neumann.
Stars: William Tracy, Joe Sawyer.
Service comedy; in uniform herself as Mrs. Culpepper, who addresses a meeting of the Girls' Home Defense League on vocational therapy.

RHYTHM PARADE

(1943, Monogram)

Directors: Howard Bretherton, David Gould.
Stars: Nils T. Granlund, Gale Storm, Robert Lowery.

Musical comedy; as Ophelia, sister and backer of a nightclub owner, who saves the career of a singer (Gale Storm) after the latter is thought to be an unwed mother.

THE DANCING MASTERS

(1943, 20th Century-Fox)

Director: Mal St. Clair.
Stars: Laurel and Hardy.

Comedy; as Mrs. Louise Harlan, wife of industrialist Wentworth Harlan (Matt Briggs) and mother of Trudy (Trudy Marshall), a pupil at Stan and Ollie's dance school who is in love with an inventor working at her father's plant.

UP IN ARMS

(1944, Samuel Goldwyn/RKO Radio)

Director: Elliott Nugent.
Stars: Danny Kaye, Dinah Shore, Dana Andrews.

Musical comedy; as Mrs. Willoughby, who converses with Kaye's hypochondriac in a crowded movie theater lobby, divulging that she is forty-six-years-old, married to a broker who earns $88 a week and has seven children; Kaye gives her some tablets and details of his love life, and she enjoys watching his musical number, "Manic-Depressive Pictures Presents," spoofing film credits and plots.

BATHING BEAUTY

(1944, MGM)

Director: George Sidney.
Stars: Esther Williams, Red Skelton.

Musical comedy; as Mrs. Allenwood, member of the faculty of an all-girls school, who discovers Skelton in one of the dormitories.

SEVEN DAYS ASHORE

(1944, RKO Radio)

Director: John H. Auer.
Stars: Wally Brown, Alan Carney, Gordon Oliver.
Musical comedy; as Mrs. Croxton-Lynch.

THE HORN BLOWS AT MIDNIGHT

(1945, Warner Bros.)

Director: Raoul Walsh.
Stars: Jack Benny, Alexis Smith.

Fantasy comedy; as Madame Traviata, solo singer (dubbed) on a radio show and (in Jack Benny's dream) as the woman in a park who accuses Benny of stealing a trumpet from some boys and who falls into the bear trap they have dug. [She is billed as Miss Rodholder.]

BILLY ROSE'S DIAMOND HORSESHOE

(1945, 20th Century-Fox)

Director: George Seaton.
Stars: Betty Grable, Dick Haymes.

Musical; an appearance in glorious Technicolor in a comical dream sequence, playing the very regal Mrs. Sylvester Standish of Newport who sings a greeting to Grable ("so good of you to come to my reception") when the latter arrives as a guest, and who then introduces a line of celebrities to her.

SUNSET IN EL DORADO

(1945, Republic)

Director: Frank McDonald.
Stars: Roy Rogers, George "Gabby" Hayes, Dale Evans.

Western with music; as Aunt Dolly, who wants her niece to marry a casino operator but the niece makes her own choice.

LITTLE GIANT

(1946, Universal)

Director: William A. Seiter.
Stars: Bud Abbott and Lou Costello.

Comedy; as Mrs. Henderson, soot-covered victim of a vacuum cleaner demonstration in her home by Lou's door-to-door salesman.

SUSIE STEPS OUT

(1946, Comet/United Artists)

Director: Reginald Le Borg.
Stars: David Bruce, Nita Hunter.

Comedy; as Mrs. Starr.

THREE FOR BEDROOM C

(1952, Brenco/Warner Bros.)

Director: Milton H. Bren.
Stars: Gloria Swanson, James Warren.
Farcical comedy, entirely set aboard the Santa Fe Super Chef en route from Chicago to Los Angeles; as Mrs. Hawthorne, a passenger who talks to herself.

STOP, YOU'RE KILLING ME

(1953, Warner Bros.)

Director: Roy Del Ruth.
Stars: Broderick Crawford, Claire Trevor.
Gangster comedy set in 1930s, remake of *A Slight Case of Murder* (1938); in one of her most substantial roles as the sensitive Mrs. Whitelaw, a wealthy resident of Saratoga Springs and mother of a state trooper (Bill Hayes) who is invited to a party given by a retired beer baron (Crawford), mauled about on the dance floor and closeted for a rest with four corpses.

SHAKE, RATTLE AND ROCK

(1956, American International)

Director: Edward L. Cahn.
Stars: Fats Domino, Lisa Gaye.
Musical comedy; as Georgianna, who with her husband (Raymond Hatton) is part of a group campaigning against rock 'n' roll as a detrimental influence on youth.

AUNTIE MAME

(1959, Warner Bros.)

Director: Morton Da Costa.
Stars: Rosalind Russell, Forrest Tucker.
Musical; as Woman at Party [no lines, just a fleeting appearance].

ZOTZ!

(1962, William Castle/Columbia)

Director: William Castle.
Stars: Tom Poston, Julia Meade.
Comedy; as Persephone Updike, wife of a college Dean (Cecil Kellaway).

WHAT A WAY TO GO!

(1964, Apjac-Orchard/20th Century-Fox)

Director: J. Lee Thompson.
Stars: Shirley MacLaine, Paul Newman, Robert Mitchum, Dean Martin, Gene Kelly, Dick Van Dyke.
Comedy; in a meaty end to her big screen career in 'scope and color, as Mrs. Foster, mother of Louisa (Shirley MacLaine), seen early in the film. She is self-centered, greedy, pushing her daughter into marriage with the slimy, rich Dean Martin character (who says that she couldn't be Shirley's real mother, they must have found her on the doorstep one stormy night in a cage). When MacLaine rebels against her mother's wishes and marries Dick Van Dyke's simple storekeeper, Dumont screams "Oh! Oh! Oh!" with outrage.

FREE!
Citadel Film Series Catalog

If you like this book, you'll love the other titles in the award-winning Citadel Film Series. From James Stewart to Moe Howard and The Three Stooges, Woody Allen to John Wayne, The Citadel Film Series is America's largest and oldest film book library.

With more than 150 titles--and more on the way!--Citadel Film Books make perfect gifts for a loved one, a friend, or best of all, yourself!

We'd like to send you, free of charge, our latest full-color catalog describing the Citadel Film Series in depth. To receive the catalog, call 1-800-447-BOOK or send your name and address to the address at bottom.

If you know what books you want, why not order now!
It's easy! Just call 1-800-447-BOOK and have your MasterCard or Visa ready.

STARS
Alan Ladd
Barbra Streisand: First Decade
Barbra Streisand: Second Decade
Bela Lugosi
Bette Davis
Boris Karloff
The Bowery Boys
Carole Lombard
Cary Grant
Charles Bronson
Charlie Chaplin
Clark Gable
Clint Eastwood
Curly
Dustin Hoffman
Edward G. Robinson
Elizabeth Taylor
Elvis Presley
Errol Flynn
Frank Sinatra
Gary Cooper
Gene Kelly
Gina Lollobrigida
Gloria Swanson
Gregory Peck
Greta Garbo
Henry Fonda
Humphrey Bogart
Ingrid Bergman
Jack Lemmon
Jack Nicholson
James Cagney
James Dean: Behind the Scene
Jane Fonda
Jeanette MacDonald & Nelson
 Eddy
Joan Crawford

John Wayne
John Wayne Reference Book
John Wayne Scrapbook
Judy Garland
Katharine Hepburn
Kirk Douglas
Laurel & Hardy
Lauren Bacall
Laurence Olivier
Mae West
Marilyn Monroe
Marlene Dietrich
Marlon Brando
Marx Brothers
Moe Howard & the Three Stooges
Norma Shearer
Olivia de Havilland
Orson Welles
Paul Newman
Peter Lorre
Rita Hayworth
Robert Redford
Sexbomb: Jayne Mansfield
Shirley MacLaine
Shirley Temple
The Sinatra Scrapbook
Spencer Tracy
Steve McQueen
Three Stooges Scrapbook
Warren Beatty
W.C. Fields
William Holden
William Powell
A Wonderful Life: James Stewart
DIRECTORS
Alfred Hitchcock
Cecil B. DeMille
Federico Fellini

Frank Capra
John Huston
Western Films of John Ford
Woody Allen
GENRE
Bad Guys
Black Hollywood
Classics of the Gangster Film
Classics of the Horror Film
Cliffhanger
Divine Images: Jesus on Screen
Early Classics of Foreign Film
Martial Arts Movies
Great Adventure Films
Great French Films
Great German Films
Great Romantic Films
Great Science Fiction Films
Great Spy Films
Harry Warren & the Hollywood
 Musical
Hispanic Hollywood: The Latins
 in Motion Pictures (English &
 Spanish edition available)
The Hollywood Western
The Incredible World of 007
The Jewish Image in American
 Film
The Lavender Screen: The Gay
 and Lesbian Films
The Modern Horror Film
More Classics of the Horror Film
The Pictorial History of Science
 Fiction Films
Second Feature: "B" Films
They Sang! They Danced! They
 Romanced!: Hollywood
 Musicals

Thrillers
The West That Never Was
Words and Shadows: Literature on
 the Screen
DECADE
Classics of the Silent Screen
Films of the Twenties
Films of the Thirties
More Films of the 30's
Films of the Forties
Films of the Fifties
Lost Films of the 50's
Films of the Sixties
Films of the Seventies
Films of the Eighties
SPECIAL INTEREST
Bugsy (Illustrated screenplay)
Dick Tracy
Favorite Families of TV
Film Flubs
Film Flubs: The Sequel
Forgotten Films to Remember
Hollywood Cheesecake
Hollywood's Hollywood
Howard Hughes in Hollywood
More Character People
The Nightmare Never Ends:
 Freddy Krueger & "A Night
 mare on Elm Street"
The "Quantum Leap" Book
Sex In the Movies
Sherlock Holmes
Son of Film Flubs
They Had Faces Then
Those Glorious Glamour Years
Who Is That?: Familiar Faces and
 Forgotten Names
"You Ain't Heard Nothin' Yet!"

Citadel Film Series/Carol Publishing Group
Distribution Center B
120 Enterprise Avenue
Secaucus, NJ 07094